Political Stability and Development

Political Stability and Development

A Comparative Analysis of Kenya, Tanzania, and Uganda

Dirk Berg-Schlosser
Rainer Siegler

Lynne Rienner Publishers • Boulder and London

Published in the United States of America in 1990 by
Lynne Rienner Publishers, Inc.
1800 30th Street, Boulder, Colorado 80301

and in the United Kingdom by
Lynne Rienner Publishers, Inc.
3 Henrietta Street, Covent Garden, London WC2E 8LU

Library of Congress Cataloging-in-Publication Data
Berg-Schlosser, Dirk.
  Political stability and development : a comparative analysis of
Kenya, Tanzania, and Uganda / by Dirk Berg-Schlosser and Rainer
Siegler.
    p.   cm.
  Includes bibliographical references.
  ISBN 1-55587-165-8
  1. Political stability—Kenya. 2. Kenya—Politics and government.
3. Political stability—Tanzania. 4. Tanzania—Politics and
government—1964- 5. Political stability—Uganda. 6. Uganda—
Politics and government. I. Siegler, Rainer. II. Title.
JQ2947. A91B47   1990
320.9676—dc20   90-8249
                                                       CIP

British Cataloguing in Publication Data
A Cataloguing in Publication record for this book
is available from the British Library.

Printed and bound in the United States of America

The paper used in this publication meets the requirements
of the American National Standard for Permanence of
Paper for Printed Library Materials Z39.48-1984.

Contents

PART III   COMPARATIVE STUDIES

Diagrams and Tables

Social Indicators

Indicators of External Economic Relations

Political Indicators

Analysis of Social Structure

Abbreviations and Acronyms

ANC	African National Congress
ASP	Afro-Shirazi party
ASU	Afro-Shirazi Union
CIA	Central Intelligence Agency (U.S.A.)
CID	Central Investigation Department
CCM	Chama cha Mapinduzi (Party of the Revolution)
COTU	Central Organisation of Trade Unions
CPK	Church of the Province of Kenya
CUT	Co-operative Union of Tanzania
DP	Democratic party
EAC	East African Community
EC	European Community
Fedemu	Federal Democratic Movement of Uganda
FKE	Federation of Kenya Employers
Foba	Force Obote back again
FUTU	Federation of Uganda Trade Unions
GDP	Gross domestic product
GEMA	Gikuyu, Embu and Meru Association
GNP	Gross national product
GSU	General Service Unit
IMF	International Monetary Fund
JUWATA	Association of Workers of Tanzania
KADU	Kenya African Democratic Union
KANU	Kenya African National Union
KAU	Kenya African Union
KCA	Kikuyu Central Association
KCGA	Kenya Coffee Growers' Union
KFL	Kenya Federation of Labour
KNFU	Kenya National Farmers' Association
KPCU	Kenya Planters' Co-operative Union
KPU	Kenya People's Union
KY	Kabaka Yekka
LSK	Law Society of Kenya
MP	Member of Parliament
NCCK	National Council of Churches of Kenya
NMC	National Milling Corporation

NEC	National Executive Committee
NRA	National Resistance Army
NRC	National Resistance Council
NRM	National Resistance Movement
NTC	National Trading Corporation
NUTA	National Union of Tanganyika Workers
OAU	Organization of African Unity
PCEA	Presbyterian Church of East Africa
PMB	Produce Marketing Board
PQLI	Physical Quality of Life Index
PTA	Preferential Trade Area
RC	Resistance Council
SADCC	Southern African Development Coordination Conference
SDA	Special District Assistant
SRDP	Special Rural Development Plan
TAA	Tanganyika African Association
TANU	Tanganyika African National Union
TDPF	Tanzania People's Defence Force
TFL	Tanganyika Federation of Labour
UDC	Uganda Development Corporation
UFM	Uganda Freedom Movement
ULC	Uganda Labour Congress
UNLA	Uganda National Liberation Army
UNLF	Uganda National Liberation Front
UNRF	Uganda National Rescue Front
UPC	Uganda People's Congress
UPDM	Uganda People's Democratic Movement
UPM	Uganda People's Movement
UTUC	Uganda Trade Unions Congress
ZNP	Zanzibar National Party

Preface

This study, the first of its kind, originally was commissioned by the German Ministry for Economic Cooperation. (The German version was published by Weltforum Verlag, Munich, in 1988.) The sole responsibility for all findings and opinions expressed here lies, however, with the authors.

In conducting our research, we contacted a great many institutions and individuals, who are too numerous to be listed here and who in some cases preferred to remain anonymous. Among these were representatives of governments, parties, universities, churches, the press, and bilateral and multilateral donor organizations, together with many "ordinary" people. All of them can be assured of our continuing gratitude for their cooperation and hospitality.

The largest part of the translation was done by Ann Nassauer. At Philipps-University, numerous people were involved in the technical implementation, including the statistical parts of the project: they include Bettina Gawinski, Renate Maulick, Inge Seifert, Sigrid Weber, Folko Arends, Norbert Kersting, and Kai Schmerer. We are very grateful for their help.

All remaining errors are, of course, ours.

Dirk Berg-Schlosser
Rainer Siegler

Introduction

It often seems obvious that there are links between political and economic development: lasting economic development is unthinkable without a certain amount of political and legal order; conversely, economic development can contribute to the stabilization of a political system. Yet, economic success cannot by itself safeguard the survival of a regime, as was shown under particularly spectacular circumstances in Iran in 1979. Nor is the mere continuation of a particular form of government (as in Stroessner's Paraguay, for example) a guarantee of economic and social development in a wider sense. The links are therefore more complex than they appear, and it is all the more surprising that they have been subjected so far to relatively little detailed analysis within the general development discussion.

For a long time, notions prevailed within the framework of modernization theories (for a discussion of different schools and paradigms, see, e.g., Nuscheler 1985b) that the social and economic prerequisites for more-democratic political systems were insufficiently fulfilled in Third World countries, and that rapid economic development needed an authoritarian form of government. Richard Löwenthal's (1963:187) statement concerning this antinomy is particularly succinct: "for each degree of freedom there is a slackening in the pace of development, for each degree of acceleration there is a loss of freedom." The advocation of a strong state in the form of a development-oriented dictatorship relied completely on the willingness of elites actually to pursue such a modernization and on their ability to bring about concomitant sociocultural changes and to concentrate resources on centrally assigned priorities in the economic field. Warnings that such authoritarian political structures, intended to be only temporary, might become more durable and mainly self-serving remained unheeded (Rüland/ Werz 1985:211ff). And actual developments during the last three decades failed to live up to more-optimistic expectations in many respects (see Berg-Schlosser 1985b).

The change to a dependency-oriented paradigm, which examined the external conditions of underdevelopment, ignored most of the internal political aspects of the problem, thus relinquishing the possibility of a differentiated analysis of the interactions of political and economic factors. Only in more recent years, has there been a renewal of interest in the scope of action of political systems and the elites acting within them (see Elsenhans

1

1981; Menzel/Senghaas 1986). Yet, the proclaimed thesis of the incompatibility of the state functions of modernization and stabilization denotes a virtually insoluble dilemma here, as well (Simonis 1985:176). Further, when it is formulated in such an absolute way, this thesis can be only of limited use for a productive line of inquiry. The Third World, faced with obvious shortcomings and deficiencies, has no serious alternative to socioeconomic development, nor can it do without some degree of regular state intervention and political continuity. The only feasible way to escape this contradiction is to attempt a more precise definition of the notion of stability: forms of political stability must be found that are both sufficient to set economic and social reforms in motion and yet flexible enough to withstand self-induced changes within the political framework. Since this balance has rarely been achieved—in reality, there are only cases with mixed results—the comparison of some suitable states is a particularly useful way of examining the links between political and economic development more closely.

The balance between stability and development is of particular interest in the cases analyzed here: Kenya, Tanzania, and Uganda. With regard to certain central factors (e.g., geographic and climatic conditions, availability of natural resources, ethnic composition, type of colonial development, international economic dependencies, a period of institutionalized cooperation in the East African Community), they show considerable similarities, indicating that a systematic comparative analysis, in the sense of a most similar systems design (see Przeworski/Teune 1970) may be particularly rewarding. On the other hand, the developments that have taken place since independence, in respect to political systems, economic policies, and socioeconomic development, are widely different. The three states can to a certain extent be regarded as prototypes that typify development paths, with their specific strengths and weaknesses, taken elsewhere. Tanzania has long been regarded as a model of an independent African socialism (see e.g. Rosberg/Friedman 1964; Pfenning/Voll/Weber 1980). Kenya has followed a clearly peripheral-capitalist development path, with semicompetitive features on the political level (see Leys 1974; Berg-Schlosser 1979a; on the concept *semicompetitive* see Hermet et al. 1978), while Uganda has embodied a torn praetorian society with political chaos and economic decline (see, for example, Mamdani 1976; Wiebe/Dodge 1987; on the concept *praetorianism* see Huntington 1968).

In view of the small number of cases and the multitude of variables to be considered, however, both extensive macro-quantitative analyses on a statistical basis and narrowly conceived quasi-experimental designs, (as in the method of difference of J. S. Mill), which have the objective of directly isolating a few factors, must be discounted as unsuitable for any comprehensive study (see Aarebrot/Bakka 1987). Instead, we use a differentiated interaction model, which does justice to the complexities of the contexts.

This model leans on a systems approach, but one that consciously includes concrete influences, in a structural-comparative and historical sense, such as colonialism, class structures, and continuing world economic conditions. The systems model offers an important frame of reference for an essential first step: a configurative analysis of each case, which gives suitable consideration to the complexitiy of the particular constellation of factors and the specifics of their interrelationships in the historical process.

In a second step, systematic paired comparisons (Rokkan 1970) allow the common features and, more especially, the differences to be determined, even where, as here, there is a limited number of cases. It is then possible, in a third stage, to make an overall comparison and isolate some characteristic key variables, which in turn offer important points of reference for the evaluation of the chosen development paths and the factors determining them.

The information gained has to some extent a paradigmatic character with regard to this methodology: it can illustrate the degree to which a differentiated analysis of political conditions is capable of determining the requisites for concrete development efforts with regard to both internal and external aspects. It therefore goes much further than the commercial political risk analyses that have frequently been undertaken but are often of questionable value, from the point of view of both method and content (see, e.g., Ruloff 1987). Nevertheless, we must draw attention to certain limitations of our method and the results obtained.

The number and quality of data sources available are necessarily linked to the subject of the study itself. Political conditions and development in Kenya are relatively well documented, (with the usual reservations of the trustworthiness of the data). This is also true of the corresponding time series, regional distributions, and similar aspects. In Tanzania, however, the amount of up-to-date statistical material is clearly limited, and in Uganda data of this kind are frequently nonexistent or are inconsistent in many respects, so that one has to be content with more or less rough estimates and extrapolations. The presentation of the Kenyan case demonstrates what would have been desirable in all cases—for example, in the differentiated social structural analysis, chronological documentations, and regional distributions. Nevertheless, the literature used here is extensive and includes a large amount of relatively inaccessible "gray" material, such as the Conference on the Arusha Declaration in December 1986 in Tanzania, and the meeting of the African Association of Political Science on Constitutionalism and Political Stability in the East African Region in Kenya in January 1987.

Equally, the generalizability of our results remains limited, in view of the fact that the study has been restricted to three cases. However, insofar as the states in question can be classified into general system types, it is possible to formulate more-concrete hypotheses (though it would be desirable to check the results using a systematically varied—e.g., West African francophone—context). Individual conclusions that might be more universally valid could also be tested in a most different systems design (Przeworski/Teune 1970).

A final reservation must be expressed regarding the concrete, prognostic nature of these analyses. Studies of this kind can be carried out only at the level of concrete structural analysis and specific processes and tensions, which limits to a certain range the potentialities of possible developments. We cannot anticipate the level of concrete actions to be expected from the groups and persons concerned. They have, ultimately, the chance to turn our analyses into self-fulfilling or into self-defeating prophecies!

I
Specification of Analysis

1
A Model of Interaction

In order to identify the factors that constitute political stability and to understand the reciprocal effect between these factors and the level of development that has been reached, it is necessary first to establish an appropriate theoretical framework for the categories to be used. With the highest possible degree of operationalization and sufficient universality, these categories must be applicable to various political orders and phenonema, so that it is possible to use them as a basis for determining characteristic differences and comparable aspects.

These requirements are particularly well met by the concept of the political system that authors such as David Easton (1965), Karl W. Deutsch (1961), and Gabriel A. Almond (Almond/Powell 1966) have developed for the empirical analysis of political phenomena. A systems model, which relates different dimensions of political reality to each other in a classificatory way, enhances understanding of individual cases and the multifaceted interrelationships of political determining factors. Used in this pretheoretical sense, the model is not yet able, by itself, to define causal relationships in social reality. However, this kind of framework is necessary before we can consider any particular historical case more abstractly, conducting comparative analysis and identifying relevant variables. The systems model is based on a notion of politics that Easton defines as "the authoritative distribution of possessions and values within society." In this sense, a political system is a system of decisionmaking, wherein the decisions concerning distribution assume a binding character on all members of the society. This is further underlined by sanctions that are potentially valid for the whole of society (Easton 1965: 21, 153).

The word *system* must be understood as a complex of interdependent, interacting parts with definable limits; as a fitting together of mutually dependent parts. The reciprocity of all the parts means that if one element is altered, there is a more or less pronounced change in the whole system. All in all, a system can be seen as a whole that preserves its identity in a complex and changeable environment (Almond/Powell 1978:5ff). As in cybernetic processes, one can consider the reciprocity between political system and society or environment as a circulation of inputs and outputs (see Diagram 1). The inputs, which in a way form the raw material of the political, process and set it in motion, are turned by the transformation processes of the political system into outputs that result in actions directed toward the society.

7

These outputs can then become the basis for new inputs, which refer more or less directly back to the previous outputs. Through this feedback the system can react successfully and flexibly to the demands placed on it (Easton 1965:18, 29; Almond/Powell 1978:9).

Diagram 1 shows the continuous flow of influences from the environment to the political system. Only the effects that are relevant to the political system operate as inputs, which, according to Easton (1965:29), always take on the form of demands or supports. The demands made by society on the political system are concerned with distributing or extracting resources, for example, or with regulating behavior, gratifying the need for political communication, or allowing for participation in the political process. Without, at the same time, social support in the form of taxes, services, obedience, loyalty, participation in political acts, and so on, the system would be unable to function (Almond/Powell 1978:10ff.; Hartmann 1987:31f). The transformation initiated by these interests and demands is carried out within the political system by the authorities through institutions provided with special powers to decide how and to what extent individual demands are to be granted. They undertake the distribution, obligatory within the society, of resources, both material and immaterial, that come to them through the support mechanisms.

The corresponding outputs can be characterized as distributive, extractive, regulative, or symbolic (that is, useful in the broadest sense of the word for political communication [Easton 1965:31; Almond/Powell 1978:11]). Insofar as these outputs signify the gratification or nongratification of demands, they contribute to a strengthening or weakening of the supports that accompany demands. Political systems have to rely in the long run on sufficient supports and these can be optimized with the aid of feedback mechanisms. Outputs are transformed by the overall social system; thus, demands can again arise, for a further cycle as it were, and reach the political system as feedback (in Diagram 1 this aspect is shown by a broken line). These further demands provide the authorities with information on the consequences of previous outputs and enable decision to be corrected. In this way an autonomous system arises which can regulate itself. It is therefore necessary, when analysing the conditions for the stability of systems in a rapidly changing environment, to pay particular attention to the ability to form this kind of "feedback loop" (Easton 1965: 31 f).

If the authorities are unable to produce and consolidate sufficient permanent supports, they can try for a limited time to counter lack of support through repression. In the long run, however, this will lead to a buildup of dissatisfaction, and an increasingly high price will have to be paid for superficial stability. The results are crises or breakdowns of the system. The latter is particularly the case when the system's legitimacy has been undermined in the course of its development and demands of a different quality are being made. This is, for example, true of the transition from forms of traditional legitimacy to a rational-legal type wherein large numbers of the population are demanding increasing participation (see Huntington 1968).

SOCIAL BASES

Despite Easton's comprehensive use of the term *environment*, the immediate social surroundings doubtless have a particular significance for the analysis of political systems. To specify the social bases of political processes, we find it useful to employ the AGIL-schema developed by Parsons, in which actions and their structural embodiments, or roles, which go to make up social systems, are used as basic units. The typology contained in the AGIL-schema of general fields of action deriving from its general problems of orientation can also be applied to the political system (see Diagram 2). The two dimensions—contingency of action and complexity of symbols—whose scopes range from reduced to extended forms, are the basis for an action space that is divided into quadrants. Contingency of action denotes the range of various possible actions, while symbol complexity describes the hypothetical background of action that can be expressed in symbols (terms of speech). If both dimensions are present in their extented form, they describe an extensive opening of actions directed toward the environment (adaptation). In the opposite case, Münch (1982), who has modified Parsons's schema for the analysis of sociocultural aspects, refers to a closing against the system's surroundings (integration). The task of determining a particular action when symbol complexity is extended (goal attainment) is associated with specification. The use of existing cultural formulae in order to justify decisions that open up new fields of action is represented by the action-type generalization (latent pattern maintenance); Pappi (1986:282) characterizes its achievement as the expansion of possibilities of action through a greater possibility of subsumption under a particular code.

When the whole society is taken as the system of reference, it is possible to identify not only a political subsystem but three other subsystems: economic; community; and social-cultural. This division into four subsystems of social action can be seen as a concretization of the four types of action defined in the action space. The political subsystem serves to bring about and implement decisions that obligate the whole of society and so complies with the characteristics of specification; the economic or exchange subsystem is meant to ensure an efficient distribution of all resources while taking individual preferences into consideration; the community subsystem is responsible for generating a subjective sense of solidarity and guarantees the integration or closing of the society to the outside world; and the social-cultural subsystem is built up around intellectual discourse, which by means of the construction of obligatory symbols for society performs the duty of generalization (Pappi 1986:281f).

As far as the social bases are concerned, there are social-structural and political-cultural elements to be examined in particular. This procedure follows the central distinction between structure and culture in the theory of political systems. Whereas structures constitute the objective dimension of politics, culture relates to the subjective dimension. This dimension, in the form of values, perceptions, and expectations of the people who are concerned with the political events at any one time, represents an essential aspect of political reality (Almond/Powell 1978:12f).

Categories of social structural analysis. The kind of structural differentiations of a society can be determined both horizontally, referring to groups that exist side by side, and vertically, referring to groups that exist in a hierarchical relationship. Structural analyses in the tradition of social stratification theories, however, remain arbitrary in their descriptions because of the haphazard way in which their categories are formed (see, e.g., Warner 1960). Through lack of a basic social theory they also fail to give an insight into the number and extent of the most important political conflict groups at any one time, or to show how they have evolved historically in the vertical dimension or are latent as a result of objectifiable opposing interests. In contrast, the model used here employs a differentiated class analysis that relates directly to Third World situations and provides categories that are theoretically meaningful and empirically controllable without lapsing into dogmatic constraint and the rather undifferentiated perspectives of many Marxist authors (for substantiation and criticism, see Berg-Schlosser 1979b).

The essential determinant of the categories used here lies in the relationship of individuals and groups to the means of production as an expression of an interest that must in each case be ascertained objectively and that can be considered to be dominant for the establishment of these groups (see Diagram 3). Following Marx's example, a distinction is made regarding the ownership of means of production. On the one hand, there is the proletariat (without ownership), on the other, the bourgeoisie (with ownership). A second facet of this relationship goes beyond formal ownership and refers to the actual powers of decisionmaking over means of production. The pure capitalist, who is exclusively an owner of capital, can thus be distinguished from the managing director. A third element to be considered is the power of disposal on the grounds of political control (e.g., immediate control in nationalized concerns, parastatals, etc.), or through the setting up and shaping of a framework of political, legal, or other conditions. On this basis it is possible to define a bureaucratic bourgeoisie (Shivji 1976) or state class (for this term, see Elsenhans 1981), which—depending on the political system—differ both in structure and in importance.

For the owners of means of production there is a second differentiation that rests on the dominant source of income. Here we have three groups: (1) those who receive their income almost exclusively from capital rent;

(2) those whose income results in more or less equal parts from their own work and their ownership of means of production; and (3) those who rely almost exclusively on their own work if they are in a formal sense self-supporting. We follow Geiger (1932) in calling the last group "proletaroids." They earn their living as day laborers on their own account or as small shop owners with no assistance from paid employees. The proletaroids can thus be analytically separated from the proletariat, as—although they share broadly speaking, the same chances in life—the former can be formally distinguished by their independence and often by their degree of awareness.

Persons without ownership of means of production are categorized according to the extent of their powers of decisionmaking over means of production. The spectrum extends from top management across a middle level where we find among others, master tradesmen, heads of departments, and members of the technical and commercial wage-dependent "intelligentsia," down to the proletariat, which has no powers of decisionmaking. In this way we can avoid a subsumption of these groups under the uniform heading of wage dependents as this tends to gloss over the objective opposing interests among these groups and their usually different forms of political organization. Persons without a fixed income or without any other definable relationship to the means of production, often to be found as marginalized groups in the Third World, are covered by the term *subproletariat*.

In the last step of our analysis we differentiate according to economic sectors. As managers of public utilities (parastatals) are closely linked to the state class, there has to be a distinction within this group between public and private sectors. Particularly relevant to less-industrialized states is the further subdivision of the private sector into agricultural and nonagricultural spheres. The middle and lower levels of decisionmaking in the public sector are comparable with the corresponding categories in the private sector. The wage dependents with a medium capacity for decisionmaking are referred to here as the "salariat." In other studies, which often remain rather vague in their definitions, this category is often termed the new middle class as opposed to the old middle class of the petite bourgeoisie. The owner entrepreneurs characterized in our classification as petite bourgeoisie can be defined in the agricultural regions of East Africa as having more than two hectares of land, in contrast to the agricultural proletaroids who are first and foremost concerned with growing enough to live on. Large-scale farmers and landed proprietors, who have come into existence only through colonial influences, own more than twenty hectares. In the nonagricultural sphere the petite bourgeoisie can be defined by the ownership of a business with up to ten employees.

There are not only antagonistic relations between these groups, but one can also reckon with symbiotic-complementary relations (as, for example, between capitalists and managers) or autonomous ones (such as for agrarian proletaroids and the subproletariat). Furthermore, there is in reality often an overlapping of categories (e.g., through a mixture of forms of ownership and employment or through family ties). The aim must always be to augment the establishment of quantitative changes and the degree of intra- and intergenerational mobility with an analysis of the capacities for conflict and organization and the reciprocal, objective areas of interest, so that the social and political processes which are developing along this basis can be adequately understood (see, e.g., Olson 1965; Offe 1969). A concrete interaction of horizontal and vertical aspects of social stratification can also be particularly significant for the formation of political conflict groups. Thus, whichever class structure we look at must be brought into relationship with racial, ethnic, and confessional patterns. It is very seldom a question of ethnic or religious conflict per se, as these usually concern economic or political matters. A careful analysis of conflict groups will therefore need to pay very special attention to these interactions of various social-structural dimensions.

Political-cultural aspects. The subjective dimension of politics is usually termed *political culture* nowadays. It relates to the sociocultural framework of political systems and the concrete forms of its historical character. Political culture can be defined here as the collective whole of all beliefs, attitudes, and values that refer to, and give meaning to, the political process and that enter political reality as subjective predispositions. Seen as a collective, political culture depicts the psychological and subjective dimension in politics in, as it were, an aggregate form (Pye 1968; Elkins/Simeon 1979:129; Reichel 1981:21; Berg-Schlosser 1985c).

If one accepts Almond's classification of various aspects of political systems, then important features of political culture can be grouped together in the following way: on the system level (polity), questions concerning the manner and extent of the political system's legitimacy, as well as the national and social consensus, play the major role; on the process level (politics), the main emphasis is on the orientations that determine the manner and extent of participation in political life; the policy level, on the other hand, spotlights preferences regarding political issues and how these preferences are distributed (Almond/Powell 1978:25ff). An important premise of this concept is the assumption that political behavior is for the most part acquired. That is, in political socialization, political culture develops through a continual interplay between the historical and topical experiences that influence both the outlook of a society and each individual life history of its members. In this way it is possible to determine, approximately, the characteristics of a political culture by using the assessments of those who know the country well and the analysis of symbols, rituals, and traditions of public life, even if the results of survey research are not available (see Pye 1968; Kaase 1983:153ff).

The founders of political-cultural studies strove to identify conditions under which democratic regimes could be stable in a phase of social modernization. They believed stability could be guaranteed wherever a specific political culture was combined with an adequate system of government. More recent authors formulate this idea more cautiously and refer only to the independent contribution the subjective dimension can make in explaining continuity or change in political systems. They see political culture as a grid that gives structure to the perception of situations and consequently to the perception of areas in which action can take place (Elkins/ Simeon 1979:127ff.; Pappi 1986:280; Reichel 1981:28f., 36ff.).

We can attempt to place political culture in its social environment with the aid of the AGIL-schema (see Diagram 4). Within this classification political culture corresponds essentially to the action-type specification. At its core it can be defined as "consent to the legitimacy of the political order of a system, a consent that is on the one hand upheld by consensual norms and loyalty to the political community and anchored on the other hand in political value orientations" (Pappi 1986:282). The ability of political systems to function is always revealed sooner or later through asking how far members of the system who disagree with particular political decisions are obliged to accept them, tolerate them, or, under the influence of forces that we characterize in more detail for our three cases, submit to them. Tensions and conflicts can arise among the various social subsystems, and these can have a politically destabilizing effect or can in the long run even lead to the collapse of the system. If acceptance can be won only by gratifying concrete demands and expectations (in the sense of specific supports) then it is part of the political system of exchange and must be kept separate from the core of political culture. This does not exclude the possibility, however, that long-term satisfaction with the economic and political balance of achievement becomes as it were capitalized and, taking on the form of consent to legitimacy, acquires permanence. Political loyalty and a political sense of values are, however, essential components of political culture, as they both act as agents for basic patterns of orientations. If individuals take their membership in the system completely for granted, a demarcation between the group, in the sense of a community, and the outside world is ensured. Political loyalty means basically that political support is rooted in the community system. It consists of common symbols and rituals and of norms founded on consensus. Political values are generalized in social-cultural systems with the aid of discussion and argument. Decisions made by the political institutions must be justified by checking them against the elementary pattern of values, and discursive strategies must be developed to subsume decisions under central values of political order. While considering this functional perspective, we must not lose sight of the destabilizing potential that can exist in these processes (Pappi 1986:284ff.). Thus, the analysis of political-cultural aspects must always establish how far the social subsystems are in agreement with the political subsystem.

INPUT STRUCTURES

The particular suitability of the structural-functional approach for comparative analysis arises from the definition of universal functions that are prerequisites for all political systems and whose accomplishment can be identified and compared in concrete political structures (e.g., unions, political parties, parliaments, law courts, bureaucracies). Following the cybernetic model, we must differentiate among input, conversion, and ouput structures: input structures convey demands and supports to the central political system; conversion processes—by which the flow of inputs is transformed to outputs—run through four stations, each of which is defined by universal functions, and articulation of interests and their aggregation belong in the input area. Both of the other part functions of the political process—that is to say, ultimate course directions and the decision for a particular policy and its implementations—already come under the central political system. The political process comes into motion when individuals or groups register political demands and reinforce them by using the resources at their disposal within society, either as promises (referring to future action or accompanied by present action) or other means of pressure (e.g., violence). As these demands must be made publicly, institutional and organizational arrangements are needed for the formulation and articulation of interests.

In the same way, the aggregation of interests needs specialized structures according to social level of development. The manifold individual interests must be aggregated to form more complex alternatives of political action, but they will have a chance to succeed only if they manage to mobilize sufficient social resources for this purpose (existing or potential seats in the legislature, civil rights, possibilities of economic influence, etc.). This is true also of other organized interests that have been brought together by means of a complex process and, temporarily at least, remain under one heading. In the case of competitive multiparty systems, aggregation processes can lead to temporary pacts and the formation of coalition governments (Almond/Powell 1978:14f.; Berg-Schlosser/Maier/Stammen 1985a:185f).

It often happens that the structures that serve both these functions are also concerned with the realization of the third important function in the input area: the recruitment of personnel for political office.

Intermediary groups. Groups that act for major economic interests (employers' associations, trade unions, organized groups in the agricultural field, etc.) and that have their own apparatus and organizational regulations, represent today the most important structures for the aggregation of interests, but the significance of less-specialized networks of social communication should not be underestimated. Systems of patronage, for example, whereby a particular clientele ensures politicians political support in return for guarantees of particular advantages, represent an essential factor of political reality (Jackson/Rosberg 1983–1984). At the same time there are often intermediary groups of a different kind, rooted in traditions of informal social structures and used only occasionally to articulate demands. The degree of organization and the ability to provoke conflict (including the potential for refusing to give what is due) in all these groups are important factors in their ability to gain ground. Both the modern organizations and the forms of interest aggregation linked to intermediary groups and concerning for example, the influence of ethnic factors and precolonial traditions are of interest for our analysis (Almond/Powell 1978:143ff., 170ff).

The more differentiated and specialized structures of interest aggregation are, and the more complex the network of channels that lead to the elite (personal contacts, representatives in the various institutions and the mass media), the more flexible are the system's possibilities of response. The degree of autonomy enjoyed by these structures—that is, their independence or their control and regulation by the political leadership—has an important influence on the efficiency of communication between society and the political system. Wherever their field is substantially limited by control from above, a considerable deformation of the flow of information and a subsequent possibility of destabilization must be reckoned with (Almond/Powell 1978:149f., 178ff., 193). When analysing organized groups in any political system, there are further concrete matters to be dealt with concerning their position and function in society, their inner structure, their programs, what actions they take when asserting their goals, and their importance for citizens' participation in the political process.

Political parties. Structures that are already involved in the articulation of interests are often also concerned in their aggregation. Additionally, in complex political systems, independent organizations have often developed in the form of political parties. These differ from associations or unions in that their aim is to influence political decisionmaking in an immediate and exclusive way. The influence of bureaucracy and the army on the aggregation of interests can sometimes be considerable, but they are often rejected because their hierarchical organization, designed for specific duties, cannot sufficiently fulfil the requirements of aggregation.

The comparison of political party systems is concentrated on their competitive character, apparent not only in the relations between different parties but also in internal party relationships or in aspects of political action in parliaments and in the executive. The competitive nature of parties constitutes the core of Dahl's (1971) polyarchy concept, which emphasizes the pluralistic character of the party system, with its basis of regular political competition and its generally accepted mechanisms of election and change. One-party systems that use mechanisms of open competition to fill a considerable part of their political positions, and multiparty systems in which there are restrictions concerning the admission of parties, both fit into Hermet's (1978) category of semicompetitive systems. The other extreme on this continuum is represented by one-party systems without regular mechanisms of competition and by political systems without party structures. Alongside the internal decision structure and readiness of access we must also analyze in this context the regulations for elections and succession in office (Berg-Schlosser 1984d:11f; Almond/Powell 1978:205ff., 220ff).

The degree to which parties can act successfully depends on their actual procedures for solving conflict, and these can be founded in the respective groups of people and in the political culture of a society. "Historical-communalistic lines of tension," which uphold racist, ethnic, or religious conflicts as relevant forces over a long period of time, can be expressed on a party political level in such a way that they curtail parties' ability to compromise and thus prevent an open contest for "floating" voters. Not only the number of parties, however, but also their specific basis and structure is important in order to judge their respective capacity for competition.

THE CENTRAL POLITICAL SYSTEM

The major function of the political system as far as society is concerned is handled by the government, in that it transforms politically relevant demands into authoritative decisions. It is important to distinguish analytically between the phase of political decisionmaking (policymaking) and that of converting policies into concrete acts (policy implementation), which is often carried out by the bureaucracy, although in fact, it is not always possible to make a clear separation between the two.

Institutional aspects. The three functions of the central political system—namely, rule-making, rule application and rule adjudication—are similar to the classical categories of legislature, executive, and judiciary, but enable us to analyze the horizontal divisions of authority without losing sight of the actual divisions of competence among those institutions. Authoritarian systems (Linz 1975) can chiefly be distinguished by two features: (1) the main supporting forces behind the system are not required to stand for election; (2) there is no regular delegation of authority to forces outside the immediate circle of leadership or any other form of institutionalized separation of powers (Almond/Powell 1978:237). Measured against the extensive separation of powers in many presidential democracies, parliamentary-democratic systems (wherein executive and legislature are closely connected) present a limited form of separation of powers. An independent judicial system guarantees, however, both civil rights and liberties as well as control over the processes of legislation and administration, if the parliament does not entirely fulfil these functions itself.

The degree of institutionalization and the formalization of duties, relationships, and methods of recruitment determine on the one hand the transparency of the procedures used to settle conflicts and, on the other hand, represent an important factor in determining the efficiency of a system. In a typological sense, a distinction has to be made between violent usurpations (e.g., in military dictatorships) or traditional arrangements (e.g., succession by inheritance in monarchies) and the recruitment of a circle of leaders by election. In contrast to competitive-democratic procedures, there are also concordant-democratic methods (Lijphart 1977) by which an attempt is made in the appointment to high positions of state to limit conflicts arising from subcultural tensions (e.g., between denominational or ethnic groups) through institutional arrangements (e.g., proportional rights, rights of veto).

The concrete right to vote for institutions of public representation defines the chances of participation for wide circles of the population and so determines the extent to which political systems and their powers of integration are firmly established in society. Furthermore the social basis of a regime is partially reflected in its ideological orientation, which is shown in the recruitment of leading representatives from particular sociocultural groups and classes (which we have defined earlier in this chapter; see also Berg-Schlosser 1984d:5ff).

Actual power structure. Analysis of actual power structures deals with the combination of different social groups that, together, form the top of the political system, and with the nature of political relationships at the top. As a result of traditional influences, politics in African societies often appears as a hierarchical mesh of personal connections; for example, between influential politicians as patrons and their various clienteles. There are further forms of actual power structure: a structure may be confined to a small, self-contained collective (e.g., a military junta) or it may be built up in a wider and more representative way and thus try to integrate the most important social groups in a pluralistic sense (see for examples, Berg-Schlosser 1984d). Political corruption and rivalry between leaders of groups, kept for the most part out of the public eye and not primarily based on common social interests or political strategies, should also be considered. Taken from this perspective it seems important to judge carefully the forms of corruption and nepotism often found in various degrees in developing countries, which can cause considerable damage to the efficiency of their systems (see Jackson/Rosberg 1983–1984:431ff).

OUTPUT STRUCTURES

The bureaucratic apparatus carries out extractive, distributive, regulative, or symbolic actions (outputs); that is, it implements policies. To do its job, it must be granted the competence to decide its own rules for implementation. The administration thus has an important role in the execution of laws, and in extreme cases it can counteract the intentions of the political leadership. It is important here to differentiate between the actions (outputs) and their concrete social effects (outcomes) (Almond/Powell 1978:283ff).

Administrative structure and behavior. Generally speaking, the effectiveness of the administration grows in proportion to the differentiation and specialization of its structures, and also with the degree to which its structures penetrate society. Increasing problems of communication can, however, reduce administrative effectiveness considerably. The payment of personnel, the freedom of decisionmaking for each civil servant, and the controllability of administrative rulings are factors that must be considered when assessing corruption and nepotism. The "gray" zone, an area that is felt to be more or less permissible between plain corruption and administrative dealings that keep strictly to the rules, can be defined primarily in a cultural way. In view of the ethnic heterogencity in most African states, the patterns of recruitment contribute strongly to the degree to which the bureaucracy is accepted by society.

The repressive apparatus. The execution of the monopoly of state power in the output field is the task of the security forces. Either as police, army, paramilitary organization or secret service, such forces have various duties and structures. The experience of many states in the Third World has shown the army to be—contrary to its originally intended uses—an internal political danger for many regimes. Often, as a result of failed military coups, civil regimes have tried to develop structures that balance the concrete advantage the army possesses; namely, the legitimate power of disposal over weapons. Paramilitary militias or special units that are separate from the army can counterbalance this factor. Forms of subjective control can be achieved by means of specific recruitment through which it is ensured that military personnel and the political leadership have the same interests in mind. In African states a key aspect, which has come into existence since colonial times, lies in the ethnic composition of the army. Subjective controls can also be achieved, however, by means of a professional ethos in the army that enables it to accept subordination to political leadership.

Effective control over the repressive apparatus also manifests the ability of a system to enforce universal normative standards. It can easily be seen in many military dictatorships and repressive regimes that massive violations of human rights and a considerable curtailment of participation and democratic legitimacy are closely and complexly connected (Rüland/Werz 1985:223ff.; Illy et al. 1980). The behavior of security forces in respecting human rights is a strong indicator of a normative evaluation of a political system, but it also illustrates the quality of its procedures for dealing with conflicts.

FEEDBACK TO THE SOCIAL SYSTEM

The output of a political system returns through its social consequences, is transformed through the political-cultural conditions into input, and can, in an ideal situation, enable a gradual optimization of political strategies. In many respects a political system's field of action is determined by its social bases, but long-term policies, if they are constantly adhered to, also help to shape these structures. In this way outputs can mainly benefit particular social groups, either preserving the status quo or introducing social-structural changes. Agricultural structure, which is a most important area for developing countries, can be directly influenced through the stratification policy of a regime, by for example, land reforms, or taxation, or through the intervention of the state in the marketing of products, parastatal agricultural credit and extension services, and so on. If state policy leads to economic successes that can be felt by wide strata of the population, and if these positive results continue, they can lead to a permanent gain in legitimacy for a political system in the political-cultural field.

EXTERNAL FACTORS

Within the dimensions of the world economy, with its manifold forms of economic dependence, there are specific differences between countries that can be seen as subject to political interventions in order to overcome remaining colonial structures. For some years now, the obstructive and destructive potential of resources flowing from bilateral and multilateral development aid has also been under discussion (see e.g., Nuscheler 1987). The world-political dimension of the Third World becomes evident in its relationships to the world's political blocs, in its activities in international organizations, in the North–South dialog, or in the informal continuation of former colonial dependencies. In many regions there are also attempts to achieve regular cooperation in economic, political, cultural, and infrastructural matters. Nonetheless, regional conflicts, which are often severe and include not only open warfare but also hidden support for insurgent movements in neighboring countries, must not be overlooked as a security risk.

2

Identification
of Central Notions

POLITICAL STABILITY IN THE
FRAMEWORK OF SYSTEMS THEORY

A differentiated concept of political legitimacy in a dynamic sense is of
major importance for understanding stability in the context of systems
theory. Starting from a more general, development-theoretical context, the
notion of stability must be operationalized more concretely in the present-
day, real situation in Africa. The stability of a regime always rests on its
ability to deal successfully with actual or potential conflicts and challenges,
and the prognosis of stability equally rests on our reading of a regime's
capabilities (see Dowding/Kimber 1983:237, 241). Since the 1970s and
especially after events such as the Islamic revolution in Iran or the downfall
of the Marcos regime in the Philippines, which demonstrated that business
abroad can be carried out only on the basis of an adequate estimation of
political risks, multinational corporations have increasingly demanded such
prognoses. A great many recipes have been applied, put together according
to the specific requirements of various customers, that attempted, in
particular, to detect risks at a level below regime breakdown.

The terminology used in such assessments, which are supposed to give
quick, pragmatic, and intersubjectively controllable results, usually implies a
systems-theoretical background. Overholt (1982:326ff.), for example, claims
that the method recommended by him has the advantage of integrating many
different observations and interpretations of phenomena. His "organizational" approach sees politics as organized conflict and establishes an
analysis of politically relevant organizations divided into three categories: (1)
quality of personal leadership; (2) quality of institutional structure; and (3)
quantity and quality of the mass base of these organizations. All this is
reminiscent of structural-functional model analyses, but the use of a
simplified "check list" definitely limits the depth of assessment. Although
the "Issue-Actor-Analysis" (Rayfield 1982:343f.) and the "Prince model"
(Coplin/O'Leary 1982:333ff.) make use of the theory of interaction and
communication, they both deal almost exclusively with political events
linked to concrete issues and persons. Other patterns of analysis (e.g., Nacht
1982:348f.) recommend a list of questions that, although they seem plausible
in individual aspects, have a fragmentary, divided character that exhibits a
lack of logical stringency and theoretical consistency. The superficiality of

such analyses is shown in the results; for example, one report on the stability of the Marcos regime, for 1980, forecast a 60 percent probability that it would withstand the next eighteen months (Coplin/O'Leary 1982:335ff). Prognoses on this level venture to forecast developments that depend to an incalculable degree, just as the fates of individual leading personalities do, on historical "accidents" and coincidences. This kind of analysis may suit some specific interests, but on the whole it implies a largely static notion of stability, confined to continuity in political leadership (see Ruloff 1987).

In contrast, stability in a wider, systems-theoretical sense means a dynamic balance that is distinguished by a synchronous course of structural and cultural changes that are adjusted to each other. A well-functioning political system does not react only by refusing or fulfilling demands; it can also make flexible and creative use of a repertoire of alternative actions, including limited changes within the system (Huntington/Domínguez 1975:7; Easton 1965:19ff.; Almond/Powell 1978:64). Thus, stability means the continuity of a system in its fundamental components, but it explicitly permits a gradual change in less-important aspects (Dowding/Kimber 1983:233f). The problem for the observer is to decide whether a change remains within the framework of the elements that constitute the system, or whether it has already begun to go beyond the system (for a brief survey of the notion of stability, see Svensson 1986:129ff). A system's stability becomes, in a concrete sense, its endurability; the system is able to regulate, by means of its own authoritative decisions, conflicts that threaten its existence. Such regulation cannot take place over long periods of time if it does not have the support or the consent of sufficiently large parts of society, even if brute force and institutionalized acts of terror are directed at important sections of the population in order to enforce obedience.

Easton's notion of support refers both to actions such as paying taxes, observing laws, and taking part in elections, and to attitudes that evaluate the political system functionally and normatively. The spectrum of these attitudes ranges from rejection through passive acceptance or indifference, to strong consent and personal identification (Easton 1975:436). According to the kind and degree of such supports, the central political system can assess the quality and quantity of supportive acts it may expect. The basis of legitimacy of a political system thus defines the field of action for the exchange of inputs and outputs with society and also has a decisive influence on the efficiency of its central institutions (Easton 1965:153; Kaase 1985: 101f). If support arises from satisfaction with the daily outputs and their effects, Easton speaks of "specific support." "Diffuse support," on the other hand, refers to a consent that is given to political institutions and personalities for their own sake and not because of any immediate action. One can compare diffuse political support with a reservoir of goodwill that either exists or is lacking, but that, in the short run, is independent of disappointments caused by the nongratification of demands (Easton 1975:436f., 444ff).

In a vertical sense, levels of support refer to the political community, the regime, the authorities, and the incumbents. "Political community" means all the members of a political system, in a wide sense, living together in a nation-state. Among its essential features is a certain amount of national and social consensus. A set of basic values, norms, and provisions for institutional structures is considered to be a constituent component of a regime. Values, in this context, formulate the general political aims that are accepted by society, whereas norms determine the field of action of operational rules and procedures. Thus, a regime is not defined by constitutional norms alone, and neither is it to be seen as a fixed structure. Its flexibility, which is of great relevance to systems theory, becomes evident in the course of continual but limited change. The authorities consist of the government and its supporting forces, the political parties, and other institutions at the top of the political system. As they are conceived as a conglomerate of authoritative roles, each actual incumbent must, strictly speaking, be considered on his or her separate level (Easton 1965:177, and passim).

Only the authorities and the incumbents can enjoy specific support as a reward for political achievements; for example, in the form of popularity of parties or politicians (Easton 1975:437). Diffuse political support is, however, possible at all levels. If it sinks below a critical point, there is the danger that the authorities will not be able to cope with the processes of transformation and implementation. Because there is always some delay before the social effects of outputs appear and because all systems have limited capacity, and there will always be some members whose demands have not been fully satisfied, systems cannot exist permanently without diffuse support for the regime and the political community. The diffuse supports for a regime, independent of its daily outputs, constitute its legitimacy. Because diffuse support can penetrate to the higher levels, national consensus and political loyalty to the political community are of great significance for the stability of the regime and the authorities as well (Easton 1975:450). Legitimacy is rooted in the individual's conviction that the regime's ethical values correspond to his or her own, and that it is therefore right and proper to accept the authorities' decisions on the grounds that they are embedded in the regime. Another form of diffuse support—trust —arises from the generalization of output satisfaction. As trust is by nature a long-term commitment, it can be distinguished from specific support, which is orientated to short-term gains (Easton 1975:447ff).

Weber's (1964:157ff.) typology of the forms of legitimate authority defines three ideal-types: legal-rational, charismatic, and traditional legitimacy. In reality, we come across only mixed forms. As the ideal of constant, immediate, and critical reflection is conceivable only in a direct democracy within very small political units, the indispensable advance support consists to a great extent of habitual acceptance. With all forms of rational legitimacy, therefore, the institutionalized and regular mechanisms of change recruitment of the authorities play an important role. These feedback mechanisms, which ensure that the demands of the members of the system are taken into account, make rational legitimacy the essence of "modern" politics. This kind of legitimacy stipulates the political system's ability for constant renewal and vice versa; legitimacy in this sense is a fundamental prerequisite for political stability.

A strong basis of legitimacy gives the authorities a relatively secure position: as long as they keep within certain limits they can basically expect that their decisions will be accepted. On the other hand, it is a political necessity that the authorities do not try to gain this acceptance exclusively by force, and the social costs of doing so are formidable. Those in power must try to identify with at least some principles that the political community will recognize as a justification of their power (Easton 1965:278ff). Consent to legitimacy and national consensus develop in a "historical, collective process of learning that is transformed on the individual level by socialization mechanisms" (Kaase 1985:103). A continuous record of achievements can, when generalized, bring about not only an increase in trust but also a genuine increase in legitimacy. The fact that it is not dependent on outputs, at least for a certain length of time, guarantees that the authorities' mistakes and failures do not have much effect on the acceptance of the political order. The diffuse political support for the political community is even less susceptible to disturbances stemming from short-term disappointments.

As generally true as the preceding comments may be, the young states of African developing societies, most of which gained their independence in the early 1960s, face the task of nation-building. Because they are the artificial creation of the colonial powers, an explicit political strategy was needed to develop a national consensus and awaken a sense of national solidarity that could refer back to a common culture, language, and history, in spite of the great number of ethnic groups, most with little in common. If the citizens' loyalty is impaired by conflicts stemming from ethnic fragmentation, this is a potential threat to the legitimacy of the political system. And here lies the social-structural reason for the one-party systems to be found in many African states. In the cases where many political parties were active, the division along communalistic cleavages often proved disastrous (as, for example, in Nigeria and Uganda). In this context the main task of one-party systems is to institutionalize loyalty and authority. If institutionalized mechanisms are made available for ordered participation in the internal affairs of these systems, then the people's demands for participation can be canalized, given permanence, and serve the stabilization of the regime (see Apter 1965). The charismatic legitimacy of individual politicians can also become an important factor of national integration. Where leaders of independence movements took over the highest offices of state, their personal authority could be used to create a reservoir of diffuse political support for the regime and the political community (Easton 1965:304f).

One can imagine constellations wherein regimes are stable even if acceptance by the mass of citizens is either very low or altogether missing. Whether this rare condition is fulfilled where stability is guaranteed solely and exclusively by the legitimacy of the regime in the opinion of the elite, can be decided only by considering the complex interactions beween the degree of mobilization within the whole of society and the distribution of politically relevant resources among its most important groups. It would be premature to state that this is a characteristic phenomenon of developing societies in general.

With the aid of an index of social mobilization that measures the industrialization, degree of literacy, urbanization, and development of the mass media within a society, Deutsch (1961), among others, analysed the effects of these phenomena on the level of development of a political system. Macro-quantitative studies of this kind tried to prove the assertion that socioeconomic modernization goes hand in hand with political development in the sense of cultural secularization and structural differentiation. They confirmed a strong, positive correlation between a high social level of development and a distinctively competitive political system. Multiparty systems, a high level of participation, and a certain measure of rational legitimacy became the essence of political modernity (see, e.g., Huntington/Domínguez 1975: 33 ff). It turned out, however, that it is not always justifiable to equate political development with democratization. Political development, therefore, is mostly used in a more limited sense that refers to the differentiation and specialization of political institutions and their increasing complexity, or to the administrative capacity of regimes in general. Yet there are some who adhere to this paradigm of modernization theory and insist that secularization and differentiation, on the whole, heighten the efficiency of a system, even if there is a critical point beyond which these processes have a destabilizing effect (Almond/Powell 1978:358, 372). Huntington (1968), among others, has tried to come to grips with the instability that characterizes many regimes, despite processes of modernization, in his concept of transitory societies. Transitory societies are confronted, mainly through the effects of global demonstration, with demands for participation that cannot be fully realized for lack of adequate institutions. The consequent overloading of the political systems accounts for their instability.

Political stability includes both features of social tranquility and order and the possibility of gradual change within the boundaries of the system (Hurwitz 1973:449). Tranquility and order can be gauged with "political events" data (Taylor/Jodice 1983b), for example, which register expressions of instability such as unrest, armed rebellions, deaths as a result of violent internal struggles, or public protests. Such data, which are collected in a purely additive way and refer to a given time and place, by necessity leave out the underlying tensions that precede the events. Because these tensions can undermine stability, even when they are not manifested in tangible incidents, the use of such data should always be embedded in a historical-qualitative analysis that is able to give additional indications of the origins of critical situations and can point to more-significant social changes. Data concerning the size of the security forces also give a certain indication of the perception of internal stability by the authorities.

The extent and the efficiency of the feedback mechanisms constitute the main element of the second aspect of stability, the possibility of gradual change. Data on participation in elections, on the regular replacement of elected representatives (rotation of elites), and on the correctness and impartiality of election procedures must be examined against this background. Other forms of participation, such as taking part in self-help projects (for example, the Harambee projects in Kenya), are also to be considered in their quantitative aspects (see, e.g., Verba et al. 1978). As a criterion for the citizens' political field of action one must also consider the degree to which particular normative goals are realized. Our evaluation relies on two somewhat differently accentuated sources: the Index of Political Rights annually compiled by Freedom House in New York, and an index of political repression based on the annual reports of organizations such as Amnesty International and the International Commission of Jurists, and on similar materials (see Berg-Schlosser 1984d).

Conversely, it is possible to diagnose structural tensions in systems that appear stable but in which there are insufficient feedback mechanisms. System breakdowns may then lead to a qualitative change of the system type. In the majority of cases such transitions are abrupt and often violent; for example, military coups or revolutions. There are some cases, however—for example, in the progressive opening of authoritarian systems—for which it is possible to imagine gradual transitions leading in the end to a permanent, qualitative change.

DEVELOPMENT

The notion of development also needs closer specification. On the one hand it can be seen in the context of general development-theoretical discussions and the variously emphasized internal and external factors. On the other hand it must be placed beyond purely macroeconomic data into a multidimensional, socioeconomic relationship that also takes into consideration, for example, aspects of distribution and the satisfaction of basic needs of large parts of the population.

Economic development. Theories of modernization and dependence have, in spite of all their differences, many common points of reference, and in each the evaluation of world market integration (Boeckh 1985:63) has a key function. Modernization theory considers underdevelopment a "prehistoric condition of nature" as it were. Modernity develops as a result of integration into the world market and through the spreading of Western norms and values, and special development policies and projects are aimed at speeding up this process. In its transitional phase, society is divided into a modern sector and a traditional one, and tradition is regarded as a retarding factor that must be overcome. In contrast, the advocates of the *dependencia* approach see underdevelopment as a structural deformation that begins with integration into the world market and subsequently reproduces itself. Interacting sectoral discrepancies and structural heterogeneity characterize the economies of the Third World; instead of an integrated economy, distinguished by an industrial network producing investment and consumer goods, by a well-adjusted system of supplier and processing industries, and by a comprehensive domestic market, economic sectors with totally different productivity factors exist side by side (see e.g., Elsenhans 1986). With regard to commerce and services, the wide spectrum of the informal sector (see ILO 1972) can be contrasted with the official, state-licensed companies of the modern sector. Authors following a dualistic approach start with a strict division of these sectors of the economy, but it is somewhat more realistic to analyze, in conjunction with the notion of structural heterogeneity, their interacting aspects. For example, the subsistence economy of the traditional sector contributes to lowering the cost of living and so to a lower level of wages within the modern sector, while in the towns, the informal sector functions as a reservoir of labor and thus operates in the same direction.

These considerations emphasize the fact that the relevance of most available macroeconomic indicators is rather limited. As they rely on the results of official statistical assessments, they almost exclusively reflect the conditions of the modern sector and the official economy and thus tend to underestimate severely the contributions of the informal and subsistence sectors.

Social development. Behind the widespread criticism of the exclusive use of macroeconomic indicators (see, e.g., Nohlen/Nuscheler 1982:458), there is mistrust of development strategies, exemplified in the term *growth without development.* Experience has taught that it is not growth alone that should be the objective of development, but growth linked with an acceptably broad distribution of produced values. In our social structural analysis, aspects of distribution are determined by means of GINI coefficients of income distribution, by ethnic-regional disparities, and by the share of available land owned by large estates. The Physical Quality of Life Index (PQLI), developed by Morris, is useful as a summary index for measuring the development of material aspects of the overall conditions of life. The three components of this index—average life expectancy (at birth), infant mortality (between one and four years of age), and the rate of literacy (percentage of the population over fifteen years of age)—cover major elements of a wider development, reflect indirect aspects of distribution, and at the same time do not pose any major problems in gathering the necessary data. In addition to this, the satisfaction of basic needs was determined, on the basis of the indicator catalog compiled by Nohlen and Nuscheler, using data on the per capita consumption of calories and protein, the number of doctors per person, the number of hospital beds and outpatient facilities, and the proportion of slum dwellers in the total population. Demands that go further than material needs are covered in the education sector with school-attendance figures for primary and secondary schools. Thus, the catalog of indicators is based on a multidimensional development concept, similar to that which Nohlen and Nuscheler (1982:55) referred to as a "magic pentagle" of growth, work, equality/justice, participation, and independence.

II
Country Studies

The topography, climate, and vegetation zones of the present-day states of Kenya, Tanzania, and Uganda are remarkable for their great variety. They range from the tropical coastline through hot, dry savanna to Alpine mountain ranges, and from temperate, fertile highlands to desert. Before the first European traders, missionaries, and conquerors arrived in the midnineteenth century, the mainly egalitarian-segmentarian societies of the African population had already had a great deal of contact for many centuries with foreigners—Arabian traders in particular, but also with people from Asia. Under these influences a highly developed culture arose along the coast of East Africa, which reached its peak between 1200 and 1500. After the Portuguese had temporarily taken Zanzibar and Pemba, the sultan of Oman managed to renew his control over Zanzibar. When his empire was divided in 1828, Zanzibar became an independent sultanate, and after the cultivation of cloves began in 1840, it was able to increase its already great wealth.

Demands from American plantations caused an increase in the slave trade in East Africa after 1770, and it reached considerable dimensions between 1840 and 1870. As a result, the age, gender, and reproduction profiles of many African peoples were seriously distorted; in some regions, entire populations were wiped out. During their raids the slave traders penetrated deep into the hinterland of Kenya and Tanzania. West of the East African Rift Valley, in present-day Uganda, well-organized African kingdoms participated in the slave trade.

The European conquest did not begin until 1880. The British were at first mainly interested in Uganda, with its strategically favorable position at the upper reaches of the Nile and its apparent wealth. From 1884 on the adventurer Carl Peters tried to lay claim to large areas of the Tanganyikan coast for the German Reich by means of "contracts" between local rulers and a private German–East African Company. During negotiations in Berlin between 1885 and 1890, Great Britain and the German Reich agreed to fix the limits of their spheres of interest. Great Britain was granted Uganda and Kenya so that a railway could be built to the coast, whereas Tanganyika, which at that time included Rwanda and Burundi, came under German influence. In the subsequent Heligoland-Zanzibar treaty, the German Reich also ceded Zanzibar to Great Britain, and it was governed in the name of the British Crown by the sultan until the attainment of independence. Massive resistance from the African population continued until 1907, and the German Reich sent troops to Tanganyika, which, in 1891, formally became the colony of German East Africa. The British annexed Uganda in 1894 as a protectorate, and Kenya became a formal part of their colonial empire in 1895. From 1919, Great Britain administered Tanganyika under a League of Nations mandate. Thus, Kenya, Tanzania, and Uganda were, until their independence, under a common colonial power. The increasingly close cooperation culminated after 1948 in the first economic union when the East African High Commission was formed.

3

Kenya

PRECOLONIAL AND COLONIAL BACKGROUND

At the turn of the century, Governor Sir Charles Eliot and Hugh, Lord Delamere, both large-scale farmers, paved the way for the immigration of European settlers to Kenya, influencing both the form of colonial rule and future social structures. The White Highlands in the Rift Valley became an enclave of European landowners, while African peasants were confined to densely populated reservations. Harsh taxation compelled many Africans to work as hired laborers on the settlers' farms, creating an infrastructure that guaranteed that the central area around Nairobi and the White Highlands would have a head start in development. The settlers' production was also subsidized by a system of monopolies, favorable railway tariffs, and protective customs duties at the expense of the African peasantry. Marketing boards and cooperatives controlled by European farmers were set up as parastatals. The flourishing settler economy during World War II and Nairobi's function as the center of finance and commerce in the East African region led to a first wave of industrialization in the capital city after 1940 (Leys 1974; van Zwanenberg 1975; Brett 1973). Immigrants from the Indian subcontinent tended to dominate trade and crafts.

In the beginning, the African population, partially weakened by famines and interethnic struggles, could put up only sporadic resistance to the immigration of European settlers. A relatively high poll and hut tax and the prohibition of the cultivation of marketable cash crops such as coffee and cotton forced African peasants into wage labor. The major victims of these measures were the Kikuyu, who had to surrender part of their land to the Europeans and who were themselves limited to the so-called reservations. These conditions upset the balance of Kikuyu society, which, compared with neighboring ethnic groups, was relatively elaborate. Overpopulation in the reservations and loss of land led to the disappearance of the traditional *ahoi* system that had ensured impoverished peasants a meager livelihood as tenants on land belonging to richer peasants. Landless Kikuyu "squatted" on the settlers' farms where they were allowed to cultivate a small plot of land in return for work.

The worsening of conditions for the squatters, whose dependence soon began to resemble that of serfs, and the introduction of an identity card (*kipande*) that was intended to perfect the tax system led to the formation of the first political resistance organizations. At the same time, differentiation within Kikuyu society had been intensified by the introduction of a monetary economy. The wealthier Kikuyu's interest in agricultural innovations led to the forming of the Kikuyu Central Association in 1924, which fought especially against the prohibition of coffee cultivation by Africans. Competitive thinking and a particular interest in improving one's situation through education gained a firm footing in parts of the population as early as the 1920s.

Consensual traditions, which had neither completely disappeared in the egalitarian-segmentarian social structures of the other ethnic groups nor even among the Kikuyu, and the formation of resistance against colonial rule facilitated the development of African interethnic cooperation and a "national" consensus, if only a minimal one. Resistance was expressed particularly by the Mau-Mau guerrilla movement, which was rooted chiefly among the Kikuyu. After battles with heavy casualties (ninety-five dead on the European side, more than twelve thousand dead on the African side), it was finally put down by the British in 1955. Nearly thirty thousand people were interned, among them Jomo Kenyatta. Kenyatta, who had led the Kikuyu Central Association from 1928 until it was banned in 1940, reappeared at the head of the newly founded countrywide organization that succeeded it, the Kenyan African Union in 1946. During his imprisonment he had become the generally acknowledged, charismatic leader who was to rally Kenya as a national symbolic figure along the road to independence (Rosberg/Nottingham 1966).

From 1955 onward the colonial administration tried to master the social causes of African unrest. The Swynnerton Plan centered on the registration of all land as private property and also on the consolidation of scattered fragments of land. This policy aimed at building up a wide class of smallholders, thus ensuring a petite bourgeoisie and, eventually, capitalist development in Kenya on a permanent basis (Leys 1974). At the same time the number of African members in the Legislative Council was increased. In the Lancaster House Conferences, where, beginning in 1960, the constitution for independence was drafted, the British gave support to the moderate forces in the Kenya African Democratic Union (KADU) under Daniel arap Moi, who, as an opponent of the Kenya African National Union (KANU) and the Kikuyu who dominated it, was in favor of a federal system for Kenya. The programs of Africanization and resettlement in the White Highlands that were agreed upon at this time meant the end of significant parts of the settler economy.

DEVELOPMENT POLICIES AFTER INDEPENDENCE

The bitter opposition between those who sympathized with, or fought for, the Mau-Mau guerrilla and the Africans who fought against them as "loyalists"

Kenya
mixed economy

on the side of the British, and the rivalry between the KANU and the KADU split the society in a variety of directions. The attainment of independence (*uhuru*) and the charisma of the first state president, Kenyatta, were a sufficient basis at first for the forming of an overarching consensus, but, in the course of time, a more comprehensive, pragmatic political orientation was needed (Odhiambo 1986). Sessional Paper No. 10 of 1965 programmatically defined Kenya's African socialism as political democracy, social welfare, a mixed economy, and self-reliance, including the gradual Africanization of assets and jobs. In actual fact, Kenyan socialism consisted of a comprehensive agrarian reform that aimed chiefly at directing agriculture along lines of private enterprise and commerce, with the aid of a system of registration and consolidation of land and the transfer of settlers' land to Africans. With the renunciation of the African right of use of land on a communal basis, the introduction of private property rights, and the consolidation of scattered plots, the situation became worse for those without land and for the smallest peasants (see Leys 1974). The success of credit programs, agricultural extension services, and further measures for the promotion of an effective and progressive small peasantry cannot, however, be achieved without these structural reforms.

Favorable British credits enabled Kenya's government to obtain the European settlers' property in the White Highlands at market value. State settlement programs such as the Million Acres Scheme were intended to reduce the possibility of conflict arising from the marginalized parts of the peasantry, particularly among the Kikuyu, and at the same time to serve structural, political aims. For this reason it became a principle to sell the land and not to distribute it according to social criteria. The average size of the plots being sold was approximately eleven hectares, far larger than the usual size of an African farm. Altogether almost 100,000 families were able to settle on 1.1 million hectares of valuable land between 1960 and 1980. In this way, but also by the commercialization of small holdings, the agricultural petite bourgeoisie expanded considerably (see House/Killick 1981:160ff.; Livingstone 1986:218ff.).

Heedless of the distress of landless peasants and the numerous cases of unofficial occupation of land, Kenyatta's government completed implementing its land policy between 1964 and 1966. The first development plan was not primarily concerned with the redistribution of settlers' property, but it offered the prospects of considerable credit for the transfer of intact, large farms to Africans. The political and economic elite of Kenya were thus able to acquire large estates—in all 30 to 40 percent of the 1.4 million hectares of former "white" farmland—and often made commercial use of them as "telephone farmers" from Nairobi. More than half of the European property—approximately five hundred plantations and ranches covering 1.6 million hectares—was not included in these transfers, however. Although Kenya's smallholders supply over 70 percent of marketed agricultural products, the owners of large farms have, proportionally, a greater influence in farmers' associations, marketing boards, and other parastatals because of their political standing. The government's producer price policy, carried out through these organizations, has nonetheless been, on the whole, an effective stimulant of agrarian production.

The hierarchical structure of top jobs—formerly reserved for Europeans and Asians and correspondingly well paid—and of lesser jobs was also retained during the Africanization of personnel in the civil service and in private enterprise (see Bigsten 1984:16ff). Since the members of the new state class were expressly allowed to take part in economic activities, as confirmed once again by the Ndegwa Commission of 1971, they could either become large-scale farmers, change over to the top management of international corporations, or buy parts of companies that had been officially separated from the main corporation and then offered to Kenyans (e.g., the field of transport in the case of the oil companies). The *watajiri* (rich people) thus became separated from the previously more homogeneous African peasantry. Their power can be traced back to political connections, and they now dominate the state (Leonard 1984:145ff).

The refusal of trade licenses during the Africanization of trade and commerce proved to be the most important instrument concerning Asians who had not become Kenyan citizens. After rapid success with transfers in the retail trade, difficulties soon arose in areas where specific know-how was needed. The state helped Africans in these areas with credit and training schemes, and they also received a great deal of protection from, for example, parastatals who were engaged in trade (Leys 1974). A wide range of people from the agrarian and nonagrarian petite bourgeoisie and the salariat benefits in this way from the regime and forms its mass base (Currie/Ray 1984; Leonard 1984:145ff.; Godfrey 1986:28). The boundaries between these people and the watajiri are not clearly defined and there is high social mobility. Because of this, even a moderate limitation of landownership, suggested by critics many times, has not been politically feasible.

Kenya's African socialism has thus turned out to be a capitalist market economy in which growth takes precedence over distributive policies. Credits and other aids such as "industrial estates" serve the advancement of national industry, whereas guarantees of the repatriation of profits (e.g., the Foreign Investment Protection Act of 1964) and exemption from taxes have been very successful in attracting foreign investors. As a result there is still a 70 percent foreign share in the industrial capital of the country (Stewart 1981:75ff). Customs duties and a system of import licenses safeguarded the industrialization strategy of import substitution, which continued until the mid-1970s. The capital-intensive production of foreign firms, relying on the importation of modern technology, ended up by actually increasing dependence on imports. The requirements of this small modern sector meant that the more highly developed regions were given preference for infrastructural investments, thus contributing to the increase of regional inequality (Stewart 1981:78ff).

The nationalization of some central areas (e.g., some banks, electricity) was carried out unobtrusively from 1969 onward by obtaining shares at the London Stock Exchange. Numerous joint ventures—joint projects with state and international capital—and a wide range of semistate companies (parastatals)—engaged in the marketing and manufacturing of agricultural products, and in trade, tourism, and insurance, and were active in finance companies, leading to considerable state influence on economic development in the context of a mixed economy. In addition, compared to the Western industrial nations, the Kenyan state performs several central regulatory functions. With its well-prepared development plans Kenya has, however, limited itself to a chiefly indicative planning framework (Hofmeier 1982).

Since Kenya's state class has become established with the expansion of the public sector as an economic factor, there has been close cooperation with international capital. The Kenyanization of top management, the sale of shares in foreign companies to Africans, as well as the Kenyanization of part of their shares in investment funds was intended to ward off more-radical criticism, but in effect it served to strengthen the amalgamation of watajiri interests with those of foreign capital (see Leys 1974; Leonard 1984). Nonetheless, there is good reason to believe that the Kenyan element has been strengthened and that the trend is toward a higher potential of political control over international companies. Without doubt, the number of entrepreneurs with larger, or several, firms, and of directors who have a share in the capital of their companies and who owe their positions chiefly to their own accumulation, has increased. In recent years the core of a small, indigenous industrial bourgeoisie has developed (Swainson 1977; Kaplinsky 1980), but it is by no means in a position yet to face up to the dominance of foreign capital. The policies that control further economic and infrastructural development will presumably, however, be influenced more strongly in future by national and local interests (for a summary, see Berg-Schlosser 1983b).

With both pressure and support from the International Monetary Fund (IMF) and the World Bank, the regime reacted to high deficits in the balance of payments and the budget, arising from the world debt crisis that made itself felt in Kenya after 1978, with a comprehensive policy of stabilization and structural adjustment. The Fourth Development Plan (1979–1983) shifted priorities from industry to agriculture, and from import substitution to production for export. Rationalization of parastatals; the closing of a few, highly unprofitable units; and a budget policy that makes the acceptance of new development projects dependent on the financibility of their running costs and that will accept suggestions and aid for projects from donor countries only if these correspond with the regime's own priorities: all these measures are aimed at, among other things, a sharp reduction in public borrowing. Realistic rates of exchange, the liberalization of imports, the raising of interest rates, and limits on pay rises are intended as supporting measures to stimulate economic growth. Sessional Paper No. 1 of 1986 presents this policy reform in the context of the challenge Kenya faces as a result of its high rate of population growth, its shortage of agricultural land, and the threat of mass unemployment, particularly among the better-qualified, younger parts of the population (see Godfrey 1986:6ff). The new significance given to the district planning committees by the strongly emphasized district focus can be traced back to President Moi's attempt, announced in 1978, to draw closer to the goal of regional equality.

SOCIAL BASES

Social Structure

Between 1970 and 1980 Kenya's population increased by 40 percent to 15.1 million inhabitants, of whom only about 3 million belong to the male working population (this includes all able-bodied men between fifteen and sixty years of age but excludes secondary school pupils and students who are still engaged in formal education). A growth rate of up to 3.9 percent per year has led to a population structure in which 48 percent of all inhabitants are under fifteen years of age, but urbanization has remained behind the forecasts made in the early 1970s, based on tendencies that had continued since independence. Between 1962 and 1969 Nairobi, on an annual average, increased its population by 15 percent (ILO 1972:49); according to the last census, however, only about 12 percent of all citizens live in towns. The decreasing expansion rate of Kenya's two major cities—Nairobi and Mombasa—which is evident in these figures, shows the surprising ability of the agrarian sector to absorb a large part of the additional labor force (Livingstone 1986: 6ff).

Large-scale farms, which in 1960 were exclusively in the hands of Europeans, show a considerable change. More than half of Kenya's arable land was divided up for the settlement of progressive smallholders, and one-third of farmland was handed over undivided to eleven hundred African owners, until by 1980, less than one hundred European large-scale farmers remained. The Africanization of the formerly purely European state class was already completed by the end of the 1960s. The group of twenty-nine hundred capitalists, in 1970 mostly Asian, increased through the rise of successful African entrepreneurs from the petite bourgeoisie, or through members of the state class who had transferred to industry, to approximately four thousand members. Some Asians had also changed over to the management of international companies during the 1960s. Because of Nairobi's function as a stronghold of international capital in the East African region, the number of Europeans actually increased in this area, despite the reinforcement of the African element. Since 1970, therefore, there are still about forty thousand Europeans living in Kenya (see Diagrams 5 and 6; Table 57).

Since only about 17 percent of the entire area of Kenya has sufficient agricultural potential, the distribution of land has a decisive influence on social stratification. Just 0.1 percent of all agricultural holdings are plantations and large farms of more than one hundred hectares; these account for more than 14 percent of the 5.6 million hectares of good land. Together with forty thousand holdings that can be classified above smallholder level, these farms and plantations represent 2.5 percent of all agrarian landowners but more than a third of the available land in cultivation (see Livingstone 1986:294ff). The remainder is distributed among the 1.7 million smallholders, who are themselves very much stratified. Three-fourths of them belong to the group of agrarian proletaroids who own less than two hectares of land per household and who all together cultivate about 22 percent of agricultural land. Among these are the smallest landholders with less than 0.5 hectares each, who form the bottom 30 percent of the smallholding spectrum; the top quarter of prosperous smallholders cultivate farms of two to five hectares on the average (see Livingstone 1986:165).

Whether an increasing concentration of land leads to further impoverishment of the lower strata is one of the controversial issues of a debate that has focused criticism of the entire development model on an analysis of these social-structural aspects (for a summary, see Cowen 1981; Kitching 1985). Recent studies of this process of concentration show the bottom 40 percent of smallholders to be the losers and the richest 30 percent to be the winners in Central Province and in Nyanza (Collier/Lal 1986:252f). Land speculation and the division of former European farms into several units are responsible for the fact that the number of units designated as large-scale property reached 3,735 as of 1980 (see Okoth-Ogendo 1981).

Since independence, the agricultural bourgeoisie has increased fourfold, to 470,000 households in 1980. This is 15.8 percent of the population (Collier/Lal 1986:253ff.) and shows the consolidation of the middle peasantry and a considerable social mobility as far as the rise from the class of agrarian proletaroids is concerned. As the absolute number of proletaroid households has not risen above 1.2 million since 1960, their proportion of the population has been reduced from 69 percent to 42 percent as of 1980. According to the present trend, the various smallholder classes' shares in consumption and income are developing parallel to the change in land distribution. It is true, however, for the whole of Kenya that yields per hectare decrease with the size of the farm. Through intensive cultivation and a high concentration of labor even the smallest plots (under 0.5 hectares) in regions with good soil can make an essential contribution to the upkeep of a household. The ability of rural districts to absorb the increase in population has been based up to now on this potential (see Chege 1986; Livingstone 1986; Barkan/Holmquist 1986).

In addition, there have been increasing cultivation of lucrative cash crops such as tea and coffee, improvements (seed, fertilizers, etc.) in common food crops (maize, millet, sorghum, beans, etc.), and further innovations. Although all in all only just under 10 percent (Livingstone 1986:170, 183) of all smallholders plant "pure" cash crops—in Central Province this figure amounts to about 45 percent—and nearly all smallholders cover their own subsistence needs, half of their total products reach the market. Still, supplementary income, often from the informal sector (including temporary work as local craftsmen) is essential for the agricultural proletaroids. The chances of further advancement and social mobility today are determined less by the size of a farm than by the children's school certificates, as these raise the prospects of a member of the family finding paid employment in town. Because of strong family ties a good part of the income earned in towns comes back to the rural areas and can lead to further investments. Education thus becomes the determining factor for the capacity for innovation in the case of many smallholders (Collier/Lal 1986:252ff).

About two-thirds of the society profit in this way from the country's economic growth. Thirty percent of the population, however, still live under the subsistence level and receive 6 percent of the gross national product (GNP). The share of the richest 25 percent of the population amounts to 67 percent; approximately 27 percent of the GNP falls to the middle group (45 percent) of the population. The available indicators point to the fact that the already low standard of living among the bottom third is sinking even further (Collier/Lal 1986). The mass of the rural poor inhabitants is composed of more than 100,000 families without land, the bottom third of the smallholders and the nomads of the semiarid regions in Eastern and Northeastern provinces. Eighty percent of the poor smallholders come from Eastern and Western provinces as well as from Nyanza (House/Killick 1981:160ff.; Livingstone 1986:301ff). With the extremely high population density in both western provinces—29 percent of the entire population of Kenya live there on 4 percent of the total land—the limits of landholding capacity seem to have been reached. As a similar development is becoming noticeable in Central Province, the social conflict potential is being heightened by the lack of land, an atypical factor for an African state (see Collier/Lal 1986:25f.). In contrast the social importance of the rural proletariat (mostly laborers on large farms and plantations) has been reduced; in 1970 it made up 14 percent of the population, in 1980 only 7 percent. Until 1970 the large increase of workers on smallholdings was able to compensate for the decline of rural paid labor on large farms.

As in 1970, less than one-fourth of the male working population in 1980 found employment in the modern sector; these include rural workers on large farms, the nonagrarian proletariat, the salariat, and the nonagrarian bourgeoisie. Policy initiatives to create employment could scarcely keep pace with the high increase in population, but such policy caused in particular an above-average expansion of the public sector (from 268,000 employed in 1970 to 472,000 in 1980) and thus raised its share in formal employment from 40 percent to 50 percent. The significance of the salariat (administrative employees, technical and commercial employees, teachers, etc.), which in 1980 accounted for 7 percent of the employed, and the nonagrarian proletariat, which encompasses 15 percent of all households, is growing steadily but only very moderately in comparison with the structural changes in the rural areas. Against the background of a general fall in real wages between 1975 and 1984, analyses indicate that it is mainly the people with agrarian and informal incomes that have profited from the recent developments (Bigsten 1984; Collier/Lal 1986:92f). Kenya's high degree of social mobility is based in the decisive influence that level of education has on attainable incomes. As long as it was possible within the framework of Kenya's highly competitive society for the able-bodied person to work his way up, this factor had a stabilizing effect. At least since the early 1980s, however, the disappointed hopes of highly qualified young people, whose prospects of adequate work have dwindled, have contributed a great deal to the growing potential of student and other youth unrest.

By 1970 there had already been a considerable change in the racial composition of both the salariat and the nonagrarian bourgeoisie. Whereas an increasing number of Asians were forced into either the industrial sector or the informal sector in the towns through the withdrawal of licenses for trade and crafts, or into emigration—of the 140,000 Asians in Kenya in 1970 there were only seventy-eight thousand left in 1980—the number of Africans in the nonagrarian bourgeoisie increased tenfold during the first decade of independence (Leys 1974). The "farmers-cum-businessmen"—that is, farmers who invest their profits in a nonagrarian business (for example, in the fields of transport and gastronomy) and who are a particularly dynamic element—must also be mentioned (Berg-Schlosser 1979a:323, 343ff). In contrast to these accumulating owner-entrepreneurs there are the nonagrarian proletaroids (day laborers, hawkers, shoeblacks, *matatu* [private transport]– contractors, etc.). Their low percentage (2.2 percent) of the working population is a result of the still very limited chances of expansion in the informal sector (see House 1981:357ff.), but its productive segments are being specifically encouraged in the rural regions, for example in the Rural Industrial Development Programme. The persecution of Nairobi's street tradesmen and kiosk owners, who have begun to develop a form of collective resistance, still continues, however (Livingstone 1986:363ff). The boundaries between the nonagrarian proletaroids and the subproletariat are extremely fluid, as seen in the slum areas of Mathare Valley or Kangermi in Nairobi. The considerable growth of the subproletariat—300 percent between 1970 and 1980—accelerated even more during the depression of the early 1980s. Social problems and their accompanying phenonema, such as criminality and prostitution, have now reached such proportions that official politics can no longer ignore them.

Against the background of these class structures and racial differentiations, differences and conflicts among ethnic groups are gaining in political significance. Ethnic settlement areas still mostly coincide with the administrative boundaries of districts and provinces, despite a certain amount of intermingling in the towns. The Kikuyu (20 percent of the population) in Central Province, the Luo (12 percent) in Nyanza, the Luyia (13.8 percent) in Western Province, the Kalenjin (10.8 percent) in Rift Valley Province, the Kamba (11.2 percent) in parts of Eastern Province, and the Mijikenda in Coast Province constitute the larger ethnic-regional units. Central Province, with its above-average productivity in the agrarian sector and a high proportion of cash crop production, coupled with infrastructural advantages in schools, health centers, roads, water supplies, and so forth, and long favored by a more generous allocation of state resources, contains a high proportion of the agrarian petite bourgeoisie. The Kikuyu, who as a group were already more developed during the colonial era, were able to further this advantage through their dominant role in the Kenyatta years. In contrast, the densely populated provinces of the Luo and Luyia, both of whom were largely excluded after 1966 from the dominant alliance among the leading groups of the Kikuyu, Kalenjin, and Kamba, suffered neglect for a long time. This political constellation, together with a development strategy that tended to favor the more developed areas rather than counterbalance them, created structures that led to a concentration of poverty in less-developed regions (Bigsten 1980:148ff.; Livingstone 1986:294ff.). Consequently, it is not only due to the fact that the capital, Nairobi, is adjacent to their region that the Kikuyu have a particularly high proportion of members of the nonagrarian classes, especially the middle and higher ones.

Political Culture

"We help those who help themselves": with this motto President Kenyatta not only popularized a type of self-help that is typical of Kenya—the so-called Harambee projects—but he also used it to formulate the basic idea of his rural development strategy, an essential element of his policy of nation-building. "Harambee," similar to the English expression *Heave-ho!*, signifying a common effort or struggle, became the slogan of a regime that tried to develop a feeling of solidarity up to the national level but did very little to counteract social or regional inequality (see Bigsten 1980:160ff.) when it promoted the launching of individual initiatives or furthered local groups, as in the self-help campaigns. The popularity of the Harambee projects has not decreased to any great extent. A survey carried out in 1985 showed that 90 percent of the population (almost the entire rural population and many in the towns) have already taken part in these projects. Self-help in local communities has meant in particular the building and improvement of schools, health centers, cattle dips, and water supplies. These installations are shared by all community members, irrespective of their contribution to them. Most of the initiative, finance, and organization is provided by the community; outside assistance is often needed, especially for larger projects, yet the bulk of these works, about 80 percent, is so small that no state aid is necessary. This autonomy is one reason for the great impact and resilience of the Harambee movement (Barkan/Holmquist 1986:2f., 17f.; Holmquist 1984b).

Soon after independence it became evident that ideological, ethnical, regional, and personal rivalries and conflicts within the KANU and Parliament were causing severe tensions. In order to diffuse these conflicts, President Kenyatta attempted to convey a new conception of the members of Parliaments' (MP) function, telling them to make themselves useful and suggesting they give intensive support to self-help projects in their constituencies. This support was received with enthusiasm by farmers and it has up to the present day greatly affected electoral campaigns and the intensive competition for positions on projects in most constituencies (Barkan/Okumu 1978). The initial weakness of the bureaucratic apparatus meant that a pragmatic approach to local rural development was needed, and by referring back to a tradition of self-help that was not merely anticolonial, Kenyatta created an institutionalized framework for initiatives "from below." People living in a particular locality knew which projects were most needed there, and obtaining materials and building installations was organised on the spot. Money and labor, given by community members as a result of often quite considerable social pressure, offered the bureaucracy the chance to spend less for such investments. Seen from this angle, the Harambee projects almost assume the character of an additional tax (Holmquist 1984a:174ff.; see also, Ngethe 1984).

The reward promised for self-help—namely, the prospect, held out by the state, that it would pay the running costs for larger projects—has had a corrective effect that should not be underestimated. As running costs are far higher than building costs in the case of schools, which are among the most popular Harambee projects, self-help can ultimately be used by local communities as an instrument for pulling more resources away from the center to the periphery than would normally be the case. At the same time this kind of self-help has contributed to the aggravation of regional imbalances, for the developed areas were on average far more active in organizing projects (see, e.g., Holmquist 1984a:85ff). In both frequency of participation and amount of contributions, the agrarian proletaroids and the agrarian petite bourgeoisie, together 72 percent of the rural population, provide the social basis for the Harambee movement. Whereas the landless very rarely participate in self-help projects, the owners of larger farms often contribute out of a sense of social obligation or to obtain political favors on a scale that makes for, on the whole, a moderate redistribution in favor of the poorer classes (see Thomas 1985).

The high rate of general acceptance of this instrument can be seen in the fact that 90 percent of the rural population expect to profit from future projects. They are often considered to be the only method of attaining anything in the way of local development and can, at the same, time be controlled from below. The agreement of the rural population with the values embodied in the Harambee movement and the accompanying development policies constitutes a considerable source of legitimacy for Kenya's political system (Barkan/Holmquist 1986:2). Each MP performs important functions for these self-help projects, particularly for larger ones, in that he can use his connections in the ministries and bureaucracies of Nairobi when trying to procure financial aid from the state. By making use of this patronage, MPs and their potential rivals try to win over local communities, and within these clientelistic structures these contributions form an important basis for each candidate. They do not, however, always mean an inevitable obligation for those at the receiving end as long as the whole process remains strongly competive in the framework of regular and orderly elections (Holmquist 1984b:86ff., 1984a:185).

On the whole, these distributive aspects, personal factors, and local issues form the foundation for electoral decisions instead of problems concerning national policy. In the 1983 elections an average of 47 percent of the population registered as voters and 39 percent actually voted (see tables 53 and 54). The high rate of MPs who lose their seats—50 percent on the average—shows both the fierce competition and the high potential of dissatisfaction being voiced. Participatory attitudes, the level of political information, and support for the system are, all in all, more strongly developed in rural regions than in the towns, and the greater interest of the agrarian population in their MPs leads to a considerably higher turnout for elections, compared with the towns (see Berg-Schlosser 1981b; 1982b) where often only a third of those entitled to vote actually do so (ACR 1983–1984:166). Frequent and active participation is at its most widespread in the agrarian petite bourgeoisie and in ethnic groups with a particularly high proportion of people belonging to this class (the Kikuyu and Kalenjin, for example). In contrast, the political participation of agrarian proletaroids, and in the regions dominated by them, as for example the Luo country, is weaker and based on a lower level of political interest and information. The egalitarian and participatory traditions of almost all ethnic groups in Kenya form a basis that can be made use of in the present electoral system in a "modernized" form. This relatively high level of participation is also transformed into relatively strong support for the system as a whole, especially among members of the agrarian and nonagrarian petite bourgeoisie.

Since the end of the Shifta War in North-Eastern Province in the 1960s and the failure of the Somali population's attempted secession, the pragmatic acceptance of the country's boundaries as an established administrative and economic unit can no longer be doubted, and memories of the struggle for freedom, which lasted several decades, and the era of the Mau-Mau movement serve, among others, as a unifying bond in the sense of a national identity. Nonetheless, the role played by ethnic-regional lines of tension in creating conflicts and influencing their perception has scarcely diminished in spite of the campaigns by presidents Kenyatta and Moi against so-called tribalism. The condemnation of such attitudes for the purpose of nation-building—which, however, was also used to divert attention from the main core of conflicting economic interests (see, e.g., Leys 1974)—was not able to break through the influence of traditional ties, which can be seen both in the great social significance of solidarity within the families as well as in the still mostly unbroken power of the clans in some ethnic groups (Berg-Schlosser 1979a:367ff). The great significance of appeals to ethnic identity was shown by the events following the assassination of the then–KANU general secretary, Tom Mboya, in 1969. Although at that time the majority of the Luo had been excluded from the governing alliance for some years and felt themselves to be at a disadvantage in many respects, the death of this Luo politician mobilized a wide movement of protest among the Luo against the Kikuyu who dominated the regime. The fact that Mboya was a Luo meant more than the fact that he was a leading politician in Kenyatta's regime. In turn, as in other cases when they felt their position to be threatened, important Kikuyu groups organized a series of oath-taking ceremonies in Central Province in order to ensure their people's solidarity by referring back to the tradition of the Mau-Mau era, and to give an outward appearance of readiness for action.

In 1978, Daniel arap Moi succeeded Kenyatta as president with the motto *Nyayo* (footsteps). Although this referred at first to the continuation of Kenyatta's course, in time the motto was interpreted as an appeal to follow the new president (ACR 1979–1980:232f.; 1980–1981:214f). Corruption, nepotism, poverty, and "tribalism" were all part of the abuses that Moi denounced and against which he promised to fight for the good of the "ordinary citizen" (Godia 1984:7ff). His name began to be connected with the hope that many injustices of the Kenyatta era could be avoided in future (see Hofmeier 1982a:149). President Moi's endeavor to surround his policies with the aura of his own philosophy, "nyayoism," is aimed at keeping a hold on the national and social consensus attained so far. Moi does not enjoy a charisma comparable to that of Kenyatta (see Godia 1984; Moi 1986), but by attaching general values such as his favorite "peace, love, and unity" to essential policy initiatives, he attempted to extend the regime's basis of legitimacy in the sense of diffuse support. These intensive, ideological endeavours are quite understandable in view of the ruptures in Kenya's social consensus, reflected both in a constantly high crime rate over many years and in the potential for student protest and similiar manifest or latent forms of social unrest. Those in power still enjoy a considerable measure of legitimacy, but the increasing sensitivity toward justified criticisms, including reports on human rights violations by foreign media and the wave of arrests and convictions in 1986–1987 of regime opponents who were presumed to belong to the subversive organization Mwakenya (see ARB, Political Series, 1986, 1987) give the impression of an insecure political leadership whose basis of power has diminished.

There is evidently a growing anger in Kikuyu circles as they believe their position is being menaced on all levels, and that they are being pushed aside in favor of the smaller ethnic groups, in particular the Kalenjin, within the new alliance. Some Kikuyu are thus increasingly expressing a radicalism rooted in their more recent history, which was already noticeable under the surface in their critical attitude to powerful figures of the Kenyatta era. This radicalism can be traced back to the time of the Mau-Mau struggles, when the Kikuyu suffered bitter divisions into loyalists and armed homeguards of the colonial masters on the one hand, and the guerrillas and their sympathizers on the other hand (see, Mutiso 1975). It also stems from the neglect of the Mau-Mau fighters when the former White Highlands were being distributed. Fueled by the many rumors characteristically circulating in the country through conversations in the matatus and at funerals and similar social events, such attitudes can quickly reach a popular level (Odhiambo 1986:39ff).

INPUT STRUCTURES

Intermediary Groups

It is necessary to differentiate between organized groups that represent specific interests, such as trade unions, employers' organizations and farmers' associations, and structures such as the church that, as a mainly social institutions perform only sporadic input functions, or those such as ethnic organizations that represent diffuse conglomerations of interests. Finally, the press as a public organ must be considered as a structure for the expression of interests.

Trade unions.   The first trade union activities began in the 1930s. After independence, a more radical opposition group developed around Dennis Akumu and was partially directed against Mboya, the undisputed leader of the Kenya Federation of Labor since 1953. Mboya was minister of labor in Kenyatta's first cabinet and had excellent connections to both domestic and foreign enterprises. After the ideological struggles of 1964 had led to a rift in the trade unions, the regime intervened: a law passed in 1965 established the newly formed Central Organization of Trade Unions (COTU) as the one central body for all trade unions. With an organization according to branches of industry and not according to professional skills (as for example in England) or to ideological alignment (as for example in Italy), Kenya's trade union system is similar to that of the Federal Republic of Germany. Twenty-eight of the thirty-three registered single trade unions belong to the COTU, and and the central body represents altogether 300,000 members. The COTU's program and activities are concentrated on the general social and economic problems of employees, their representation in official commissions, arbitration in local labor disputes, and the improvement of trade union organization and education matters.

On the whole, the ability of the trade unions to fight for their interests is rather limited, as can be seen, for example, from the number of strikes (Bigsten 1984:7ff.; see also table 56); since 1965 it has been well below the level of the Western industrial nations. Institutionalized control—shown, for example, in the fact that all elected top functionaries of the COTU must be confirmed by the Office of the President—is further to be seen in the legislation concerning industrial relations. On the initiative of the employers' organization, Federation of Kenya Employers (FKE), the Trade Disputes Act, was passed in 1965, and this, as a reaction against the frequency of strikes since 1960, changed the situation further to the disadvantage of the trade unions. They possess a certain amount of autonomy in negotiations, but the minister of labor can declare strikes illegal if the lengthy negotiating procedures, culminating in the industrial court (the highest arbitration tribunal), have not all been correctly adhered to. As proceedings in this court are often delayed and the panel of judges is appointed by the government, the trade unions have up to now regularly given in. On the few occasions when the COTU has announced a one-day general strike to obtain a rise in the minimum wage in times of political tensions, as in May 1975 or June 1982, a brief warning from the president was enough to make it abandon its plans (ACR 1975–1976:224, ACR 1982–1983:191; Collier/Lal 1986:92ff).

In periods of grave economic and political crises, so-called tripartite agreements among the government, COTU, and FKE were concluded. In 1964, private and public employers guaranteed for the first time a 10 to 15 percent increase of personnel, while the trade unions accepted a twelve months' wage freeze and agreed to renounce all strikes for that period. This initiative, which led to forty thousand new jobs, was intended to subdue high unemployment, which in 1964 had led to a wave of unauthorized squatting by landless farmers. Agreements in the years 1970/71 and 1979/80, practically identical in structure and motivation, followed the same strategy: the extremely high unemployment rate was to be counteracted by a long-term reduction in wages (Stewart 1979). Although ninety thousand new jobs were to be created in 1980, the actual reduction in unemployment was very slight. Both the lack of long-term controls and the redefinition of temporary jobs as permanent limit the efficiency of such agreements.

According to the regulations, the representatives of the individual trade unions elect the top functionaries of the COTU every five years. Both the dispute over Juma Boy, the general secretary for many years, which began in 1980 (ACR 1980–1984/85), and the long struggle of Joseph Mugalla, who was elected in the face of considerable opposition in 1986 and who has still to assert his power in the individual trade unions, show that the central body has been weakened by continual leadership crises. At the same time, the individual trade unions are increasingly proving to be dominated by competing factions and their clientele systems. This is why in the mid-1970s, for example, radical trade unionists such as Kimani wa Nyoike called for a reactivation of the trade unions; that is, more-frequent trade union elections and a stronger political orientation (ACR 1975–1976:224). Kimani's trade union, the Union of Kenya Civil Servants, the largest and most powerful single union, was dissolved by presidential decree in 1982 because of its "militancy."

Employers' organizations.   As an organization that caters to the interests of all medium-sized and large enterprises in Kenya, the FKE today represents approximately twenty-three hundred employers in industry and commerce and approximately five hundred large-scale employers from the agrarian sector. However, the management of the FKE is dominated by representatives of the Africanized management of foreign corporations and the large parastatals. In the 1970s the president of the FKE was reported to have free access at any time to the minister of labor and other cabinet members who dealt with economic issues (Leys 1974:140f). During the disputes between the COTU and FKE, which often went on for months (as, for example, in the course of the tripartite negotiations in 1979/80 or during the attempted implementation of the five-day week in 1986/87, which ultimately failed), political leaders and top civil servants avoided giving an official opinion for a long time, but both the course and the final result of these developments allow the conclusion that the FKE is on the whole in a considerably better position of power, albeit an informal one, compared with the COTU (see ACR 1978–1979:275, 1979–1980:238; *Weekly Review* May 1, 1987:20).

Agricultural organizations.   Agricultural interests are also strongly represented, particularly in general organizations such as the Kenya National Farmers' Union (KNFU) or those with reference to particular products, as, for example, in the Kenya Coffee Growers' Association (KCGA). Apart from giving assistance in such areas as further education and insurance, and in the sale of seed, fertilizer, and similar means of production, their work includes representing agricultural producers in their negotiations with marketing boards (for example the Kenya Planters' Co-operative Union [KPCU] or the Kenya Co-operative Creameries) that process and market raw products. The policy of the KNFU, successor to the Kenya Farmers' Association founded in 1946 by European settlers, was determined for a long time, even after the Africanization of the White Highlands, by large-scale farmers. The strong position enjoyed by these closely linked organizations, cooperatives, and marketing boards continued after independence (Leys 1974:36, 103f.; Zwanenberg 1975). The KNFU is now, however, trying to increase its membership from its present thirty-seven thousand to 100,000 with an extensive program of recruitment, in order to strengthen the claim that it represents a majority of Kenyan farmers (*Weekly Review*, March 20, 1987:24f).

It is in part due to the influence of these organizations on producer prices, which are negotiated by the government bureaucracy and the parastatals responsible for the marketing of products, that a considerable share of the export revenues of these products comes back to the "progressive" smallholders as well (see, e.g., Amey/Leonard 1979:31ff). The retreat into subsistence production, typical for many African countries, was avoided in this way, as the Kenyan model left farmers enough material resources and gave them incentives to increase their production. The attempt by the Kenya Coffee Board in 1986, for example, to alter the distribution of profits among coffee producers so that a larger share of the revenues could be retained by the marketing board, was successfully blocked by Kenya's coffee planters. As they elect representatives into the coffee board's management through the KCGA and as they also have behind them a second strong organization—the KPCU, encompassing 180 cooperatives with a total membership of 450,000 farmers—they were able to mobilize such strong and prompt resistance that the minister of agriculture ultimately abandoned the final confirmation and implementation of this plan (*Weekly Review* April 3, 1987:12ff).

Ethnic organizations. In the struggle for government allocations for regional development projects and infrastructural measures, as well as in the distribution of jobs in the public sector, one of the standard arguments has always been the demand, never completely fulfilled, for ethnic-regional equality, or, in other words, the complaint of unjust treatment. Anyone wishing to make political and economic capital out of ethnic tensions, however, must reckon with disciplinary action from the political leadership. The solidarity of ethnic groups continues to be an important political factor; nonetheless, campaigns against "tribalism" are a part of President Moi's political arsenal just as they were of Kenyatta's. Ethnically oriented interest groups began to unite from the late 1960s onward in the guise of tribal welfare organizations, and groups such as the Maasai United Front, the New Akamba Union, the Luo Union, or the Gikuyu, Embu and Meru Association (GEMA) often took over the task of organizing local Harambee projects and similar communal enterprises (see Hofmeier/Schönborn 1987:152ff).

The GEMA took great pains to avoid being considered by the public as the instrument of Kikuyu claims to power, but in 1973 its inner circle was already looking for an acceptable successor to Kenyatta, and until 1978 it took part in various attempts to prevent Moi, then vice-president and a Kalenjin, from constitutionally assuming the presidency after the death of the incumbent. The GEMA became a meeting place for cabinet members and other top politicians, bankers, and influential entrepreneurs—in other words, the political and economic establishment of the Kikuyu, Embu, and Meru—where they were able to consolidate and increase their power and influence; a financially strong holding company gave them in addition a powerful economic backing (ACR 1973–1974:169; see also Odhiambo 1986:38). When President Moi finally dissolved all organizations referring to ethnic links (including football clubs) at the end of 1980, he had the GEMA particularly in mind, although he mentioned no names (ACR 1980–1981:210ff). Nevertheless, there is no doubt that ethnic forces still represent an important element of power at an unofficial level.

Churches. The churches of Kenya have seldom relaxed their long-established reserve toward political issues after independence (Hofmeier/Schönborn 1987:152ff). Since the failure of the attempted coup in 1982 and particularly since the changes in the constitution and the introduction of preliminary elections within the KANU in 1986, well-known representatives of individual churches—for example, the Church of the Province of Kenya and the Presbyterian Church of East Africa—and the church confederation—the National Council of Churches of Kenya—have criticized various aspects of the regime's policies (see *Weekly Review* October 17, 1986:3ff., November 11, 1986:3ff., and April 24, 1987:3ff). Claiming to be the advocates of the weak and oppressed, they have taken up the causes of expelled politicians such as Oginga Odinga and Charles Njonjo, in the same way that they have denounced the blatant contrast between rich and poor, or developments that they feel imperil freedom and civil rights guaranteed by the constitution (see *Weekly Review* January 30, 1987:15). Despite considerable pressure from the political leadership, a relatively independent channel of information has developed within these institutions over the last few years and has put them into a position to convey to the regime limitations on acceptance of particular policies.

The press. Kenya's press, consisting of two daily newspapers both in foreign hands, *The Standard* and *Daily Nation*, the *Kenya Times*, which is published by the KANU, and, in particular, the magazine *The Weekly Review*, report—openly within certain limits—on political rivalries and disputes, errors made by the bureaucracy and parastatals, and other significant social and economic issues. In dealing with individual cases, criticism is allowed, but the press cannot afford to examine critically and with the same candor basic social power relationships, the political interests of the political alliances at the heart of the regime, or, above all, the president (see Hofmeier/Schönborn 1987:152ff).

Party System

Political organizations in Kenya, particularly in Kikuyu country, have a tradition going back to the 1920s. From the great number of mostly ethnic-regionally defined parties legalized by the British in the late 1950s, two rival parties, the KANU and KADU, came to the fore on the eve of independence. Whereas the KANU represented mainly an alliance between the Kikuyu and the Luo, KADU was the party of the smaller groups—the Luyia, Maasai, Mijikenda, and Kalenjin. In order to forestall the threat of Kikuyu domination, the KADU wanted a federal constitution, but in the elections of 1961 and 1963 it suffered major defeats. The KANU government that led the country to official independence on December 12, 1963, with Kenyatta as prime minister, aimed from the very beginning at altering the federal *majimbo* constitution, which had been forced upon them in the negotiations for independence, as quickly as possible (Berg-Schlosser 1979a; Odhiambo 1986:9).

After a number of KADU members had crossed over to the KANU, the KANU general secretary, Mboya, managed to persuade KADU leaders to accept the final amalgamation of both parties. In 1964, parallel to the first important constitutional changes, the KADU decided to dissolve itself, the decision accelerated by the evolution of a new political constellation. The quarrel over the federal structure of the state was of secondary importance compared with the adapted development strategy of the newly independent country (Leys 1974). The demand for land reform in favor of the landless and the Mau-Mau fighters, who had received little during the distribution of former European properties, divided the "radicals"—for example, Odinga, Bildad Kaggia, and Akumu—from the "conservatives"—for example, Kenyatta, Mboya, Koinange wa Mbiyu, and Moi—who were in command of the central institutions of the young state and in a position to reap the benefits of the British-controlled decolonialization. Odinga, whose position can be characterized as populist, became the figurehead of this opposition within the party. He criticized the increasing social inequality in Kenya and the capitalist path of development that President Kenyatta, in fact, was propagating. Parliament provided a forum for this dispute: radical backbenchers launched attacks on the government benches, which were more concerned with defending and increasing the newly acquired property (Odhiambo 1986:28ff).

The KANU leadership hoped to find a permanent solution by means of a widespread depoliticization of such issues. Sessional Paper No. 10 of 1965 prepared the way, ideologically speaking, for the removal of the "left-wing" critics with a concept of African socialism that claimed to be working toward an egalitarian society but that served primarily to justify policies that were backing a development strategy principally oriented to maximal economic growth and a peripheral-capitalist development (Odhiambo 1986:30f.; Mohiddin 1981). At the first national KANU delegates' conference in Limuru in 1966, Mboya, an experienced tactician, managed to silence the radicals around Odinga.

Odinga left the KANU and founded a new party, the Kenya People's Union (KPU). In the following by-elections all the MPs who had resigned from the KANU together with Odinga, except those who were Luo, lost their seats. Although the KPU considered itself as the organ for all the forces that were dissatisfied with Kenyatta's course, its sphere of influence was thus restricted mainly to the Luo region. The place in the alliance with the Kikuyu from which the Luo had now largely withdrawn was subsequently taken over for the most part by the Kalenjin, and it was from their ranks that the vice-president, Daniel arap Moi, was chosen (Leys 1974; Berg-Schlosser 1979a). After the murder of Mboya, a Luo but still closely loyal to the regime, an angry mob threatened to stone Kenyatta in 1969 in the main town of the Luo country, Kisumu, and he seized the opportunity to ban the KPU. From then on the nomination of candidates for general elections took place only inside the KANU. Former KPU members were not allowed to stand for election (see e.g., Barkan/Okumu 1978:100).

Apart from this key function before elections, the KANU kept very much in the background, and the party conferences and elections—which according to the statutes should have been held annually—did not take place. Thus, the national KANU elections, which had long been announced for April 4, 1977, were postponed indefinitely two days before this date, as the intense rivalry over the most promising positions in the succession to Kenyatta was threatening to reach destabilizing dimensions (ACR 1977–1978). As a consequence of the political demobilization under a de facto one-party system, there were during the 1970s neither regular meetings of a legitimized party executive committee nor an apparatus of functionaries, right down to the party basis, could guarantee the KANU's continual presence in the political life of the society. To speak of a "no-party system" at that time in Kenya is certainly justifiable (see, among many others, Okumu/Holmquist 1984:61). Shortly after President Moi took office, he announced that he would help the KANU to regain greater political importance both through a massive campaign to recruit new members and through new party elections at all levels. These elections gave Moi an opportunity in the spring of 1979 to drive his most prominent opponents out of the party organs that still formally existed. Instead of serving the worthy aim of reactivating the ruling party as a political institution and thus giving political participation a new forum, these elections, carried out with relative speed, served primarily to strengthen the position of the new regime (ACR

1978–1979:269). It is therefore not surprising that in spite of the repeated announcements of dates for party elections, the delegates were not able to elect the KANU national committees until 1985.

In all the developments and events linked with the intention of giving the KANU a stronger position, there recurs to a greater or lesser extent the intention of disciplining those who are politically active (Okumu/Holmquist 1984:66). In the face of criticism of the political leadership by representatives of some churches and by the Law Society of Kenya, President Moi even postulated the KANU's supremacy over the constitution. The political significance of this decree, which was intended to subordinate both Parliament and the highest courts to the party, became apparent in a dispute raised by Shariff Nassir, the KANU chairman in Mombasa, who was displeased that the elected MP for Mombasa had criticized local issues in Parliament. As leader of the local party council, Nassir tried to call the member to account. The danger—which became more concrete in 1986 by the creation of a special KANU disciplinary committee—that this notion of party discipline under the conditions of a one-party system can lead to the undermining of parliamentary immunity and to the erosion of the safeguards of freedom of speech in Parliament, which have been laid down in the Powers and Privileges Act, remains imminent. Most of the cases brought before the disciplinary committee in 1986 and 1987, however, were the result of attempts by local party leaders to suppress criticism or to eliminate rivals for the next parliamentary elections in 1988. But even in cases where the person in question had publicly criticized the president's policies, no further action was taken. The hierarchy of the party organization in this way sometimes counteracts such trends with considerable opposition (Okumu/Holmquist 1984:66).

As party membership is a prerequisite for any official political position and only KANU members can stand for Parliament, the suspension of membership, in extreme cases for life, means the end of a political career. It is only when seen from this perspective that the relevance of the change in 1982, when Kenya officially became a de jure one-party state, becomes evident (Odhiambo 1986:35f). The fate of Odinga, whose candidacy was once again refused in 1982, illustrates this development. The change in constitution prevented his plan of forming a socialist party together with George Anyona, who was afterward arrested under the Detention Act (Currie/Ray 1984:581). Outside the KANU, however, Odinga was unable to defend his position as political leader of the Luo. The joint statement made against Odinga by important Luo politicians in 1987 shows to what extent he had lost ground. His name was also mentioned in connection with the clandestine Mwakenya movement to the Central Investigation Department. Since he refused to deny all connections with this secret organization, which was alleged not only to be taking part in revolutionary activities but also aiming at founding a socialist party, all Luo members of parliament including cabinet members such as Robert Ouko and William Omamo publicly renounced him.

One function has always been fulfilled by the KANU, however: the selection of candidates for parliamentary elections (Khapoya 1980:19; Okumu/Holmquist 1984:66). Normally, it sufficed that neither the applicant's life history nor his conduct gave grounds for doubting his suitability, but former KPU members and politicians who had alleged or proven connections with the subversive underground group Mwakenya faced political obstacles. Up to now, because of the inefficiency of party structures, an actual screening of candidates with regard to their political persuasions has not taken place. There has always been room for a great number of candidates, under the name of the KANU, representing a wide variety of policies.

With the "first past the post" electoral system of relative majorities, MPs—elected from a large number of candidates—often did not represent more than 20 percent of the voters in any one constituency. The decision in 1986 to introduce internal primary elections was therefore a logical step, similar to the majority system with two ballots that was at certain times practiced in France. Yet the method decided upon by the KANU proved to be very controversial: voters have to queue up in each polling station behind the symbol or representative of their candidate; whoever receives support from fewer than 30 percent of the constituency's party basis is eliminated as a candidate for the general election. This method, which in view of the frequent irregularities and manipulations experienced at elections is defended by its supporters as a "typically African" solution that can be controlled by anyone who so wishes, has been judged by some church representatives, such as Manasses Kuria, Timothy Njoya, and Alexander Muge as the abolition of the secret ballot. The massive way in which the regime has disputed the competence of critics from the church and the law society to express a political opinion criticizing this method of voting suggests a loss of confidence within the political leadership. Thus, the intensified political control that can now be observed has also resulted in a changed voting system that, under different circumstances, might have been accepted more easily.

The strongly competitive nature of parliamentary elections in most constituencies in Kenya is reflected during the preliminary stages of elections in the public struggles for positions and in the rivalries within KANU committees. Since the 1970s at the very latest, one of the prerequisites for a political career has been the planning and setting up of a political base in one's chosen constituency, and this may be done, for example, by organizing Harambee projects, procuring favorable loans, making large donations of money, exposing corruption, or finding other ways of gaining a good local reputation. Even MPs who have been voted out of Parliament or candidates who have made several failed attempts can in the long run change the situation to their advantage by such methods, as experience has shown in the constituencies of Mathare Valley or Dagoretti in Nairobi.

"Mobilization parties" such as the KANU nowadays ensure political support by means of demonstrative acts, such as recruiting as many members as possible. This shows the system's capacity for integration, but despite the fact that since 1984 civil servants have been under a certain amount of pressure to join the KANU, the aims of the recruitment campaigns carried out since 1979 have not been reached (ACR 1984–1985:267). In addition the fee of KShs 1,000 for lifelong membership is beyond the financial means of the lower classes, so that the KANU's efforts are directed more toward the agrarian and urban petite bourgeoisie (Currie/Ray 1984:573).

Regulations concerning the highest government posts have been laid down in the KANU's statutes: each candidate for the presidency must belong to the party leadership. In 1979, the National Delegates' Conference appointed Moi as president of the KANU without there being any other candidates. This involved the ingenious feat of a "regional strategy," even more polished for the next elections in 1985, which ensured the realization of consociational structures in the KANU leadership (see ACR 1976/77–1979/80ff). Such a balanced structure is meant to neutralise regional and ethnic disproportions and thus to contribute to the formation and strengthening of a national consensus (see Berg-Schlosser 1985a). Because the leadership of both party and state rests on a personal identity, the KANU has scarcely appeared as an independent organ in a political-programmatical sense. Points in the election manifesto or principles of policy announced by the leadership during party meetings always correspond with the decisionmaking in the central political system (ACR 1983–1984:164).

CENTRAL POLITICAL SYSTEM

Institutional Aspects

The constitution at the time of independence in 1963 guaranteed regional parliaments and an independent administration (majimbo) for the provinces. By December 1964, provincial administration had already been made directly responsible to the president who replaced the British Queen as head of state but also remained the leader of the government. The Westminster model was finally abandoned when the Senate, as the "federal" chamber, was dissolved, the president was provided with extensive emergency rights in 1966, and direct election of the president became part of the constitution in 1968. The KANU had managed to realize the long-term goal of a centralized presidential system by means of a peaceful reconstruction of the constitution (see Gertzel 1970).

Kenya African National Union

From 1969 onward national elections—in 1974, 1979, and 1983—took place regularly within the framework of the one-party system. The process of the elections and their results, which have become routine by now, conform to the basic structure of a semicompetitive system (Hermet et al. 1978). Because of the KANU's relatively unrestricted nomination procedures, there has always been a very great number of candidates; in 1983, for example, there were more than nine hundred competing for 158 seats. Instead of competition between different parties, the strong competition within the single party acts as a forum for public participation. As also indicated by participation in Harambee efforts, the voters see their MP chiefly as a lobbyist who is sent from the rural periphery to the center. Election campaigns are rarely influenced by national issues and policies but are dominated by local matters and by the candidate's effectiveness in obtaining allocations of state money for the area. The fact that a very high number of MPs, usually more than 50 percent, lose their seats each election shows how uncompromisingly they are held personally responsible. Younger politicians who have been able to acquire the necessary potential of economic and political influence can in this way be recruited into the elite and integrated into the president's system of patronage, which also serves as a control over their activities (Barkan/Okumu 1978).

In order to check the dangers to the national consensus that may result from the fragmentation into forty-two distinct ethnic groups, there is on the one hand an electoral system that guarantees almost proportional representation, at least in the rural areas, and on the other hand a consociational composition of cabinets since 1963, which takes into consideration both the economic importance of the regions and the "political weight" of the politicians and their relationship to the regime. Kenya's regime has thus attempted to continue to a certain extent the consensual traditions of egalitarian African societies in a system that is aimed at national unity. The additional large number of assistant ministers (forty-three in 1983, for example) means that nearly half of Parliament are members of the government and extends the consociational principle down to the district level (Berg-Schlosser 1985a). The presidential system of patronage is thus significantly enhanced (see, e.g., Barkan 1984c). Since positions in the government also involve access to a wide spectrum of financial resources, both legal and illegal, and the power to appoint civil servants, the prospect of having an influencial MP or even a minister is sufficient to subdue regional or local disputes and is becoming a significant source of legitimacy for the regime. The office of president has up till now been the only post not subjected to regular checks during elections or to institutionalized change. After his renomination as unopposed candidate by the sole party, the incumbent has always been confirmed in office.

The controversial debates at the time of the KPU and the wave of populist criticism that was articulated in 1974/75 by such MPs as John M.

Seroney, Joseph Martin Shikuku, and Josiah Mwangi Kariuki ("the three JMs") have earned Kenya's Parliament the reputation of being one of the liveliest in Africa. In a number of cases the government's motions for legislation have been rejected or at least modified. The annual budget legislation, the right to set up commissions of inquiry, and the freedom of debate, protected by law, guarantee the backbenchers in particular considerable scope for activity, although it is occasionally threatened by attempts at disciplinary action (see Leys 1974; Barkan 1984c; Odhiambo 1986). Detailed press reports contribute to the strengthening of the position of Parliament. Since there is no organized opposition, however, the independence of the judiciary, which has not always been respected, takes on an additional and essential controlling function within the framework of a limited separation of powers.

Actual Power Structure

The real political center is the presidency. During Kenyatta's era his closest advisers, Mbiyu Koinange—his brother-in-law and minister of state in the president's office—Njoroge Mungai—another relative and foreign minister—and Charles Njonjo—attorney general and member of the cabinet—formed the core of the Kiambu group (named for Kiambu District) among the Kikuyu politicians, who largely controlled political decisionmaking. When necessary, other political leaders of the greater ethnic coalition were consulted (Leys 1974:244ff). In 1978, influential Kikuyu politicians, strongly supported by the GEMA, started a campaign to safeguard the presidency for the Kikuyu on a permanent basis. Njonjo, however, was able to prevent the change in constitution that was being demanded. It was also mainly due to his intervention that the transfer of the presidency from Kenyatta to Moi in 1978 went so smoothly, although it became known in 1979 that the transfer had been threatened by the so-called Ngoroko conspiracy. Njonjo, minister for constitutional affairs from 1982 onward, and vice-president Mwai Kibaki, both Kikuyu, ensured that Moi received support from the Kikuyu population after 1978. Njonjo was particularly skilled in accumulating political and economic influence and placing his protégés in suitable posts, and he became in this way the regime's "gray eminence" without at first appearing to rival Moi. When his ambitions were unmasked in 1983/84 by an official commission of inquiry that condemned him as a conspirator and traitor (*msaliti*), dismantling his apparatus of power proved to be difficult.

By calling early national elections in 1983, President Moi effected some important changes in the composition of the cabinet and outwardly legitimized his actions (Berg-Schlosser 1983a). He increasingly relied on supporters from his own ethnic group, the Kalenjin, but also on representatives of the Maasai, Luo, Luyia, and Mijikenda, which in part constituted the former KADU coalition, at the expense of the Kikuyu.

Parallel to this, the weight within the class basis of the regime was also shifted. The importance of national entrepreneurs and the petite bourgeoisie increased, at the expense of the comprador bourgeoisie that had been more strongly represented by Njonjo.

OUTPUT STRUCTURES

Administrative Structure and Behavior

President Kenyatta and his team of advisers were able to rely on the background work of capable, loyal Kikuyu who held key positions in the bureaucracy, in the parastatals, and in the army. The strong position of the output structures (i.e., the top of the ministerial bureaucracy) corresponded to the relatively small influence that Parliament, the party, and pressure groups had on political decisionmaking. President Moi has basically kept to this distribution of influence, but he has concentrated more powers in the Office of the President with several ministers of state and the chief secretary as the head of the administration. To the great indignation of the Kikuyu, a new policy of staffing has emerged whereby representatives of smaller ethnic groups, and in particular Moi's own, are being appointed to positions of leadership.

The regime first made the attempt to institutionalize elements of decentralization in development planning in 1968 with its Special Rural Development Plan, but the lack of suitable personnel, confusion over the distribution of competence between central and provincial administrations, and the absence of independently administered funds prevented it from attaining much success. In the same way, the District Development councils created in 1972 were mostly unable to set up appropriate regional plans or to hold their ground in the face of the central administration (Oyugi 1986). Moi's renewed district-focus policy has kept to the same planning principles but has now provided these councils with the backing of presidential authority. By allowing support for Harambee projects in future only when they correspond with official priorities, the leadership hopes to limit the explosive increase in running costs that has partly been caused in part by various self-help projects such as schools (Barkan/Holmquist 1986:29f). At the same time, this focus should lead to a regionally more even development that, to a certain extent, will be at the expense of the more advanced districts—for example, those of Central Province.

The goal of keeping the dramatic rise in foreign debt and the continually growing budget deficit under control has also been pursued by the fifth Development Plan (1984–1988), which proposed cuts in official investments and services, privatization of some parastatals, cost-sharing (e.g., in hospitals and schools), and an improvement in efficiency in the public sector, in order to lower the state quota of the gross domestic product (GDP) from 30 percent to 25 percent (see Godfrey 1986:12f). The Ndegwa Report of 1982 had criticized not only this increased share of the public sector but also the distorted personnel structure. On the one hand there is a mass of underemployed people with few qualifications, and on the other there is a lack of technicians and experts and a completely overburdened leadership. For this reason it is intended to restrict state activities in order to relieve the leadership's capacities (ACR 1982–1983:187f).

There has been some opposition to this concept by vested interests that developed during the Kenyatta era. Together with the numerous parastatals there arose a large number of sinecures. Public employees were expressly allowed to carry out private transactions (Hyden 1984), and the whole of society was permeated by large-scale corruption, nepotism, embezzlement of funds, and so on, as an unwanted side effect (ACR 1984–1985:285ff). The wide general support that Moi's policies initially received in 1979 was based on the expectation that he would correct such abuses, some of them blatant, but, after new affairs and scandals were exposed in 1980/81, it became obvious that the attempted coup of 1982 was in part an expression of a renewed crisis of legitimacy. As a result, Moi announced the drafting of a national code of conduct that was to apply to all elected politicians, top civil servants, and parastatal managers, but its effectiveness in reducing the extent of corruption and abuse of office should not be overestimated, as patronage is very firmly rooted within the society.

Structure and Behavior of the Repressive Apparatus

Shortly after independence in 1964, there were mutinies, as there were in neighboring Tanzania and Uganda, among dissatisfied army units, and these could be quelled only with the help of the British. Kenyatta tried to guard against further attempts of this kind by creating a counterweight in the form of the paramilitary General Service Unit. Its ethnic composition, with a relatively high proportion of Kikuyu, differed from that of the army in which the Kamba and Kalenjin were dominant. A deliberately slow process of Africanization and improved professional training on the one hand, and generous pay and other material privileges on the other ensured the building up of a largely loyal officers' corps during the 1970s. It was the army in particular that put a swift end to the politically motivated coup attempted by the air force on August 1, 1982. Moi was thus able to show generosity toward the armed forces in 1983 and decreed the closing of all outstanding court cases and an extensive amnesty for soldiers in cases where judgment had already been passed (see Berg-Schlosser 1982a). The only executions carried out were those of twelve coup ringleaders in 1985. Although the army has almost doubled in number since 1970, an increase spurred mainly by the dangerous situation during the Ogaden conflict between Ethiopia and

Somalia and the threats from Idi Amin in Uganda, Kenya has a relatively small fighting force of fifteen thousand soldiers (see Table 55).

Repression of opponents and MPs who overstep the tolerated limits of criticism—and whose popularity could endanger that of the political leadership or who are becoming too powerful in any other respect—is mostly carried out by means of preventive detention, a legal procedure borrowed from colonial times. As long as Parliament is kept informed to a certain extent, a person can be detained for years without trial. Sporadic attempts at a formal examination of this procedure by the courts after 1982 failed and in two cases, resulted in the banishment of the lawyers involved (*Weekly Review* March 6, 1987:3ff). Events such as these have led to recent massive criticism, by Amnesty International among others, of the increasing violations of human rights in Kenya (AI 1987).

TIME SERIES ANALYSIS

Political indicators. Time series for single events such as riots, armed attacks, deaths following internal strife, protest demonstrations and political murders show that 1969 (anti-Kenyatta demonstrations and Mboya's murder), 1974/75 (several corruption affairs and Kariuki's murder), and 1982 (failed coup) were the culminating points of destabilizing tendencies (see Tables 48 and 51; Diagram 9). The number and level of strikes always increased at the time of these crises, but they never again reached the extent of the phase from 1959 until 1965; 1974 and 1985/86 both show a distinctly higher level of strike activity than the usual low level (see Table 56). With distinctly higher ratings in the aforementioned indicators, the years between 1963 and 1967 appear as a phase of consolidation marked by the war of secession in the Northeast (Shifta War), by the murder of Odinga's adviser Pio Pinto, by unauthorized possession of land, and by political-structural changes. In the time comparison the indicators for 1966/67 reflect the onset of a stabilizing process within the regime. Although a number of plots were discovered in parts of the military in 1971, 1978, and 1982, neither Kenyatta nor Moi felt it necessary to increase the numbers of the General Service Unit (see Table 55).

The extent of repression used to check momentarily acute crises of stability and legitimacy can be clearly seen in the wave of banishments that affected the entire KPU leadership after 1969; regime critics such as Shikuku, Seroney, and Anyona after 1975; and, among others, two lawyers, a journalist, and a politician after 1982. The fact that Kenya had on average up to thirty political prisoners often led to international criticism of its human rights record. In 1975/76 Kenya's classification on the Freedom House Index scale of civil rights was lowered. Moi's general amnesty in 1978 and the suspension of further banishment for four years were part of a policy that was increasingly intended to broaden the basis of legitimacy, and it had an effect on the development of the voting rate: whereas in 1974 only 40.5 percent of registered voters went to the polls, in 1979, 65.7 percent took part in the election and in this way demonstrated their confidence in the new regime (see Tables 53 and 54). With the same idea in mind, Moi tried to overcome the attempted coup and the Njonjo affair of 1983/84 with the help of amnesties and reprieves, early elections in 1983, and policy initiatives, but pressure on the press and the number of detentions have once again reached the same level as before 1978. In the 1983 elections only 48.3 percent of registered voters went to the polls. Authoritarian tendencies—as, for example, in the conflict over the supremacy of the KANU in 1986 and the hard line taken over Mwakenya—indicate that the leadership is attempting to gain confidence by a demonstration of severity. At the moment these developments are not laying the system open to serious doubt, nor can they present a threat in the immediate future, but they are certainly a reflection of rapidly increasing social tensions and the larger potential of dissatisfaction.

Macroeconomic indicators. The phase between 1964 and 1973 is marked by GDP growth rates of, on average, 6.5 percent. Import-substituting industrialization and the high yields of the progressive smallholders brought about the "Kenyan economic miracle." In 1974/75 the first oil price shock, global inflation, and a drought led to a greatly reduced growth rate, so that GNP per capita decreased for the first time. The world market price boom for coffee and tea from 1976 to 1978 led to another increase in growth rates, up to 7 percent, before the second oil crisis, the beginnings of the debt crisis, and the worldwide recession limited economic growth to about 3 percent per annum between 1979 and 1984 (see Table 8). In addition to the unfavorable external conditions, two droughts—in 1980 and 1984—and the internal troubles in 1982 were significant stress factors. Consequently, GNP per capita fell from U.S. $420 in 1980 to U.S. $310 in 1984 (see Table 9). Both growth rate and per capita GNP has recovered somewhat since 1985.

Roughly a third of GDP comes from agriculture, which—apart from bottlenecks between 1980 and 1982—has been able to feed the growing population, produces almost two-thirds of Kenya's export earnings, and provides 70 percent of all employment. The main products are coffee and tea, but pyrethrum, sisal, and cotton are also grown for export, and maize, wheat, rice, and sugar for the domestic market. Highly developed dairy- and cattle-farming also belong to the important areas of production. Although the agricultural share in GDP has decreased since 1960, the primary sector, whose growth has maintained a considerable rate (in 1965–1973, 6.2 percent per annum; in 1973–1984, 3.5 percent per annum), still dominates and forms the basis for the country's economy. The secondary sector's share in GDP has remained almost constantly at 18 percent since 1960. Kenya's manufacturing industry produces a wide selection of consumer goods but suffers from a lack of heavy industries and investment goods production, which have seen only very limited structural change since 1960 (see Tables 11 and 12).

The inflation rate, unrelievedly high since 1973, reached its highest ratings of more than 15 percent in 1974/75 and between 1981 and 1983 (see Table 15). During this phase, wage earners suffered massive reductions in real wages. On the whole, wages have tended to decrease since 1975, apart from a more favorable development between 1978 and 1980. The officially fixed minimum wage has encouraged low levels to such an extent that even drastic rises in 1975, 1978, 1980, and 1985 were not able to compensate. In contrast, agricultural producer prices, which in a certain way can be taken as an indication of the development of agrarian incomes, have increased steadily over a long period.

On an average, the quota of new investments—just 12.42 percent in 1964—amounted to 20 percent. The rise in investment between 1977 and 1981, a result of the price boom for coffee and tea, led to investment quotas between 20 and 25 percent. After the effects of the global recession also reached this field, however, the share of new investments fell to 18 percent, the lowest level since 1970 (see Table 16).

Social indicators.   The time series analysis of the PQLI, which measures the degree to which basic needs are fulfilled, confirms a break around 1980, when for the first time there is a stagnation in the period up to 1985. The rise in the level of social development, which still had a PQLI rating of 35 in 1960, took place mainly between 1970 and 1980 with an increase from 40 to 55 points on the PQLI scale (see Table 28). With slight variations in different phases, the best ratings in the course of their development were reached by: infant mortality in 1975 (eighty-three per thousand); life expectancy in 1980 (fifty-five years); and alphabetization (literacy) in 1980 (47 percent) (see Tables 17, 18, and 19). Calorie consumption per person has gone in the opposite direction: after a sufficient supply was guaranteed for the first time between 1965 and 1975, it has fallen back to almost 80 percent of the standard rating since the late 1970s and has thus returned to the level of 1960 (see Table 20). The main phase of expansion in the public health sector took place in the second half of the 1970s, judging by the number of doctors (1980: 133 doctors per 100,000 inhabitants) and the supply of hospital beds (1980: 174 per 100,000 inhabitants) (see Tables 23 and 25), but here, too, successful developments are threatened by the ever-increasing population.

The proportion of children between the ages of six and twelve who receive primary school education grew from 54 percent in 1965 to 86 percent in 1977, and there was a further considerable increase after Moi abolished fees for primary schools in 1978, so that a rate of almost 100 percent was reached during the 1980s (see Table 26). Although many private secondary schools were built with the help of Harambee funds in addition to the public secondary schools that already existed, the demand is still far greater than the capacity. The quota of secondary school pupils in a school year has risen, however, from 4 percent in 1965 to 18 percent in 1983 (see Table 27). Since the state usually carries the high costs of staffing the Harambee as well as the public schools, expenditure in the education sector has for years constituted about 20 percent of the central government's budget (see Table 2).

EXTERNAL FACTORS

Foreign political relations. Kenya's foreign relations have developed along peaceful lines on the whole. Immediately after independence there was the threat of secession of North-Eastern Province, when Somalia, using as grounds the Somali peoples living there, laid claims to this area. Armed conflict between Kenya's army and the so-called Shifta rebels was settled in 1967 through the mediation of President Julius Nyerere of Tanzania and President Kenneth Kaunda of Zambia. During the Ogaden War between Ethiopia and Somalia, when old fears were reawakened, Kenya was officially neutral but unofficially supported Ethiopia. Since Somalia's defeat, the danger of secession has more or less been eliminated, and after 1983 there was a gradual but noticeable improvement in relations with Somalia.

The East African Community (EAC), founded in 1963, was based on the common history of the colonial era, on joint transport systems (East African Railways, for example), a monetary union, and a joint tax system. Kenya was in a particularly strong position with regard to Nairobi's increasing industrial capacity, and without any compensatory measures it would presumably have received the lion's share of new investments within the EAC market. For this reason it was decided in 1967, after Tanzania had withdrawn from the EAC at short notice in 1965 and separate currencies had been introduced, that extensive mechanisms for the regulation of such disproportions (e.g., customs duty compensation) and joint panels for control and administration (permanent secretariat, council of ministers, parliament, and law courts) should be set up, in addition to the institutions the EAC already shared.

Uganda's development after the 1971 coup, Amin's territorial demands on Kenya after 1975, and above all the tensions that arose from the different directions in which Kenya and Tanzania were developing led to the closing of their borders and the final collapse of the EAC in 1977. A change in the relationship to Uganda took place only after Kenya had welcomed Milton Obote's second presidency in 1980 and offered its support in rebuilding the country. Kenya's political isolation in East Africa after 1977 has since relaxed. Participation in the Preferential Trade Area (PTA) agreement of 1982, which is aimed at forming a common market in Southern and East Africa by the gradual abolition of customs duties; the start of a reconciliation with Tanzania in 1983; and the agreement over the distribution of former

EAC funds in 1984: all signal an improvement in Kenya's relations with all neighboring states. More recently, however, its relationship to Uganda after Yoweri Museveni's takeover has been beset with renewed irritations and tensions.

Kenya's foreign policy is officially oriented toward the principle of nonalignment, but in fact it has pursued a definitely pro-Western course since more left-leaning elements such as Odinga and others were largely eliminated. This tendency has increased on the whole under President Moi, as can be seen in the political, economic, and military cooperation that has developed with the United States. A special status is given to relations with Great Britain, which still plays an exemplary role in the social and cultural life of the elite. Only since Moi's chairmanship of the Organisation of African Unity from 1981 to 1983 has Kenya extended its policies, which had been mostly moderate in spite of a clear rejection of South African apartheid, in a more pronounced African and North-South direction.

Foreign economic relations.   Over the years the rate of imports and exports has remained at between 20 and 30 percent of GDP (see Tables 34, 35, and 36). Apart from the strong orientation toward foreign trade, the second constant is the structural deficit in the balance of payments. With an export quota of 20 percent (1984: $985 million) and an import quota of 30 percent (1984: $1,359 million), not even Kenya's considerable revenue in the area of services, especially in tourism (the third most important source of foreign income), could quite compensate for the deficit, which reached more than KShs 400 million in the 1980s. With regard to exports, coffee (1984: $259 million or 27 percent of export sales) and tea (1984: $239 million or 25 percent of export sales) have always been far ahead of other agrarian products such as sisal (1984: 1.7 percent) (see Table 30). The re-export of crude oil products from the refinery near Mombasa (1984: $181 million or 17.4 percent of exports) must be considered as a special case, as Kenya imports the crude oil—the largest item among its imports—at high prices. The other imports, however, consist chiefly of industrial goods, machines, and vehicles for transport (1984: $1,171 million or 84 percent of imports), and only a relatively small amount of consumer goods is imported (1984: $209 million) (see Table 31).

After 1978 Kenya's trade deficit took on threatening proportions, aggravated both by the slump in coffee prices and by the continuing rise in prices for imported goods (see Tables 39 and 46). The measures taken within the framework of structural adjustment programs managed a certain amount of success, but the effect of the 1980 and 1984 droughts on the import quota reflects Kenya's dependence on the world market and modifies the significance of such policies (see Table 35). The increasing trade deficit is rooted in an alarming long-term tendency of deterioration of the terms of trade, which fell from 112 in 1960 (1970 equals 100) to 84 in 1984 (see Table 37).

Apart from the revenue coming from tourism, Kenya was able to use its profits from trade with Tanzania and Uganda in order to settle its balance of payments. Compared with the relatively small number of imports (1980: $3.96 million in raw materials, food, etc.), there were considerable exports (1980: $189 million) (see Tables 32 and 33). The collapse of the EAC, and with it the loss of the Tanzanian market, was a hard blow for Kenya's industrialization, but Kenya's importance in providing Uganda with crude oil products or manufactured foods, for example, and the supply of electricity from Uganda to Kenya remained largely unaffected.

Kenya's trade is chiefly oriented toward the Western industrial countries. For exports, Great Britain is by far its most important trade partner, followed by the Federal Republic of Germany ahead of the other European Community (EC) states; the EC receives almost half of Kenya's exports (see Table 32). Kenya's imports come from the oil states in the Middle East, the EC, the United States and Japan (see Table 33). Until 1978 Kenya was able to compensate for its constantly high balance of payments deficit with the help of a strong influx of capital from abroad.

Favorable conditions for foreign investors attracted a great many multinational enterprises, which in 1976, for example, provided about a fifth of Kenya's entire capital formation (see Table 42). Consequently, almost 70 percent of the entire industrial capital still is in the hands of foreign companies who were allowed generous conditions for retransferring investments and profits. In addition, Kenya was very successful in its application for development aid and was able to use this to finance roughly half of all public investments. By far the greatest share of funds come from Great Britain and, more recently, from the United States (see Table 41); Kenya now occupies first and second place respectively among these industrial nations' receiver countries.

Kenya's national debt, which has experienced dramatic growth since 1979 (1984: $2,801 million), has resulted in a ratio of debt servicing to level of exports that is unacceptable in the long run; in ten years it rose from 3.5 to 27 percent in 1985 (see Table 44). Kenya was forced to fall back on support credits from the IMF and the World Bank several times between 1978 and 1985. With the decline of surpluses in public transfers (see Table 40) and falling private investments on the one hand (see Table 42), and the retransfer of profits or the shifting of profits within multinational companies ("overinvoicing" in the company's internal accounts) as well as the increasing transfer of private domestic wealth abroad on the other hand, Kenya has now become a net exporter of capital.

OVERALL SYSTEM EVALUATION

The Kenyan state leadership reacted to every political crisis by raising the level of repression, which, on the whole, nonetheless remained relatively low by African standards. The air force's attempted coup in 1982 presented a real threat to the regime, but, as before, the political system proved flexible enough to overcome the crisis, in spite of all the internal tensions.

Conflicts flare up particularly in connection with the growing inegalitarianism in distribution of income and wealth. Although about two-thirds of society participate in the growth of the economy, the concentration of ownership has led to an increasing lack of land for the rural poor. In the towns this discrepancy can be seen in a rapid increase of the subproletariat, whereas at the same time a small class of very rich persons (watajiri) has developed. The widespread agrarian petite bourgeoisie has so far been able to contribute to a certain balance through its growing purchasing power. Together with the urban middle classes and the watajiri, who have become powerful through top economic and political positions, they form a stable basis for the regime. Major policies have consistently promoted their growth and consolidation. Because of its record of success over many years Kenya's political system can count on the diffuse support of these groups, although their differential ethnic-regional distribution presents an additional factor of tension.

Individual competition as a motive for economic activity became established particularly among the Kikuyu people when they were forced to take part in the monetary system of the settler economy. This principle, used by President Kenyatta at the expense of egalitarian goals as a basis for his policies of economic development and the Harambee projects, thus corresponded to already existing attitudes among parts of the rural population, and through these policies the system was able to strengthen its basis of legitimacy. At the same time, the violent form of decolonialization both promoted the development of a national consensus and divided the Kikuyu into loyalists and radicals, thus contributing further to the potential for class conflict.

The ethnic alliance within the actual power structure consisted mainly of Kikuyu, Kamba, and Kalenjin and for a long time excluded Luo and Luyia from important positions. This factor intensified regional imbalances, as shown by the advantage that the Kikuyu were able to exploit under Kenyatta because of the inegalitarian tendencies of Harambee efforts. President Moi's district-focus policy is attempting to approach the goal of an urgently required regional equalization through a stronger control over the Harambee movement. Furthermore, there are unmistakably certain shifts of ethnic emphasis in favor of members of his own group, the Kalenjin, but also in favor of the Luyia and Mijikenda, former partners in the KADU alliance.

In the field of input structures Kenya has a broad spectrum of organizations at its disposal. Economic interest groups and agrarian cooperatives draw a major part of their strength from the informal relations that have arisen among the political leadership, the bureaucracy and the small sector of enterprises with large-scale capital—mostly in foreign hands—or the large farms. In this way, agrarian groups have so far always been able to stand up to the marketing boards and insist on producer prices that offer sufficient incentives to expand production. Apart from temporary interruptions, caused mostly by climatic problems, Kenya has always been able to produce enough food for its own needs. There is, however, no adequate equivalent to this differentiated organization of particular interests on the party level. The KANU has remained a mostly passive institution, supervising the nomination of candidates for parliamentary elections. This gap is partially filled by the relatively free and abundant press, the churches, and, up till 1980, ethnic organizations. The churches succeeded in taking on the role of advocate for civil liberties in 1986, for example, and in bringing the discussion over institutional changes that aimed at the disciplining of political forces out into the open, in the face of considerable opposition from the state leadership.

In the cooperation among such institutions, a few courageous MPs, and an independent press, the vertical separation of powers does have real significance. During the course of these troubled phases, however, it became evident that the position of the executive, and above all of the president, is dominant. A harsher recourse to repressive methods has regularly narrowed the scope of opposition and quelled criticism, which has never been allowed to shake the foundations of the system with impunity. Yet, regular, strongly competitive parlimentary elections and the role of the MPs as mediators between the central bureaucracy and local development initiatives have maintained a delicate balance among these forces and have up till now provided an outlet for the voicing of political dissatisfaction.

Since the president holds a key position within the actual power structure that controls access to the politically significant centers of bureaucracy, the lack of effective regular mechanisms of replacement and control of the president shows a decisive weak spot in the political system. Even Kenyatta eventually had difficulty in controlling this potential for conflict, in spite of his great personal authority. The improved ethnic-regional balance in the formation of the cabinet under Moi has proved to be a certain countervailing factor so far.

The personal enrichment that has long since reached intolerable dimensions among top politicians and bureaucrats is undermining the efficiency of the administration and the public sector. The small amount of redistribution that follows from the social obligation to donate money (e.g., for Harambee projects) cannot compensate for the loss of transparency and controllability of administrative and planning procedures. The measures taken to set up controls over the armed forces after their mutiny in 1964—professionalization and the founding of a special unit, separate from the army—proved to be relatively efficient.

Since Moi's presidency Kenya's foreign relations have been marked by more pronounced support for the interests of the Third World and opposition to the South African apartheid regime. The withdrawal from its earlier, markedly pragmatic attitude is also a result of the greater significance given to populist elements in Moi's policies, but there is no doubt whatsoever about Kenya's pro-Western orientation, which is founded on military cooperation with the United States and Great Britain and on strong neocolonial dependencies. With regard to foreign economic relations, the high outflow of net capital, which is a result of the transfer of profits by the numerous foreign companies and the increase of credit repayments, presents the greatest problem.

4

Tanzania

PRECOLONIAL AND COLONIAL BACKGROUND

In 1891, Tanganyika officially became a colony of the German Reich. Despite a concentrated effort to gain access to all parts of the country by building railways and roads, there was no large-scale European settlement. Colonial exploitation consisted of laying out plantations (tea, sisal) in the northern parts of the country and in establishing smallholder cash crop production (mainly cotton). Early on, in 1905, the African population reacted with massive resistance both to the coercive imposition of cotton cultivation and to the harsh system of taxation, as they felt their way of life endangered by these radical changes. The German colonial administration reserved the highest posts for Germans, Arabs were appointed at the middle levels, and local posts were mainly given to traditionally legitimized members of the native population; thus unwittingly encouraging the solidarity of these so-called *jumbe* (chiefs) with the population. Pilgrimages to the center of the traditional *maji* (water) cult in the mountains and the distribution of holy water all over the country provided opportunities for communication and unity among more than one hundred different ethnic groups, some of which formerly had been deeply hostile to each other. At first there were only spontaneous, local rebellions, but later the Maji-Maji uprising, which called for (among other things) a boycott of all taxes in the name of the cult, was organized on a countrywide basis with the jumbe taking leading roles. By 1905 the rebels had taken control of nearly the whole of the southern part of the colony, and the German colonial army was at first powerless to cope with their guerrilla tactics and the widespread support they received. Only after the sources of the population's food supply had been systematically destroyed and some regions had been partially or totally laid waste and depopulated could the uprising be put down in 1907. The economic development of the colony had suffered a severe setback, but the traditional, egalitarian-segmentarian social structures remained mostly intact. The long-term result of the uprising, which had a lasting and extremely detrimental effect on German colonial power, was the development of widespread national awareness among the people (see, e.g., Iliffe 1979).

Great Britain took over the administration of Tanganyika in 1920 on the basis of a League of Nations mandate and continued the production of export crops (coffee, cotton) mainly among the African small peasantry. As it was not certain that Tanganyika would remain part of the British Empire, the British colonial administration did not attempt to develop the infrastructure any further. The immigrant Asian population received monopolies and privileges from the colonial administration, giving them control over the wholesale trade in raw products. African inferiority vis-à-vis the Asian trading bourgeoisie was one of the main reasons for the forming of cooperative groups that joined together the Tanganyika African Association in the 1920s.

During his chairmanship of the association, from 1953 on, Julius Nyerere set himself the goal of transforming it into a political party, and in 1954 the Tanganyika African National Union (TANU) was founded. The TANU concentrated its efforts on the struggle for independence and for a democratic state but abandoned the aim of a comprehensive social-political program in favor of reaching a high degree of political consensus. During the transition stage between 1958 and December 9, 1961 (the beginning of formal independence), the TANU developed into a countrywide organization with approximately 1 million members. In the three elections held during the relatively unproblematic decolonialization, it won all the available seats in the colonial parliament in the face of opposition from two other parties, the United Tanganyika Party which had the support of the colonial administration, and the African National Congress (ANC), which had broken away from the TANU in 1958 (Shivji 1976; Schönborn 1978).

The task of forming a widespread national alliance was made easier for the TANU by its favorable ethnic structure, comprising a number of small peoples who coexisted without any dominant groups, and by the existence of a lingua franca, Kiswahili. On the offshore islands of Zanzibar and Pemba, however, there were organizations that were ethnically linked both with the African and the Arab population respectively, and with the Shirazi, the original inhabitants of the islands. Zanzibar was able to obtain very high export revenues through its position at the top of the world clove market. The clove plantations, together with the strategic importance of these islands, made them a valuable part of the British Commonwealth. British sovereignty did not interfere with the sultan's regime and the political predominance of the Arabs, and this fact, together with the economic exploitation of the other groups, led to serious tensions. In the mid-1950s there were two opposition parties, the Arab Zanzibar National party and the anti-Arab Afro-Shirazi Union. Elections after 1957 were marked by party rifts, and changing constellations and manipulations, with the result that the Afro-Shirazi party (ASP)—which had split off from the Afro-Shirazi Union in 1959—was excluded from power toward the beginning of independence in 1963, although it had the majority of votes. Consequently, Zanzibar experienced violent unrest in 1964, followed by the fall of the national party government and the sultan. Only a few months after seizing power, the revolutionary council under Abeid Karume, the new president of Zanzibar, declared the ASP to be the only permitted party (Schönborn 1978).

DEVELOPMENT POLICIES AFTER INDEPENDENCE

In the early phase of political development, the settling of institutional problems dominated the course of events. This included regulating the relationship between party and trade unions, and reshaping the constitution. Nyerere, who as prime minister had led Tanganyika to independence in 1961 and who had been elected president for the first time in 1962, laid great emphasis on policies such as the Africanization of personnel in the civil service or the strictly anticolonial orientation of foreign policy, which brought swift and sometimes striking success and an increase in legitimacy for the regime. Economic policies followed a plan—the Transformation Approach—that had been drafted by World Bank experts, among others, and that recommended the commercialization of agriculture and the building up of import-substituting industries, and placed great hopes on the influx of foreign capital (Kahama/Maliyamkono/Wells 1986:25ff).

Resistance from the TANU had prevented land registration along Kenyan lines in the 1950s and the nationalization of all land at the beginning of the 1960s made it impossible to accumulate private holdings in future, thus stopping large farms or plantations from expanding. By 1967 Tanzania had also decided on a mixed economy, wherein only certain sectors were reserved for public enterprise but others were open to joint ventures or purely private investors (Shivji 1976; Migot-Adholla 1984). The large multinational enterprises' preference for Kenya—they mostly chose Nairobi for their branches and investments—together with a decline in the influx of development aid, influenced the TANU leadership's decision to give up this development plan in 1966 (Kahama/Maliyamkono/Wells 1986:28f).

The Arusha Declaration of 1967 outlined a new development orientation with a socialist program that had been largely influenced by Nyerere. Egalitarian structures, collective production in *ujamaa* villages, state control of central industries, satisfying the population's basic needs, and using one's own abilities and resources as far as possible (self-reliance) were all central elements of this program. Nyerere stressed that in the course of its realization, which was intentionally long-term, it was essential to bear continually in mind the goal of building up a democratic political culture and its appropriate institutions. The emphasis was intended to be on developing the agrarian sector in order to reduce dependence on foreign capital. Parallel to this, the network of social services (schools, health care, water supplies, etc.) was to be extended to rural areas. The central regulation of these development processes was to be carried out by means of five-year development plans starting from 1964 (Shimwela 1984; Hofmeier 1982b).

The policy of *ujamaa vijijini* attempted to combine the necessity of modernizing agriculture with the political aim of preventing the class divisions that could occur as a result. This slogan—ujamaa refers to the strong family solidarity within traditional African societies—is part of the ideological attempt to use elements of traditional culture for the legitimation of political strategies and for the establishment of a national identity. The ujamaa villages, with their collective living quarters and production organized mainly on a cooperative basis, were intended to replace not only the traditional pattern of settlement with its scattered plots, but also the method of individual cultivation (Mascarenhas 1979; Migot-Adholla 1984). At first the regime relied on the voluntary formation of these villages. A few were set up, particularly in the less developed regions, after the government had offered to give preference to ujamaa projects in the provision of social institutions (see Raikes 1975). Open resistance was shown only by commercial farmers (kulaks) who this plan was attempting to repress in the interests of social equality. Since only 15 percent of the rural population was living in 5,631 villages by the end of 1973, the TANU leadership decided to use force in order to complete the resettlement. The main reasons given for this action were technocratic ones—better opportunities for schooling, health care, water supplies, and marketing facilities (see Tables 18, 22, 25, and 26)—many farmers eventually became reconciled to collectivization after they had seen some progress in these sectors. In 1980, 91 percent of the rural population lived in 8,269 villages (Mascarenhas 1979; Hofmeier 1981a; Kahama/Maliyamkono/Wells 1986:42). Although in most cases political persuasion and bureaucratic intimidation had been sufficient to induce farmers to join villages, sometimes massive coercion was used (see ACR 1976–1977:351). The aim of collective production was largely abandoned, however, and consequently the strong position of the richer smallholders, especially in the northern regions, was scarcely affected (Putterman 1986).

Due to the drop in marketed agrarian production since the late 1960s and the serious food crisis that befell Tanzania in 1973/74 (arising from a combination of external factors—oil crisis, global inflation—and internal ones—mistakes made during resettlement, preference for cash crops, the technocratic aspect of the development villages prevailed over social-political transformation. The government hoped to solve the problems not only through intensifying state control, which was an immediate result of building roads to the villages, for example, but also by increasing production through a more efficient distribution of necessary inputs (seed, fertilizer, etc.) and the expansion of marketing to areas that had so far not been commercially integrated. Producer prices were far too low, however, and gave no incentive for production. On the contrary, the resulting extraction of farmers' surpluses led many smallholders to withdraw from marketing and export production. They were content to sell only the few foods they did not need for their own consumption; after 1973 even the official purchasing price for these crops was more attractive than that for export crops (Leonard 1984). Through the administrative fixing of producer and consumer prices, which affected four hundred important consumer goods after 1973, subsistence farmers and the few progressive smallholders were made to feel the power of the bureaucratic bourgeoisie—the middle and higher functionaries in the party, state, and parastatals (Shivji 1986). Furthermore, the abolition of elected district councils in 1969 and 1972 and of the existing marketing cooperatives in 1976 was directly aimed at destroying important sources of influence for the richer farmers. On the other hand, the state strengthened its hold on agrarian production with new parastatals, so-called crop authorities that were set up as central marketing bodies. Retailers, another potentially influential rural group, lost a great deal of their power in 1976 through Operation Maduka, whereby all private shops in the villages were to be replaced within a short space of time by state-controlled cooperative shops.

Since 1961 Nyerere had been endeavoring to restrict the role of the petite bourgeois classes—*wanyonyaji* (exploiters)—and of foreign capital. In 1967 the party finally decided on a collective strategy of Africanization. Extensive nationalization, which between 1967 and 1971 affected all banks and insurance companies, the entire wholesale and foreign trade, the few raw material and manufacturing industries, and large areas of the plantations, gave the state control over key economic sectors. The resulting profusion of public enterprises suffered, however, from mismanagement, embezzlements, and widespread inefficiency from the very start. Seemingly draconian measures such as the abolition of the once-omnipotent State Trading Company turned out to be merely organizational changes that protected those responsible and failed to deal with real causes. Individual self-enrichment was still, however, restrained because of the party's leadership code, which maintained the relative homogeneity of the bureaucratic bourgeoisie, the so-called *watumishi* (servants) (Kahama/Maliyamkono/Wells 1986; see also Amey/Leonard 1979).

Import substitution, the building up of manufacturing capacities for agrarian export goods, and the promotion of small, labor-intensive industries were all items of the second Five Year Plan (1969–1974), but no systematic linkage was established among these sectors. The proportion of development aid in the investment budget, which had dropped to 20 percent in the late 1960s, rose to 60 percent in 1972 owing to multilateral donors such as the World Bank and states sympathetic to Tanzania's development policies (such as the Scandinavian countries), yet there was no real support for the small industries that came closest to the goals set by the Arusha Declaration (Mramba 1984). The third Five Year Plan (1975–1981) was based on a long-term strategy of industrialization oriented toward the establishment and provision of basic industries and small-scale producer goods, but due to the high balance of payments deficits there was more investment in export-oriented industries. The economic crisis and the second oil price shock in 1979 set industrialization back even further. The extreme shortage of foreign currency hindered necessary imports (spare parts, intermediate products, etc.) and prevented industrial capacities from being used to the full. In addition, investments failed to result in a higher level of productivity (Kahama/Maliyamkono/Wells 1986:31ff., 70ff). Attempts to improve workers' discipline and reduce overemployment were unsuccessful because of the relatively strong position of the urban workers' organizations.

When, in 1977, Edward Sokoine replaced Rashid Kawawa, who had been prime minister for many years, a period of hasty and often badly prepared implementation of reforms came to an end (ACR 1977–1978:407). Private investments received renewed encouragement (ACR 1983–1984:383), but there were no basic structural corrections. The dramatic crisis since 1979 cannot therefore be explained solely by the influence of external factors or natural causes (collapse of the EAC in 1977; war in Uganda in 1978–1981; deterioration of the terms of trade; droughts) (ACR 1982–1983:278ff). The long-neglected rehabilitation of the disorganized transport system (the "strategic bottleneck"), to name but one example, urgently required foreign financial aid. As Tanzania and the IMF were unable to reach an agreement, practically no aid was granted before 1986, although the Tanzanian government had put forward a comprehensive Structural Adjustment Programme by itself in 1982, and this program did manage to save the country from total economic collapse.

In order permanently to reduce public borrowing, public auditing was improved, subsidies to balance the deficits of parastatals were limited, and management was given more authority in relation to political functionaries. Tax increases and reduced subsidies were to contribute to a more balanced budget. Since two hundred current projects were halted in 1982 (ACR 1982/83:301), priority was given to the upkeep and utility of existing production capacities. Confining price controls to the most important consumer goods, and taking measures such as a gradual devaluation of the Tanzanian shilling, were intended to help develop a realistic price system (see Hofmeier/Schneider-Barthold 1983; Tanzania, Ministry of Planning and Economic Affairs, *Structural Adjustment Programme for Tanzania* 1982). The rise in producer prices, the readmission of cooperatives, and the reintroduction of local authorities with elected district councils resulted in the creation of direct production incentives and a political framework in 1982, which considerably widened the scope of the progressive smallholders and reversed the policy directed against them since 1967 (Leonard 1984:164ff). In 1983 this change of policy led to the forming of a new concept (ACR 1983–1984:269ff.): commercial agriculture was given a secure framework through the introduction of hereditary tenancy and the admission of large private farms (see Maganya 1986). Increasing export production became one of the major goals of agrarian policy.

Since 1984 the liberalization of imports has allowed a greater number of enterprises to use half of their foreign income for imports, independently. The first positive effects can be seen in the alleviation of bottlenecks in some basic supplies and consequently in the stimulation of economic activities (see ACR 1984–1985:382). The legalization of these imports is also aimed at directing the extensive parallel economy gradually back into official channels, where it can be subjected to taxes and customs duties. The readiness for reform shown by both government and party are confronted by some opposition, however, coming from the bureaucracy's desire for power and also from long-term ideological principles of certain hard-liners (see Hofmeier/Schneider-Barthold 1983).

SOCIAL BASES

Social Structures

The realization of socially and regionally egalitarian structures has received high priority among the aims of ujamaa socialism. Lines of conflict rooted in vertical and horizontal stratification are accordingly subject to attempts at direct political transformation. Among about 120 distinct ethnic groups, the Sukuma form the largest single group with 13 percent of the total population, followed by the Makonde with 4 percent, the Chagga with 3.7 percent, and the Haya with 3.5 percent. Some peoples, such as the Chagga and the Haya, have a considerably higher level of formal education than the rest, a result of historical advantages. In the case of the Chagga, who are settled in the Kilimanjaro region, the educational advantage is linked to a relatively high proportion of progressive smallholders. Due to the large number of small ethnic groups that prevent the dominance of any single group, and due also to consistent endeavors to form a national identity capable of playing down ethnic attachments, and a socialist identity, interethnic tensions are of no particular significance, apart from occasional accusations of nepotism (Hofmeier 1982b:165ff.; Klein 1980–1981:84ff.; see also Diagram 7 and Table 58).

At the time of the population census taken in 1978 there were 17.27 million Africans (98.7 percent of the entire population), about fifty thousand Asians (0.84 percent), about thirty thousand Arabs (0.25 percent), and approximately seventeen thousand Europeans (0.17 percent) on the mainland (Germany, Office of Statistics 1984:20). Numerous Europeans left the country during the Africanization of the civil service in the 1960s. The Asian emigration mainly took place when the wholesale and retail trades, after,

1967, and rentable property from 1971 onward, were being nationalized. On the islands, however, there are still about twenty-eight thousand (5.6 percent) Asians and at least sixty-four thousand (12.7 percent) Arabs, together with approximately 370,000 Africans (74.6 percent). Arabs represent the largest non-African population group in Zanzibar and Pemba, in spite of their exodus after the bloody anti-Arab riots following the coup against the sultan in 1964. Since some parts of the Shirazi population do not necessarily consider themselves to be African, there is a potential for secessionist conflict here, which last flared up during the discussion over the impending constitutional changes in 1983.

With an average population growth rate of 3 percent per year, Tanzania's numbers increased from 12.3 million to 17.5 million between 1967 and 1978; approximately 500,000 live on the islands. With an expected growth rate of 3.3 percent per year, forecasts show a population of 32 million for the year 2000. In spite of the improvement of the rural infrastructure and repeated coercive measures taken against unemployed town dwellers—the most recent attempt was the Manpower Act in 1984—the urban population has steadily increased. The degree of urbanization amounted to only 5.5 percent on the mainland in 1967 but by 1978 had reached 13.3 percent. On the islands it already amounted to well over 20 percent in 1967 (Germany, Office of Statistics 1984:18ff). Yet, Tanzania has so far been able to prevent the growth of real slums in large towns such as Dar es Salaam, Zanzibar, Mwanza, and Tanga. The proportion (2.7 percent) of the subproletariat in the population did not increase any further during the 1970s, but at the same time the proportion of nonagrarian proletaroids increased fourfold, to 11 percent by 1978. They earn their living, which is always a meager one, mainly in the informal sector of the towns and are accordingly developing into the second urban problem group (Klein 1980–1981:139ff). Campaigns against street traders, who play an important role, are highly unpopular because of their authoritarian character. Although in 1983, 400,000 people in Dar es Salaam were estimated to be either openly unemployed or in makeshift employment in the informal sector (compared with 168,000 people formally employed from a total of 1.4 million inhabitants), the authorities were able to force only about two thousand town dwellers to return to the countryside (ACR 1983–1984:206f).

Since only half of the land that is suitable for good cultivation is being used at the present time, Tanzania has considerable land reserves. The distribution of the population is regionally very disproportionate, however. Overpopulation is already noticeable in the ecologically favored regions of the North, especially in Kilimanjaro and Mwanza, which, together with Tanga, Arusha, and the coastal region, belong to the relatively rich and most developed areas of Tanzania (Klein 1980–1981:110ff). On the eve of independence about one-fifth of the cultivated land belonged to 1,666 foreign owners. This land consisted mainly of sisal, coffee, tea, or wheat plantations that were partly nationalized (e.g., all wheat farms but only 60 percent of the sisal plantations) after 1967 and continued as state farms (Kahama/Maliyamkono/Wells 1986:52). Only a fraction of the old estates still existed in 1978. At no time was former European property released for settlement by African smallholders, however; in fact, agrarian policies, especially after 1967 (see Amey/Leonard 1979; Collier/Lal 1986), made expansion more difficult for farms that were producing for local markets or exports. The proportion of the agrarian petite bourgeoisie sank, therefore, from 6.7 percent in 1967 to 4.6 percent in 1978, whereas the group of agrarian proletaroids, the subsistence farmers, made up about 68 percent of the population with a strong increase in absolute numbers.

In the early 1970s, 31.5 percent of farmers had less than 0.5 hectares and nearly 83 percent had less than two hectares. By comparison 9.5 percent cultivated between two and five hectares and 7.6 percent more than five hectares of land (Kahama/Maliyamkono/Wells 1986:62f). Although farmers in the less developed regions had had to accept greater changes of locality during the forced resettlement of the rural population in development villages, the regulations of land apportionment in the new villages—and the resulting reduction in the amount of land that could be reached on foot and was therefore able to be cultivated—did not amount to an effective redistribution. The relatively egalitarian pattern, with a GINI coefficient of 0.35, was thus maintained on the whole (Collier/Lal 1986:50ff., 130). Stratification within the villages can be judged by the amount, regularity, and composition of income, and arises primarily from the differences in available labor force or possession of cattle or machines (Collier/Lal 1986). Where there is a reversion to mere subsistence farming this stratification becomes even more pronounced. The richer farmers, who have continued to market part of their produce and to hire out machines they had bought in the past, for example, earn just enough money to buy the most necessary goods (soap, cooking oil, etc.) and can in this way maintain a low standard of living. The wealthier proletaroids, however, can sell only the sporadic and minimal surplus from their food production and are also obliged to hire machines or draft animals on a regular basis. In the long run they fall heavily into debt, which results in their "selling" land and thus sinking into a poorer class (all land is officially public property but informally at least there is a market for it among local inhabitants [Hofmeier/Schneider-Barthold 1983]). Collective production plays only a small role overall, since approximately 80 to 90 percent of the land is now in effect cultivated in the form of small plots on a private basis. The profit from collective labor is used mainly for village investments and is seen more as a kind of tax (Klein 1980–1981:112; Putterman 1986; Mascarenhas 1979; Msambichaka/Ndulu/Amani 1983). At the expense of dramatically reduced productivity, the ujamaa policy has thus mainly managed to slow down the pace of commercialization and agrarian development, but it has basically not been able to avert the trend toward an increase in social differentiation.

The modern sector comprises only about 7 percent of the entire working population (approximately 8 million men and women); that is, 511,000 wage and salary earners in 1978. In 1967 at least a third of all wage earners were in the agricultural sector, which employs 85 percent of the potential labor force, but in 1978 it was only one-quarter. Not until recently has agrarian hired labor in absolute numbers regained the level of 1964 (Kahama/ Maliyamkono/Wells 1986:53, 339), but the proportion of the agrarian proletariat in the population has fallen to 2 percent. More than anything else, the expansion of the public sector was responsible for the increase in the number of wage earners from 470,000 in 1975 to 570,000 in 1981 (Germany, Office of Statistics 1984:28). In view of the mostly negative results of industrialization efforts and the dramatic underutilization or decay of production capacities, there has been all in all a slight drop in the proportion of the nonagrarian proletariat, to 7.2 percent. By comparison there has been a great increase in the public salariat, which consists of staff with a medium level of responsibility in the state administration, in the parastatals, and in other public services. Through a network of informal contacts this salariat belongs to the clientele of the state class, at the top of public decisionmaking, and together they form the bureaucratic bourgeoisie (Shivji 1976), the core of the regime's social basis. The second group of nonagrarian middle classes, the petite bourgeoisie of merchants and tradesmen, has stagnated at 0.8 percent of the population.

At the center of power is the state class, which comprises about seventeen thousand members of the political, administrative, and economic elite. Its numbers increased continually during the Africanization of the administration in the 1960s, the nationalizations after 1967, and the formation of crop authorities after 1976. In spite of the ever-dominant position of this class, the discrepancy between the highest and lowest net income, which at the end of the colonial era was 50:1, was reduced to 6:1, in part due to a strongly progressive taxation (Leonard 1984:155). Nevertheless, this is offset by numerous fringe benefits such as public housing, cars, and telephones, and many advantages regarding information and contacts that can be extremely useful in the context of a shadow economy (Hofmeier/Schneider-Barthold 1983). A small class of entrepreneurs, whose more or less illegal transactions exploit the bureaucracy's weak spots and yield large gains, has profited from the grave economic crisis since 1978 and in particular from the shortage of goods that has only recently been alleviated (Hofmeier/ Schneider-Barthold 1982b:179). Since only some specific areas of the economy are reserved for state activity, there were still about fifteen thousand larger entrepreneurs in 1978, and there are presumably still a certain number of foreigners working in the management of nationalized enterprises (Kahama/Maliyamkono/Wells 1986:33f).

The data of a World Bank study show how disproportionately incomes were distributed in the early 1970s. The upper 5 percent of all households had a third of the private income at their disposal and the upper 20 percent had two-thirds, but the bottom 40 percent had just under 8 percent. Since then a variety of pay rises have produced changes but not been able to compensate any group for high losses through inflation, and on average have caused real income to fall, so that in 1980 it had reached half the level of 1970. Whereas the urban workers with their minimum wages suffered only a slight loss in purchasing power (20 percent), the real income of the middle and higher state employees sank by more than half and was reduced to little more than the real income of the rural population (Leonard 1984:163). As the wage structure disintegrated, there was a drop in discipline and productivity in all nonagrarian fields so that it was nearly impossible to finance even modest pay rises. Consequently, all employees have to rely on additional income. Right into the 1980s the rural population suffered both from totally inadequate, state-controlled buyer prices for agricultural products and from a serious supply shortage. By withdrawing into subsistence farming they were obliged to accept a drastic reduction in their standard of living (Hofmeier/Schneider-Barthold 1983).

Political Culture

Coups and crises in other African states, an army mutiny in 1964, and internal political struggles caused the TANU leadership from about 1965 onward to combine institutional changes with an ideological offensive in order to combat possible instability. The egalitarian ideals of ujamaa socialism, its democratic principles, and the support given to all anticolonial freedom movements increased the wide national and social consensus achieved before independence (see e.g., Baregu 1987). Positive results, particularly in the social services and through a more equal distribution of wealth, also contributed toward this goal, as did the personal integrity and charisma of Nyerere himself, who was prepared to acknowledge that not everything was running perfectly and that mistakes had been made. The unifying power of this perspective finally outweighed criticism of concrete abuses and enabled the country to press ahead with a new orientation. The pressure of expectations, which had been growing since independence, found an outlet in public discussion over both internal and external obstacles in the way of development. In spite of a declining standard of living, therefore, Tanzania has not yet experienced any open social unrest (Campbell 1986b).

Campaigns against so-called economic sabotage enjoy a certain amount of popularity, as they can be linked up with agitation against the *dukawalla*—the small shopkeeper who is represented as being the incarnation of exploitation. Yet, these actions can be permanently accepted only if they are not confined to petty black market trading or smuggling but affect above all the entrepreneurs who exploit the ineffective, sluggish bureaucracy and the constant shortages in order to do business in the gray zone, or *magendo*, where they make large profits. The course of these actions so far (floods of denunciations, overburdening of tribunals, etc.) does not give cause for great hopes, however. On the contrary, it is threatening to reinforce the increasingly widespread disillusionment with ujamaa socialism (see ACR 1982–1983:377).

What voters expect most of all from their MPs is that they will work hard in the capital to win support for local development projects. The rural population in particular is adept at summing up its MP's performance and will decide whether or not to reelect him on this basis. Since Parliament plays only a more or less acclamatory role in matters of national politics, the MP is expected to concentrate mainly on development schemes in his constituency. Accordingly, he belongs to various committees, but as the party and its functionaries dominate he has very little real influence unless he happens to belong to the cabinet (Barkan 1984c:91ff). Although the elections are chiefly of symbolic importance, between 70 and 80 percent of the population have registered as voters each time since 1960. The actual polling has always exceeded 50 percent (see Tables 53 and 54). Thus, Tanzania has distinguished itself by an astonishingly high rate of formal political participation, and this has in turn given vent to a considerable degree of dissatisfaction; the quota of MPs who lose their seats has fluctuated between 60 and 80 percent since 1960 (Schönborn 1980:222ff; Martin 1978b). Despite the lack of a real alternative, the same can be said for the presidential elections, even if Nyerere had more than 90 percent of the electorate behind him between 1960 and 1980. Voters make increasing use of the possibility of casting invalid votes (there were 6 percent of these in the presidential elections of 1976) in order to voice local grievances (Barkan 1984c).

After a catalog of rigorous development aims had been decided on in the Arusha Declaration of 1967, Tanzanian farmers were obliged to tolerate a series of state-controlled experiments. In the face of constantly renewed attempts at reform, most followed rapidly by failure, and the continual appeals to increase production, farmers reacted with the same general attitude of passive resistance that they had shown toward the colonial powers (Hyden 1980; Putterman 1986). Open resistance did occur, although very rarely, as in the case of the regional commissioner who was murdered after being sent to supervise the founding of ujamaa villages in Iringa in 1971. The regime still possesses a sufficient basis of legitimacy on the whole, but scepticism in view of the numerous failures is threatening to turn into a fundamental attitude of cynicism in large parts of the population. Even in the highest circles one finds the characteristic dual morality that is becoming increasingly pronounced as the parallel economy flourishes (see ACR 1981–1982). Recently there have been doubts within the party leadership as to whether the lower party organizations are sufficiently active and whether the elected village councils have any real significance. The liberalization that began under Sokoine and was intensified in 1980 is showing a tendency to turn away from the rigid implementation that has left little room for effective participation since 1967 (Mascarenhas 1979). The greater freedom enjoyed by private economic initiatives in recent years is therefore being combined with the development of a more open political culture (some hesitant attempts at *glasnost*, so to speak).

INPUT STRUCTURES

Intermediary Groups

Trade unions.   When, in 1964, the independent trade union congress Tanganyika Federation of Labour was abolished by decree and the government founded the National Union of Tanganyika Workers (NUTA), the Tanzanian trade union movement lost its autonomy. From then on the president appointed the general secretary of the NUTA and his deputy. At the higher levels of organization, functionaries appointed by the party were sent to join the elected trade unionists, thus bringing the trade union under the political leadership's firm control. In addition, the NUTA and, after amalgamation with the Zanzibari unions in 1977, JUWATA formed an official mass organization of the party. Whereas there were over four hundred strikes with about ninety thousand workers taking part each year in 1959 and 1960 and altogether more than 2 million working days lost, which considerably increased the pressure of the independence movement, in 1964 there were only twenty-four strikes with approximately thirty-five hundred workers involved. On the other hand, the intense struggles that had flared up over Nyerere's moderate response to the issue of Africanization led to numerous strikes from 1961 to 1963 (see Table 56).

Labor laws that virtually declared all strikes to be illegal, and workers' committees or councils that were responsible for labor problems at their place of work, prevented large-scale, independent action on the part of employees until 1970. In 1971, impressed by the overthrow of Obote in Uganda and developments elsewhere, the TANU issued guidelines— *mwongozo*—that were intended to increase the mobilization of urban workers for the regime once again. The program stressed the importance of workers' participation, and encouraged criticism and, if necessary, the removal from office of "arrogant, wasteful, presumptuous and oppressive" superiors (TANU Guidelines 1971:15). This released a wave of wildcat strikes, actions against unpopular senior staff, and in a few cases the occupation of works premises (see Shivji 1976). Draconian penalties, such as the dismissal of roughly eleven hundred employees from public transport services in Dar es Salaam, brought the strike movement to an end in 1972. Although Nyerere still referred afterward to the importance of participatory structures, in practice economic necessities received priority and the demand for more discipline and efficiency was brought to the fore. After 1973, widespread demobilization began, with catchwords intended to instill long-term confidence in the leadership (Baregu 1987).

Agricultural organizations.   Since the struggle against Asian tradesmen, the smallholding masses had been organized in processing and marketing cooperatives, and after the formation of the Tanganyika African Association, later the TANU, leaders had been recruited from the African intelligentsia and African retailers. The colonial administration also supported the cooperatives eventually, as they saw in them an instrument for encouraging progressive farmers. In spite of some negative developments (high losses, embezzlement, mismanagement), the TANU preferred up till 1967 to extend the state-controlled cooperatives rather than strengthen the African retail trade. A reorganization planned within the framework of the ujamaa villages was not carried out, so that the cooperatives remained as they were, in the hands of the richer farmers and eminent members of the rural population (see Shivji 1976).

In 1976 the TANU decided to abolish the cooperative organization Co-operative Union of Tanzania. It had shown its independence by, for example, using cooperative funds to build fee-paying private secondary schools, and in so doing had undermined the official education policy. At the lowest level some of the cooperative functions were taken over by the new central villages, and duties in the field of wholesale trade, storage and manufacturing were transferred to central, semistate enterprises—the crop authorities and the National Milling Corporation (ACR 1976–1977:343f., 364). High deficits and a dramatic decline in marketed production led the Chama cha Mapinduzi (CCM, or Party of the Revolution) to reverse this decision in 1981 and to allow both local and regional cooperatives with elected boards. However, these resolutions are still carried out according to the principle that organizations and institutions that have acquired some autonomy must be paralyzed through reorganization so that the state can reestablish its control in this field (see Baregu 1987).

Church and press.   Tanzania's favorable starting point with regard to its ethnic structure and administrative reforms (which from the very beginning removed power from local institutions) has spared the country much political friction caused by ethnic or religious controversy (see Hofmeier 1982b:182f). Churches can act only as informal channels for the articulation of interests and criticism. The press has belonged exclusively to the party and government since 1970 and in recent times has increasingly been given the backing of the political leadership when it has publicly revealed scandals and illegal activities. This does not exclude the possibility of pressure on individual journalists, however; in individual cases it is sometimes possible to publish very critical reports, but basically the press is obliged to mobilize for a policy of ujamaa socialism (Konde 1984).

Party System

After Nyerere's overwhelming victory in the 1962 elections, the ANC—the party of his rival Zuberi Mtemvu—was dissolved. The multiparty system had de facto become a one-party system. The young regime counteracted a crisis of legitimacy between 1964 and 1966 (mutiny in the army, increasing unrest in the trade unions) by strengthening the position of the president and the role of the TANU. With its improved organization and the high level of acceptance it enjoyed in wide areas of the population, the party was particularly well equipped to mobilize the population for the regime (Goulbourne 1979). The one-party system was legally established in the interim constitution of 1965, together with regular elections on the mainland. Finally, in 1975, the supremacy of the party over Parliament and government was made part of the constitution, thus confirming the TANU's notion of itself as the leading political institution.

The TANU's organization, ranging from "cells" (blocks of flats), "branches" (larger localities or companies), and district and regional boards, to national organs, is constructed along the lines of a mobilization party that seeks to ensure that the population will take part in implementing its concept of development and to consolidate the national and social consensus by means of ideological conviction. Senior positions at all levels are elective, but until the 1970s the party leadership continued to appoint full-time secretaries, thus establishing a considerable amount of control and at the same time increasing the capacity of the party apparatus (Okumu/Holmquist 1984:49ff). Control, and the authorization of the party to play a leading role in development policies, were both motives behind the assimilation of political, administrative, and internal party structures that was carried out by the decentralization of the administration in 1972 and the TANU supremacy in 1975 (Mwansasu 1979). After Karume had taken over power in 1964, the ASP was the only party permitted in Zanzibar. The 1977 union of the TANU and ASP into the CCM is significant partially because of the greater integration of the islands and the mainland, but its main achievement is to be seen in the process of democratization that Nyerere succeeded in accomplishing in Zanzibar (ACR 1976–1977:341). It was only after 1977 that new party and state elections were held on the islands.

Only those who fulfil the conditions of the leadership code are eligible for membership in the TANU or, now, CCM. Although all TANU and ASP members were offered the chance to join the CCM, membership fell from approximately 3 million to 2 million. Stricter conditions of membership can be only partially responsible for this, as members of the national youth organization and the trade union congress were automatically transferred to the succeeding organizations. At the same time, there are three other mass organizations, which are intended to prevent the formation of independent groups (ACR 1978–1979:397f). Regular party elections, educational campaigns, and monthly meetings of the lowest party groups guarantee a certain amount of activity at the base. The functionaries in the branches have great difficulty in asserting themselves, however, when confronted with the development administration's advantages of competence and information. In spite of repeated affirmation of the leadership code and accompanying purges, even local party functions in the 1980s have been synonymous with informal access to material advantages (Okumu/Holmquist 1984:59).

A national party conference with about seventeen hundred delegates elects the party chairman (since 1954, Nyerere) and his deputy (from 1972 to 1984, Zanzibar's President Aboud Jumbe and after 1984, his successor, Ali Hussan Mwinyi) every five years and, since 1982, by secret ballot. It also elects 130 of the 193 members of the National Executive Committee (NEC) from a list of 261 candidates. About a third of this powerful, collective organ of leadership are either appointed by the president or become members by virtue of their office (see ACR 1982–1983:284). The NEC does not only undertake the nominations for these elections but also makes decisions on principles and priorities of national policy and has comprehensive rights of information at its disposal; it can even call cabinet members to account. Thus, decisionmaking usually takes place outside Parliament, in the NEC and behind closed doors. Since the party is so dominant, MPs have considerable difficulty gaining access to the heads of the bureaucracy and find that their chances of satisfying potential clientele in their constituency through successful lobbying at the center of the party are very limited. The party's functions are so extended, as far as the central political system is concerned, that it is doubtful in the long run whether it can exist as a democratic participatory institution intended to represent the interests of the population (Mwansasu 1979). Consequently, a change in the constitution in 1982 stressed once again the separation of state and party. As a result, local and regional CCM functionaries no longer automatically are appointed to the corresponding administrative positions, and the elected district councils that had been abolished in 1972 were reintroduced (Okumu/Holmquist 1984).

Nominations for national elections, which have taken place regularly every five years since 1960, are carried out within the party according to an ingenious system: preliminary elections held in each district supply a list of candidates whose personal and political suitability is examined by various boards and eventually by the NEC. As a rule the NEC finally accepts the district's proposal but keeps only the first two names on the list (Bavu 1986). In 1985, over one thousand applicants appeared before the district councils competing for 111 seats (out of 234 seats in Parliament altogether), so that in only four cases was a seat taken without an opposing candidate (Munishi

1987). Since the late 1970s large sums of money and the building up of clientelistic relationships have begun to play a more important part in the preparation of a candidacy, which is increasingly organized by local power groups and sometimes by a paid electioneering agent (ACR 1981–1982:274). This aspect can be expressed neither in the brief account the applicants give of themselves at the district nominations nor during the election meetings held by the party, where both candidates appear together, as it has been permitted to comment on the party's election manifesto only since 1975. On the whole, the CCM tries to guarantee a high degree of fair competition in the organization of elections. The party even undertook changes in order to eliminate the advantages a particular candidate might gain from his position on the voting slip or from the symbol he had been given (Bavu 1986). The main interest of the candidates is concentrated less on the chances of political influence, which are limited in any case, and more on the informal advantages that are linked with proximity to the center of power (Munishi 1987).

THE CENTRAL POLITICAL SYSTEM

Institutional Aspects

The institutional integration of the islands into the United Republic of Tanzania was brought to a temporary conclusion through the union constitution, which was resolved in 1977 coincidently with the founding of the CCM. Zanzibar, however, was able to secure considerable rights of autonomy for certain institutions (independent political organs) and competences (domestic and economic policies, foreign economic relations). When the president of Zanzibar, Mwinyi, was elected president of the union in 1985 and took over from Nyerere (who had been president since 1962), the prime minister of the mainland, Joseph Warioba, became the first vice-president. The consociational principle agreed on in 1977 prevented Salim Ahmed Salim, who had been prime minister up to the elections and who is of Zanzibari origin, from remaining under Mwinyi at the top of the mainland government. In addition, Nyerere's decision not to stand for reelection had been institutionally prepared since 1982 by means of a change in the constitution. Future presidents are allowed two periods of office at the most, lasting five years each. Furthermore, the president has been formally bound by the decisions of the NEC since 1982 (see ACR 1977/78–1982/83 ff.).

Nyerere regularly stood for public election in 1962, 1965, 1970, 1975 and 1980 and Mwinyi ran in 1985, after each had been nominated by the NEC as the party presidential candidate. Within the framework of the one-party system, only yes or no votes are allowed; if less than half the voters give the candidate their support, then he is considered to have been rejected. Nyerere always received between 93 and 98 percent of all votes cast and so acquired a solid base of support and confidence that was able to withstand even serious economic setbacks (Barkan 1986c; Martin 1978b).

A characteristic of the parliamentary elections, which are held at the same time as the presidential race, is the high quota of members who lose their seats. Between 80 percent in 1965 and 64 percent in 1989 of the seats go to first-time candidates. In comparison with the backbenchers, members of the cabinet have a decidedly better chance of defending their seats, however. Since approximately 40 percent of all seats up till 1970 and approximately 50 percent after 1975 have been distributed either by presidential appointment or on the grounds of a particular office (regional party chairman, Zanzibar Revolutionary Council members, etc.), the circulation of the elite remains limited. The relatively restricted influence elected members have within the central political system, the strong rivalries between party functionaries, and the consequences of the leadership code all add up to limit MPs' chances of establishing a basis of power within their constituency as political entrepreneurs and of penetrating the political elite with any permanence (Barkan 1984c:89ff). Although members have been given a leading function, together with the CCM chairman and secretary, in implementing national development policy within their constituencies since 1975, this has not been able to compensate for the lack of resources and influence. In spite of its subordination to the party, Parliament does have certain powers granted by the right of legislation and the budget law, as shown in the few heated discussions (for example, over the introduction of a poll tax in 1982). In contrast to the arbitrary justice of the people's courts that existed for many years in Zanzibar, the judiciary's independence as an autonomous factor of control has to a certain extent been maintained on the mainland (Schönborn 1978:434ff).

Actual Power Structure

According to the division of work between the NEC, as the center of decisionmaking, and the cabinet, which deals chiefly with the implementation of policies, these institutions have shown different priorities in the realization of development aims. The cabinet, which is of necessity more pragmatic, is concerned more with problems of economic growth than is the party or NEC, whose aim is in particular the realization of egalitarian structures. Political development after the Arusha Declaration has enabled the more radical elements to dominate since 1969, which has resulted in widespread nationalization or the obligatory resettlement of the population in central villages, for example. Politicians who gave priority to economic considerations were politically isolated, as in the case of Cleopa Msuya as finance minister, or given posts abroad, as in the case of Salim who was made ambassador to the United Nations. On the whole, however, Tanzania's political system possessed the ability to tolerate the coexistence of political forces with controversial ideas of development. When a change of policy became necessary after the oil crisis of 1974–1975 and during the economic stagnation to which the radical reforms had contributed, it could be done without a great deal of upheaval, as appropriate politicians were still available (see Hartmann 1986a, 1986b).

Although Nyerere's only function since 1985 has been as chairman of the party, his support for one of the two political currents is still decisive. So far, his tremendous influence within the party has been practically irreplaceable; he used it to push Sokoine's policy of economic liberalization and a greater emphasis on discipline and efficiency, as well as its continuation under Mwinyi, through the NEC and shielded both of them in the process. The NEC, however, has begun to act with increasing independence and initiatives in recent times do not always come from the party chairman (see Mwansasu 1979).

After the assassination of Karume and the attempted coup in Zanzibar, those forces that supported a more open line toward the mainland gained control. In contrast to Karume, who determined Zanzibar's political development from 1964 to 1972, and to his isolationist policy, which was intended to prevent the feared plundering of the islands' rich foreign currency reserves, his successor Jumbe was very active in union politics. He was therefore the ideal partner for Nyerere when the CCM was founded and the union constitution was ratified. In 1983–1984, however, it became evident that the opposition in Zanzibar was still very much alive when a wave of secessionist demands met with great approval among the population of the islands. Under pressure from the NEC, Jumbe was replaced shortly afterward by Mwinyi, who was elected president of Zanzibar in April 1984 with 87 percent of the vote. He introduced a political and economical liberalization on the islands that has at least taken the wind out of the sails of the isolationist forces (ACR 1983/84–1985/86).

OUTPUT STRUCTURES

Administrative Structure and Behavior

Since 1967, the leadership code has forbidden all leading members of the party, the administration, and the public sector to draw additional income from private sources; for example, from their own enterprises or from letting property. By means of this self-restraint the state class hoped to prevent the integrity of members in their official capacity from being affected by private economic interests, which would have endangered its legitimacy of power in the long run (Shivji 1976). Privileges linked with public posts, such as an official apartment, car, and office, partially compensated for these measures, yet salaries, insufficient over a long period, are forcing even top functionaries to evade these restrictions with numerous tricks and to exploit the various advantages of their position within the parallel economy. The most noticeable effect of the code was that members of the elite were obliged to behave in a comparatively modest manner.

It is true that corruption, nepotism, and embezzlement are common and basically responsible for heavy losses in the public sector, but they have been kept to a relatively low level in individual cases. When Sokoine began to deal more rigorously with corrupt politicians and civil servants after 1977, the upper ranks of the administrative and political power elite were menaced for the first time. Sokoine's death in a road accident proved to be their salvation, as his successors were less energetic in continuing his campaigns against economic sabotage (Hofmeier/Schneider-Barthold 1983), and their liberalization policy unwittingly increased the possibilities of profit in the gray zone and so raised the level of corruption again (Campbell 1986b).

Particularly among the more qualified employees there has long been a motivation crisis, in part stemming from dissatisfaction with the egalitarian salary structure and in part from the lack of consideration given to expert knowledge during the radical reforms 1967–1977. The dominant party leadership developed policies that were almost impossible for the administration to implement (Hyden 1984). The expansion of the public sector, whose various functions were often insufficiently understood by those in office, led to inefficiency and the bureaucratic domination of economy and society. Activities in the gray zone became indispensable (Hofmeier 1981a, 1982b).

Chronic deficits in the parastatal marketing societies mean low producer prices for farmers, and there are often long delays before the proceeds are distributed. Farming surpluses extracted in this way are partially absorbed by the bureaucracy and partially used to subsidize the towns. Reforms that limit public borrowing, for example, and attempts to make public auditing more efficient are necessarily a threat to the beneficiaries of these structures and are consequently opposed by them. For some time, however, progress in the educational and health sectors and in the provision of water supplies has been able to offer the rural population some compensation, but district councils lasted scarcely a decade as regional organs of representation. They disintegrated in the friction between falling tax revenues on the one hand and the burden of expensive tasks on the other. Inexperienced area and regional commissioners, who were both senior administrative officials and party secretaries, could do nothing to halt this process. After the administration had been decentralized in 1972, the village councils were the only remaining elected organs, but they served more as channels of information than as instruments of real participation. Contrary to the official image there was no scope for effective self-help (Holmquist 1984a). Instead, competences were concentrated at all levels and organized according to a strict hierarchy from top to bottom (Klein 1980–1981:94ff.; Mawhood 1983). In this way the centralist administrative apparatus gained a high degree of uniformity but left no scope for self-help initiatives within the framework of local patronage relationships.

Since the official structures did not produce any integrated development plans for individual regions, this task was transferred in some cases to individual donor countries or organizations (Hofmeier/Schneider-Barthold 1980; Kahama/Maliyamkono/Wells 1986). The readmission of district councils with financially limited independence in 1982 marked a decisive political turning point; the potential of independent initiatives can now be put to use for economic development and it will be easier to identify local interests (Hofmeier/Schneider-Barthold 1983; Holmquist 1984a).

Structure and Behavior of the Repressive Apparatus

Party cells in the Tanzania People's Defence Force (TPDF) and officers as members of the NEC or as regional party secretaries are only two aspects of the extensive politicization of the armed forces (see ACR 1982–1983), which can be traced back to the chiefly unpolitical mutiny in 1964. Thanks to the swift recruitment of a group of loyal officers from the youth organization of the TANU, the government was soon able to cope without the help of the British troops who had quelled the uprising. By paying greater attention to political criteria during recruitment, an attempt is being made to come to grips with problems of discipline and unrest in the army right from the start. The last signs of trouble were in 1983, when a few soldiers were involved in a conspiracy.

Sporadic border conflicts, for example with Mozambique, or the tense relationship to Amin in 1971–1972, and finally the invasion by Ugandan troops in 1978 led to repeated action by the TPDF, which was extended to about fifty thousand men. The main burden of the liberation war in Uganda from 1979 onward was borne, however, by a civil militia of about thirty-five thousand men, founded in 1971 as a counterweight to the army (see ACR 1981–1982; Table 55). Its internal political function soon became clear: the militia provided the necessary staff to reorganize the countrywide resettlement in central villages and to break any resistance. In individual cases these armed units, which have police authority, have been accused of torture and murder, but usually the perpetrators have been brought to justice and those responsible removed from their posts, even at ministry level in one case in 1976. Even so, this apparatus can develop a considerable potential of repression in situations of conflict (see ACR 1976–1977).

Particularly important in this context are the detentions which take place without trial according to the Preventive Detentions Act dating from colonial times, which, until 1985, did not have to be publicly announced. The change of law in 1985 allows among other things the right of appeal in such cases and grants the detained a certain amount of protection (AI 1986). Amnesty International has repeatedly criticized the excessive practice of such detentions, for example in the fight against so-called economic sabotage, and also the large number of arrests for political reasons. Approximately half of political prisoners, two hundred to three hundred on average, are foreigners who have come into conflict with the liberation movements of their home country while in exile. Among the most prominent prisoners on the mainland since 1972 was Abdulrahman Babu, a former minister in Nyerere's cabinet, with about twenty other leaders of the Umma party, whose extradition has been demanded by Zanzibar since 1972 because of their alleged participation in the attempted coup against Karume. Nyerere refused this request, referring to the death penalty that the prisoners would expect there, the often-arbitrary judgments of the people's courts, and the refusal to allow defendants an opportunity for appeal (see ACR 1973–1974). In 1978, twenty-one people were finally set free on the mainland and 154 on the islands, who had been held in connection with this affair (see ACR 1978–1979). The differences in maintaining legal standards have on the whole changed only slightly since 1977. In 1985, for example, half of approximately thirty people who had been brought to trial after a conspiracy had been discovered in 1982 were set free. It has been shown that statements made during torture or extracted by force are not necessarily inadmissible as evidence (AI 1986); however, the judiciary has always received full support from state and party leadership when dealing with massive human rights abuses committed by the police or the militia, as in the so-called Barbaig Affair of 1976, for example, when it became known that several deaths had occurred (ACR 1976–1977:350, 353f).

TIME SERIES ANALYSIS

Political indicators.   An accumulation of the accompanying phenomena of political instability is shown by the political indicators for 1964, when unrest in the trade unions spread to the armed forces and resulted in a mutiny (see Tables 47, 48, 49, and 50). Plots that followed in 1969–1970 and 1982–1983 and that involved members of the army did not present a real threat to the regime because of the efficient politicization and mutual neutralization of the armed units. The political development of Zanzibar, on the other hand, shows breaks that are marked by political force—in 1964 Karume's coup against the sultanate led to a change of regime, and Karume himself was assassinated in 1972. After Jumbe succeeded Karume, Nyerere managed to press ahead with the integration of both parts of the union and the democratization of Zanzibar through the foundation of the CCM in 1977. Secessionist troubles flared up in 1983–1984 but were overcome by a change in the presidency of Zanzibar from Jumbe to Mwinyi.

On the mainland the low variations in these indicators and the relative insignificance of the events to which they relate correspond to regular occurrences of political life, as for example, the elections for some party and state posts. The phase of institutional consolidation during which the one-party system prevailed in the face of other powerful social organizations was transformed by the Arusha Declaration of 1967 into a phase of increased mobilization of the population for a self-reliant development. After the strike movement of 1971–1972 the regime began to abandon its participatory ideals. With the decision in 1973, to resettle the entire rural population in villages by 1976, a new phase of forcible implementation of this policy began, which involved a definite loss of legitimacy for the regime. A reorientation began in 1977 that encouraged private economic activities, and from 1982 onward, under prime ministers Msuya, Sokoine, Salim, and Warioba, it was given the dynamic force of a comprehensive change of policy through which essential structural changes are being carried out. On a political level this change of direction was completed in the presidential elections of 1985 when Nyerere, state president for many years, was replaced by Mwinyi.

Macro-economic indicators. The Arusha Declaration in 1967 marked the end of a phase that was distinguished by high GDP growth rates (on average, 6.4 percent per year). Industrialization began to stagnate for the first time. Although some radical reforms subsequently impaired economic development, GDP growth still amounted to an annual average of 4.8 percent until 1973. The dramatic increase in import prices caused by the first oil crisis and the decline in agrarian production, which resulted both from the countrywide resettlement and the drought of 1973, led to a crisis in 1973/74, which the Tanzanian leadership tried to overcome by revising the structures of prices, wages, and foreign trade. The result—growth rates of 5 to 6 percent between 1976 and 1978—was, however, also due in part to a favorable development of world market prices, in particular for coffee (see Table 8). During the 1970s the GDP per capita reached U.S. $280. From the end of 1978 the economy was caught up in the vortex of another crisis that increased in intensity because of various internal and external factors. Thus, development was characterized by stagnation and in some regards even by negative growth rates until 1984, when—affected by unchecked population growth—GDP per capita fell to U.S. $210 (see Table 9). Recently, there have been signs of an economic recovery, which endorse the new leadership's reform course under Mwinyi and strengthen its specific support among the population.

In spite of ambitious development plans, the sectoral structure of the economy has scarcely changed. Since the agrarian proportion of GDP has returned to more than 50 percent since 1978, it largely corresponds once again to the level that existed at the beginning of independence. The withdrawal into subsistence production caused agriculture's proportion of GDP to rise from just under 30 percent in 1970 to 42 percent in 1980, according to official figures (Maganya 1986:27, see Tables 11 and 12). Since the marketed proportion of agrarian production also stagnated after 1967 and constantly fell short of development plans, by 1978 at the latest food production was no longer sufficient to supply the whole of the population. The production of export crops similarly declined after 1975 because of the unattractive producer prices and the poor chances of selling these crops on the parallel market, and was thus one of the main causes for the lack of foreign currency.

Foreign currency shortages had serious consequences for Tanzania's industrial sector. A lack of spare parts, intermediate products and fuel caused the utilization of capacities to drop to a level of between 30 and 40 percent; in 1978, this was still 60 to 70 percent. After 1978 production declined at a rate of 14 percent per year. Whereas in earlier years the manufacturing industry had regularly produced approximately 10 percent of GDP, its share was reduced to 6 to 8 percent after 1980 (see Table 11). Because of the considerable decrease in the influx of foreign capital, the investment rate, which up till 1980 had always exceeded 20 percent, fell to about 15 percent in 1983–1984 (see Table 16). The overburdening of budgets has also led to more than half of all investments falling to the private sector since the late 1970s. Large budget deficits, which after 1979 were aggravated by the costs of the war with Uganda, caused a noticeable rise in the inflation rate—up to about 30 percent (see Table 15). Since 1978 the population's purchasing power has been reduced by at least a third.

Social indicators. The PQLI graph (which, in 1960, registered 24) shows considerable progress in development, with an index increase from 44 in 1975 to 61 in 1980 (see Table 28). It embraces a reduction of infant mortality by one third (see Table 18), a rapid increase in life expectancy (up by ten years in 1960–1975 and by another five in 1975–1980; see Table 17), and an improvement in the literacy rate from 66 percent to 79 percent (see Table 19). Progress in the field of medical services in rural areas is represented not so much by an increase in the number of doctors (see Table 23) as by information campaigns and the foundation and improvement of a basic rural health system (about 40 percent of the approximately eight thousand development villages have a health center). Furthermore, the new settlement structure after 1973 enabled drinking water supplies to be extended and improved so that almost 40 percent of the rural population had access to tap water in 1980, compared with only 10 percent in 1970 (see Table 22).

As schools were usually set up very quickly in the villages, the proportion of primary school pupils in any particular age group had already risen to 70 percent by 1975–1976. Due to the implementation of an extensive education reform in 1977, introducing compulsory primary education (there have been no primary school fees since 1973), this quota rose to about 95 percent (see Table 26). As primary schools have been an absolute priority since 1977, secondary school capacities have expanded only very slightly, and only about 3 percent of the respective age groups receive secondary education (see Table 27). In the interest of social equality the regime has been trying since 1978 to restrict the foundation of private schools, which were used as an alternative particularly in wealthier circles.

The realization of egalitarian principles was also the reason for the limitation of private medical care in 1976. On the whole, progress has definitely been made in the assimilation of regional and social differences, at least as far as the provision of social services is concerned. Since 1978, however, financial resources have been increasingly unable to maintain the rapidly expanding facilities (this is reflected in, for example, lack of spare parts for infrastructure, water works, etc.) and to provide the necessary materials (medicine, school books, etc.), and in this way some of the achievements made were reversed by the economic crisis. Calorie consumption per person in the 1980s is still relatively favorable as a result of subsistence production among the rural population, but this should not mask the actual supply problems, which were dramatic at times, and the subsequent necessity of importing food for the urban population (see Table 20).

EXTERNAL FACTORS

Foreign political relations.   In 1965 Tanzania's foreign policy began to take a distinctly antiimperialist and independent direction. This paved the way for the temporary breaks with Great Britain over its Rhodesian policy in 1966, with the Federal Republic of Germany over the recognition of the German Democratic Republic in 1966, and with the United States, also in 1966, because of a conspiracy that was presumed to have been supported by the U.S. Central Intelligence Agency. With regard to its political principles, the regime was prepared to accept the subsequent reduction in development aid from these countries, and, all in all, this resulted in a diversification of donor countries, thus lessening the ties with the former colonial power, Great Britain (see Kahama/Maliyamkono/Wells 1986).

In international organizations involved in the North–South dialog, in the nonaligned movement, in the group of Frontline States, and, more recently, with its opposition to IMF policy, Tanzania under Nyerere was one of the outspoken representatives of the Third World. Relations to the Soviet Union were never particularly intensive, but the relationship to the People's Republic of China was much closer, especially during the course of the TAZARA railway project carried out by the Chinese. Tanzania's association with the ideas of pan-Africanism and the freedom movements resulted in its support for Frelimo and Mozambique's independence, and in its participation in the war of liberation against the Amin dictatorship from the end of 1978 together with Ugandan exile organizations. In varying degrees the frontier conflicts of the early 1970s and Amin's invasion in 1978 revealed an external threat that never actually challenged the regime but that had a lasting effect on its social development.

After the Ugandan invasion, Kenya feared that Tanzania would develop a regional hegemony. Both this ideological rivalry and their greatly conflicting economic interests, which were contested within the framework of the EAC and led to its collapse in 1977, weighed heavily on relations between the two states for many years. In 1983, however, there began a process of reconciliation that was continued in greater regional cooperation regarding the PTA. Since the mid-1970s Tanzania has endeavored to cooperate on a political, economic and cultural basis with its neighbors in the south, and for this purpose joined the Southern African Development Coordination Conference.

Foreign economic relations. From the mid-1970s onward there has been a definite deterioration in Tanzania's foreign economic relations. At the end of the 1960s the traditional trade surpluses were replaced by moderate deficits. After 1978, however, export revenues did not cover even half of the imports. In 1980 imports amounted to U.S. $1.226 billion (approximately 27 percent of GDP) and exports to $507 million (approximately 14 percent of GDP) (see Tables 34 and 35). Although drastic economy measures reduced imports by a third by 1984, the balance of payments deficit still amounted to about $500 million due to steadily decreasing export revenues (long-term deterioration of terms of trade, decline in production, etc.) (see Table 46). Since 1978 Tanzania's foreign debt has reached alarming proportions, so that in 1983 more than half of export revenues had to be used for the repayment of debts (see Table 44). The decline in export production and the obligatory import restrictions caused the share of foreign trade to drop below 17.5 percent in the 1980s (in 1970 this figure was 26 percent; see Table 36).

About 80 percent of exports consist of agricultural raw materials. The most important regular sources of foreign currency are coffee (1984: $150 million or 13 percent of exports), cotton (1984: $50 million or 4.3 percent) and cloves (1980: approximately $50 million); the proceeds from cloves comprise 90 percent of Zanzibar's income and go directly into its budget. Tanzania's other exports include tea and, with noticeable fluctuations, sisal, tobacco and cashew nuts (see Table 30). On the other hand, the import items show that the Tanzanian industrial and transport sectors are dependent on imports and that the country is not in a position to provide enough food for its own needs. The importation of oil and oil products, which alone make up one-quarter of all imports, consumed more than half the export revenues in 1984 despite genuine economy measures (see Table 31).

The EC has been the most important trade partner since independence, with a share of 40 to 50 percent of exports and imports. Great Britain and the Federal Republic of Germany are together responsible for more than half of the EC's trade with Tanzania. The United States, India, and the People's Republic of China all have relatively low shares in Tanzanian foreign trade; Japan's role as a supplier is somewhat more important (see Tables 32 and 33). Trade with Kenya and Uganda almost came to a complete standstill after the collapse of the EAC. Tanzania, however, had the opportunity of establishing more consumer-related industries after competition from Kenya had been eliminated.

In view of the large balance of payments deficits that could no longer be compensated by development aid, Tanzania was unable to pay the outstanding instalments, which had trebled within a few years, on its public foreign debt amounting to $3 billion in 1984 (see Tables 32 and 33). The shortage of foreign currency had a catastrophic influence on the entire economy. Consequently, Tanzania was obliged to rely on further foreign credit, but this ceased in 1979 after the break with the IMF, which had taken on the role of a gatekeeper for most donor countries. The largest multilateral donor is the World Bank; the largest bilateral donors are the People's Republic of China and the Soviet Union, but considerable support was also given by West Germany and the Scandinavian countries (see Table 41). The object of the vehement conflicts between Tanzania and the IMF was not so much the actual measures to be taken (correction of the price and wage system, increase of exports, cutting of subsidies, reduction of public borrowing, raising of bank interest rates, devaluation) as the timing and extent to which they were to be carried out and the consideration of the social and political consequences with regard not only to food prices, but also the distribution of income and other effects. The IMF insisted on an immediate and uncompromising devaluation, but Tanzania neither wanted to lose face in front of an international public by accepting this condition without resistance nor wished to endanger one of its most important achievements, its relatively egalitarian social structure, by extreme devaluation and thus venture along an acknowledgedly dangerous path possibly leading to "IMF riots," as in neighboring Zambia. When an agreement with the IMF was finally reached in 1985 Tanzania accepted a considerable devaluation, to be carried out in installments, and extensive structural adjustments that may enhance the chances of economic recovery, at least as far as external conditions are concerned.

OVERALL SYSTEM EVALUATION

Because of the comparative lack of intense colonial development, the traditionally egalitarian structures of the peoples of Tanganyika were mostly preserved after 1900. With the exception of a few regions in the north, the progressive smallholders who carried out the cash crop production of the colony were not able to consolidate into a dominant, agrarian petite bourgeoisie. As a result of the Arusha Declaration in 1967, central policies prevented any further development of this class. The largest group remained that of the agrarian proletaroids who evaded the state's attempts at extraction by reverting to subsistence production, but on the whole this group was able to profit from improved social services. Through the large-scale expansion of the public sector, a bureaucratic bourgeoisie became established as a central power factor and, together with the lower classes, gave the regime a broad socioeconomic basis. The leadership code limited opportunities for self-enrichment and provided the ruling strata with a certain measure of coherence and legitimacy. Generally speaking, there are less-pronounced discrepancies between rich and poor, which constitutes a central pillar for the country's overall political stability. This has not led to a significant increase in mass purchasing power, however. Recent attempts to change this through economic liberalization and the encouragement of private enterprise imply that greater social discrepancies will be inevitable in the longer run.

The central aim of the Arusha Declaration—to distribute social wealth as evenly as possible—suited the cultural traditions of a people who were chiefly oriented to the values of egalitarian-segmentarian societies. On this basis the regime acquired a high level of legitimacy that withstood even the most blatant mistakes and setbacks, rooted as it was in consensual traditions and in the authority of a charismatic leader. This tradition of consensus and self-reliance, which had previously been displayed during the Maji-Maji uprising, thus provided a major backbone to the regime. There were also hardly any ethnic tensions, a result of the largely uniform development of the great number of ethnic groups. This favorable structure was preserved by a development policy consciously aimed at regional equality.

The TANU's extended apparatus successfully mobilized widespread support for Nyerere's development concept. Through the codification of the one-party system in the constitution, the party's claims to power were permanently safeguarded. Rival input structures, such as trade unions or agrarian cooperatives, either lost their autonomy or were destroyed. This meant that farmers had no means of facing up to state and party, which in this case also involved the bureaucratic bourgeoisie and other urban groups, or of voicing their interests with regard to the level of producer prices, but regular elections both of MPs and of the president provide the system with mechanisms through which a certain amount of dissatisfaction can be expressed. Although the party controls the conditions of the elections—manifesto and nomination of candidates—these do provide real opportunities for exerting influence, with scope for local political development. The party's dominant position, the existence of the leadership code, which is also binding for MPs, and the prevention of the development of a rural middle class has so far left no point of departure for an autonomous self-help movement along Kenyan lines. Since the change of course in policy, however, a similar collaboration is starting up on a smaller scale in

Tanzania between regional representatives at the center and local innovative groups.

The greatest opposition to this political turning point has come from the more radical wing of the party, which until the mid-1970s predominated over the pragmatic forces concentrated in the cabinet. The center of political decisionmaking is still in the party's NEC; Parliament has a more acclamatory function, and the cabinet carries out the task of implementation. This means that only the judiciary fulfils to a certain extent its intended function within the formally defined separation of powers, but the balance between the NEC and cabinet and the recruitment of a new political cadre through the party provide the regime with a reservoir of politicians and institutional structures with which it was possible to introduce political changes after 1976 and carry them through with considerable consistency in the face of the profound crisis after 1980. Until recently, corruption and nepotism have appeared only in more or less insignificant forms, thanks to the party's code of behavior, but the inefficiency of the bureaucracy and the public sector represents a central, internal obstacle to development on the whole. It is therefore absolutely essential to reduce the hypertrophic public sector and to direct the extensive shadow economy back into official channels. With the resulting increase in state revenue it should then be possible to raise the hitherto inadequate civil service salaries, so that an additional source of income is no longer essential.

The politicization of the army and the establishment of a militia have proved useful in controlling the armed forces. Conspiracies have always been discovered before they were able to develop. Tanzania has had to rely on its troops, both as a Frontline State and during the war with Uganda, but there has not so far been any reason to doubt their fundamental loyalty to the political leadership. In spite of serious supply shortages in the first half of the 1980s, there has been little social unrest in Tanzania, and the regime's stability has not been fundamentally endangered. Instead, the regime has had sufficient scope to introduce, carefully and over a period of time, a comprehensive revision of its development policies and at the same time to pursue the politically difficult integration of Zanzibar.

From the very beginning the country's foreign relations were a part of its distinctly independent development. Its antiimperialist orientation increased the national consensus, and Tanzania soon took a leading and internally popular role in standing up for freedom movements and Third World causes. The long struggles with the IMF are an expression of the determination with which Tanzania opposed a policy that was threatening the egalitarian distribution of income—the very basis of its political stability—with rigorous cuts and with formulae that had often failed elsewhere.

5
Uganda

PRECOLONIAL AND COLONIAL BACKGROUND

The area covering the present state of Uganda became a British protectorate in 1894. The newly formed country showed a marked North–South divide in the socioeconomic and political level of development of its peoples. Nilotic ethnic groups in the North (e.g., Acholi, Langi) and the East (e.g., Karamojong) and Bantu groups in the far West had decentralized, segmentarian structures. These egalitarian (acephalous) societies usually had no single permanent ruler. Ecologically better conditions in the South, on the other hand, apparently favored the development of lasting hierarchical structures among the Bantu peoples living there, especially in the kingdoms of Buganda, Bunyoro, Ankole, Toro, and Busoga (see, e.g., Kabwegyere 1974; Jørgensen 1981).

The society of Buganda, by far the largest and most powerful kingdom, was divided into clans led by a respected elder (*bataka*). Elders were members of a central royal council (*lukiko*) that gathered at the court of the king (*kabaka*). There was also a second type of division, a graduated hierarchy of chiefs who were appointed directly by the king, and were led by a "prime minister" (*katikiro*) who was chosen by the kabaka. Since the kabaka was not the religious leader of his people, foreign missionaries encountered very little resistance on his part. The Anglican church dominated at the court, whereas the Baganda population was influenced to a greater extent by the missions of the Catholic White Fathers, the majority of whom came from France. Political and theological rivalries thus spread to the mission areas and became linked with the existing social structures.

Great Britain tried to make use of this situation to establish colonial power in the form of indirect rule. The Buganda Agreement of 1900 gave the native rulers a new economic basis but at the same time decisively changed the social structure and the political order of Buganda. The most eminent members of the kingdom, in particular the chiefs—most of them Anglican—chosen by the kabaka, each received several square miles of land as private property (hence the nickname "mailo system"). Only a very few of the clan elders, who had previously played a central role in the traditional religion and who had also been in control of all the cultivatable areas, were given land, so that membership in a particular religion now took on the significance of an economically and politically relevant factor. Those who suffered most from this agreement, however, were the peasants of Buganda, who had to pay a regular farm rent (*busulu*) and a portion of their marketed products (*nvujjo*) to the owners of the estates. They also contributed fees to the lukiko and were obliged to pay a poll-tax to the central government.

As a result of increasingly high payments and a continual expansion of the estates (in 1900 there were a thousand such units; in 1926, ten thousand) the peasants' situation became visibly worse. The clan elders were their most important spokesmen, and frequent protests forced the protectorate government to intervene. With the Busulu and Nvujjo Law relatively low payments were fixed from 1928 on. In addition, peasants who were in arrears with their payments could not be driven from their land if they cultivated export crops (cotton, and later also coffee). As a result of this, the appointed chiefs, instead of being estate-owners, were now simply paid administrative officials; at the same time, however, a wide class of prospering small and middle peasantry was developing in Buganda (Apter 1961; Low 1971). At this stage the British gave up most of their plans for setting up a European plantation economy. The cultivation of cash crops (cotton) was now also allowed in the North, in the land of the Acholi and Langi, whom the British had intended to use as a labor reserve, yet society in this region was and still is far less differentiated than in Buganda. The colonial army continued to recruit most soldiers from the mainly Protestant Acholi and Langi, whereas the Baganda undertook the administrative penetration of Uganda within the framework of an internal colonization. The other kingdoms had lost most of their significance by about 1900.

The colonial powers valued Asians, especially Indians, very highly as traders and craftsmen and encouraged them to emigrate to East Africa. After some strong competition with European enterprises, they managed to gain a near monopoly of the manufacture and trade, including foreign trade, of Uganda's most important cash crops. After 1945 this trading bourgeoisie, supported by capital from their Indian motherland, took an active part in the growing industries, especially in the manufacturing branches of textile and sugar production. In spite of their great economic importance the Asians remained a dependent, easily dominated intermediate class and possessed little political influence.

In 1945 and 1949 there were general strikes and violent demonstrations in the whole of Buganda, aimed not only at Asian businesses and enterprises but also at the chiefs, which underlined the demands of the African petite bourgeoisie (progressive smallholders, retailers, and civil servants). Their opposition was also directed, as a result of the batakas' influence, at the lack of regard for the kabaka and for basic values in the traditional Baganda culture. They enforced the recognition of African manufacturing and marketing cooperatives and the transformation of the lukiko into a mainly elected, representative organ with parliamentary functions. By 1955 at the latest, British policy aimed at consolidating these classes, particularly the progressive smallholders (see, e.g., the recommendations of the Royal Commission of 1953–1955 on East Africa), in the hope of safeguarding the country's integration in the world market and preserving a pro-Western orientation for postindependence. In the 1950s, therefore, low-interest loans were made available for the African middle peasantry and retailers, buyer cooperatives for African retailers were established with state support, and there was an improvement in conditions for Africans in the civil service.

The strongly regionalist attitudes, however, which had been upheld and intensified by using the Baganda monarchy as an instrument for indirect rule, prevented the development of a united, national political organization of all petite bourgeois classes. Together with the workers' movement, which was still small in number, such an organization could have been used as a foundation for decolonization. Instead, progressive smallholders in Buganda provided a wide basis for secessionist aspirations. On the fringe of independence, which was granted as internal autonomy in March 1962 and then as complete sovereignty on October 9, 1962, a party system developed that reflected the ethnic, religious, and social areas of conflict (Mamdani 1976; Weyel 1976).

DEVELOPMENTS AFTER INDEPENDENCE

Political Developments

After a National Assembly had been elected in 1962, Uganda received its independence. Its semifederal constitution gave Buganda a certain amount of autonomy, whereas the rest of Uganda was governed as a centralized state. Buganda's competences included taxation, internal affairs, education policy, and the right of its own regional parliament to appoint Buganda's members for the national Parliament. Furthermore, the kabaka was chosen as the first president of Uganda, whose powers were limited to purely representative tasks. The central government was led by a prime minister who was elected by the parliament (Apter 1961; Welbourn 1965).

Three large parties took part in the elections for the first national assembly: the Catholic Democratic Party (DP), the Uganda People's Congress (UPC), principally a party of Protestants outside Buganda, and the Kabaka Yekka (KY), which was directed at traditionally minded Anglican voters in Buganda. After the DP had suffered a clear defeat in February 1962 during the elections for the lukiko, the KY majority nominated only representatives of its own party for the National Assembly. The elections resulted in an overall distribution of thirty-two UPC members, twenty-four DP members, and twenty-one KY members.

The KY, a party with conservative and separatist tendencies, and the UPC, a more centralist party with African socialist ideas, together formed the

government. Outwardly, the coalition was justified by its mutual Protestant-
ism, but in fact it had been made possible solely by power-political considerations (Mabirizi 1986:14ff). When, in 1964, Prime Minister Milton Obote
succeeded in holding the constitutionally planned referendum in the "lost
counties," which Bunyoro had ceded to Buganda in 1895, his UPC needed
only three more seats for a two-thirds majority strengthened by MPs who had
crossed the floor from the KY and DP. The coalition with the KY had
become obsolete. The referendum constituted an important symbolic defeat
for the leading groups in Buganda (Jørgensen 1981:216ff). Against a
background of constitutional conflict concerning the taxation rights of the
national government in Buganda and a movement directed against Obote by
the UPC's right wing, the kabaka tried to overthrow Obote with the aid of the
army in 1966. Obote used the failed coup as an opportunity to suspend the
semifederal constitution and to abolish the monarchy. Five ministers were
taken into custody and the kabaka fled into exile. A state of emergency was
declared in Buganda and continued without interruption up to Idi Amin's
coup in 1971 (see Doornbos 1973:313ff).

After the interim settlement in 1966 there followed a strictly centralized
constitution in 1967. The Republic was headed by an executive president
(Obote) who had strong powers in comparison with the cabinet and
Parliament. The parliamentary opposition consisted of only nine DP
members led by Benedicto Kiwanuka and faced about seventy members of
the UPC. New elections due to be held were postponed. Obote's position,
however, was soon weakened by often purely tactical alliances between his
political opponents, and he was increasingly obliged to rely on playing off
one group against another through the gratification of special interests in
order to hold on to power (Mabirizi 1986). An attempt on Obote's life led
him to extend the state of emergency to the whole of Uganda and to ban all
parties except the UPC in 1969.

General Amin had been opposing the government's policies with
increasing openness from his position at the head of the army, and he had
been involved in various affairs, for example the murder of Brigadier Pierino
Okoya who was presumed to belong to the Obote faction. When an attempt
was about to be made to remove him from power, Amin forestalled it with a
coup in January 1971. He dissolved Parliament and all parties and suspended
substantial parts of the constitution (Mamdani 1976:290ff). The bonus of
confidence that Amin received at first for the promises he made and for his
release of all political detainees, and the support he was given for his initially
popular economic war against the Asian community, did not last very long;
they were soon stifled by the despotism of his regime and the chaos of public
life (ACR 1971–1972:226ff). During 1973 Amin finally lost the rest of what
legitimacy he may have possessed together with important sources of foreign
support from the United Kingdom, the United States, and Israel, and his
regime had to rely almost entirely on omnipresent state repression.

The military dictatorship, created exclusively by and for Amin, was noted for its intrigues, its murders, and its mutinies. Amin's power was constantly endangered, and, as has often happened elsewhere, he took refuge in provoking external conflicts. In October 1978 he ordered an attack on Tanzania and occupied the Kagera region west of Lake Victoria. After the attack had been repelled, Tanzania decided to support Amin's opponents, who were in exile in London, Nairobi, and Dar es Salaam, among other places, in their attempt to overthrow the dictatorship. At the Moshi Conference, from March 23 to 25, 1979, more than twenty opposition groups united under pressure from Tanzania to form the Uganda National Liberation Front (UNLF). About a thousand soldiers who had flown to Tanzania with Obote in 1971/72 formed the core of its armed units.

After Amin's defeat on April 11, 1979, Yusuf Lule, a conservative university lecturer from Buganda, took over the leadership of an interim government set up by the UNLF. Disputes over competences in staff and policy matters between the president and the UNLF leadership led to his dismissal in June 1979, after he had lost the support of the Tanzanian leadership as well. Similar disputes brought about the downfall of his successor, Godfrey Binaisa, who, like Lule, had connections with the DP, in May 1980. They had both tried to restrict political activity to within the UNLF and to delay the planned elections for as long as possible, in order to keep Obote's UPC from power. In May 1980 Paulo Muwanga, Binaisa's successor, announced parliamentary elections for December and allowed all parties to take part once again (see ACR 1979–1980:347ff.; Sathyamurthy 1986:660 ff).

The new multiparty system was very similar to that of the sixties, The UPC reestablished itself mainly among the northern ethnic groups together with the non-Baganda peoples in the East and West of Uganda. It represented in particular the Protestant communities in these regions, the poorer rural population, and parts of the urban salariat and proletariat. The DP was supported primarily by the less traditional and economically weaker groups among the Baganda and other Catholic sections of the Ugandan population. The conservative forces among the Baganda formed the Conservative Party, and a fourth party, the Uganda People's Movement (UPM), was based among the Bunyoro and other western Bantu groups. The UPM represented, in the main, young, educated Ugandans who had, as had Yoweri Museveni, one of the guerrilla fighters in the struggle against Amin, lost confidence in older politicians.

At the parliamentary elections in December 1980, the 1967 constitution was revalidated. The UPC won with seventy-two seats, followed by the DP with fifty-one seats and the UPM with one (ACR 1980–1981:363ff). The opposition parties claimed that the elections had been rigged, and they were evidently right in many respects. At this point, the UPM and parts of the DP resorted to armed combat against Obote, who had been elected president for the second time. His regime's reputation soon suffered considerably both at home and abroad because of the appalling human rights abuses perpetrated by the undisciplined army.

There were three underground groups in particular that fought against Obote. The first was the Uganda National Rescue Front (UNRF), which operated in West Nile District and was a rallying point for former Amin supporters. A second group, the Uganda Freedom Movement (UFM), was supported chiefly by the traditional Baganda, whereas a third group, the National Resistance Movement (NRM), consisted mainly of UPM supporters. Although Libya gave its support to an attempted unification of these rebel groups in the early 1980s, it failed because of the intense political differences among them (*Weekly Review*, September 12, 1986:13ff).

In July 1985, after a coup had been carried out by UNLF units led by Basilio Okello, the leadership was taken over by a military commission under Tito Okello. Whereas the UFM and DP joined the cabinet, the NRM turned down the offer. Negotiations took place with Kenya's president Moi playing an active role as mediator to arrange conditions for a cease-fire by December, but in the event a settlement could not be reached that was acceptable to both sides. The civil war, which had been particularly violent since July 1985 and whose excesses surpassed even the outrages of the Amin era, was brought to an end in January 1986 with a victory for the NRM. Its leader, Museveni, was sworn in as the new president.

Economic Policies

The reorientation of British colonial policy in the Worthington Plan of 1947 encouraged the development of relatively large capacities in Uganda, especially in the textile and food industries that also produced for export. The plan's most important consequences were the building of the Owen Falls Dam in 1952 at the outlet of Lake Victoria and the foundation of a state holding company, the Uganda Development Corporation, for the promotion of industrial investments. Import-substituting industrialization and the attempt to continue to attract foreign capital also characterized the first two five-year plans (1961–1965 and 1966–1970) after independence, which provided the nucleus for an indicative planning framework. The influx of capital from various Western states reduced the dominant position of British capital and led to some diversification of foreign dependence. Local, that is, Indian, capital participated increasingly in investments, for example the Madhvani and Mehta groups (Mamdani 1976:253ff).

Parallel to this, an attempt was made to gratify petit bourgeois groups through Africanization of the civil service, programs of loans for African retailers, a licensing policy especially directed against Indians, and an agrarian policy that gave preference to progressive smallholders, as could be seen in the state support for cooperatives, which were mainly used and controlled by these farmers (Mamdani 1976:230ff). The foundation of two parastatals, the National Trading Corporation in 1967, which was responsible for the export crop trade, and the Produce Marketing Board (PMB) in 1968, which was responsible for the central marketing of foodstuffs, aimed at placing the entire wholesale trade under state control. This attempt by the leading functionaries in the state apparatus to safeguard their own economic basis and thus set themselves up as a bureaucratic bourgeoisie was met with bitter opposition. As a last resort, Asian wholesalers bought up and hoarded entire stocks from local PMB agents, who usually came from the bureaucracy but worked for the PMB as independent entrepreneurs. Although producer prices dropped, the artificially created shortage of goods caused the cost of living to soar. In 1969 the agrarian cooperatives finally refused to work with the PMB. In addition to this, as a result of a heavy drainage of both official and unofficial capital and falling exports, there was a balance of payments crisis that the government tried to control with a wage and salary freeze. When the economic crisis further escalated in 1969 after nearly all significant groups had withdrawn their support, President Obote tried to overcome the dwindling legitimacy of his regime by a political and ideological offensive, the "move to the left" (Mamdani 1976:260ff).

In the Common Man's Charter of 1969, Obote outlined the framework of his African socialist policies. Strongly patterned after the Arusha Declaration of the TANU, the charter proposed to reduce social inequality, completely to reconstruct the educational system, and to develop a mixed economy wherein state, cooperative, and private property could coexist. From April 1970 onward differentiated wage increases for the lower strata were introduced, which were intended to compensate for the higher incomes of civil servants in the middle and upper ranks of the bureaucracy and parastatals. At the same time the lucrative private earnings of the latter were to be suppressed in future (Jørgensen 1981:234ff).

With the nationalization of eighty-five enterprises announced by Obote in May 1970, Uganda should finally have been in charge of the "commanding heights" of its economy. As the state holding company already had an interest in the majority of the enterprises concerned, it was mostly only a question of discussing a buildup of its shares to 60 percent and negotiating the amount of compensation to be paid. Until January 1971, when all these plans were rendered meaningless by Amin's coup, agreement had been reached in only six cases, three of them being mineral oil companies, and in each case the terms of the international enterprises had prevailed (Mamdani 1976:266ff). The disputes between the PMB and the Asian trading bourgeoisie were gradually settled, as an increasing number of joint African-Indian enterprises signed contracts with the PMB. This arrangement, which tended to put the African petite bourgeoisie at a disadvantage, stemmed chiefly from the growing seriousness of ethnic-political conflicts. The UPC made use of it to weaken the progressive smallholders in Buganda, who opposed Obote's rule.

Amin's economic policy turned out to be just as erratic as his other measures. A systematic economic development was out of the question. The decline in tax revenue and the tremendous increases of the military budget soon threw the state finances into disarray, which resulted in the collapse of the health and education systems, together with the entire infrastructure, from the mid-seventies onward. At the height of the so-called economic war, Amin gave the Asian community three months to leave the country, starting from August 9, 1972. In the interim, looting and numerous atrocities took place, and by Amin's imposed deadline all Asians (approximately fifty thousand) had left Uganda. They left behind 5,655 businesses and much real estate. A Business Allocation Committee controlled by the military bureaucracy was formally responsible for transferring this property to Africans. Just over five hundred businesses went to Amin's personal friends, while members of the army and unscrupulous speculators who were interested only in getting hold of the firms' assets took the rest, after much use of bribery and violence. As property was also given as a reward for political loyalty, there were periodic redistributions that added to the chaos (Jørgensen 1981:285ff). During the fight over the spoils a group of very rich businessmen, the *mafuta mingi* (in English, the approximate meaning is "too much oil"), began to develop; they used their rapidly acquired wealth for activities in the gray zones of the economy or even for organized crime (Green 1981). The sudden nationalization of ninety British enterprises in December 1972, together with the confiscated assets of the Madhvani and Mehta groups, doubled the capital controlled by the Uganda Development Corporation. Because of the exodus of all Asian technicians, economists, and managers, however, the corporation was no longer in a position to run these enterprises efficiently. Conditions in the public sector were similar; a mentality of unrestrained personal gain prevailed. During the seventies industrial production was reduced by 73 percent and trade by 48 percent (Jørgensen 1981:290ff).

Disappointingly low producer prices and an increasing number of military encroachments on private property caused the peasants to discontinue their cultivation of export crops and return to subsistence farming. In 1975, after Amin's Land Reform Decree, the situation of smallholders became even worse. This law suspended all traditional property rights, placed all land under state authority, and made it possible to register private property rights all over the country. Buganda's peasants thus lost the special protective rights they had been given in 1928. The implementation of the law fell to the district administration, which had been newly organized in 1975 and was now dominated by the army. Under these conditions, and also because of heavy taxation that forced an increasing number of smallholders to sell their land, the mafuta mingi began to include agricultural land in their dubious dealings and so accelerated the marginalization of the lower peasantry (Fendru 1985; Mamdani 1986).

During this period, the so-called magendo, in which semilegal and illegal economic activities (black market trading, hoarding of goods, smuggling, illegal dealing in foreign currency, corruption, theft of public property, etc.) merge into one complex system, became the dominant characteristic of the economy (Khiddu-Makubuya 1985). In 1980 it accounted for about one-half of GDP and two-thirds of the monetary economy. In view of the lack of public safety, serious shortages of supplies, and totally insufficient salaries, the mass of the population was forced to participate in the magendo. It gradually infiltrated all areas of society and wore away any form of public morale. The system established itself so completely that it easily survived Amin's overthrow in 1979, although the change of regime caused a few alterations to be made in leading magendo circles, and there was a short-term rise in the flight of capital as many mafuta mingi fled abroad. A large proportion of this dubiously acquired wealth, had been being transferred abroad since 1972 (Green 1981).

When Obote took over the leadership of Uganda as president for the second time in 1980, his government faced the task of guaranteeing a sufficient supply of goods to cover the basic needs of the population, of restoring the infrastructure, and of rehabilitating the health and education systems. In agreement with the IMF it produced in 1981 a crash program for the stabilization of the economy that planned, among other things the abolition of state price controls, higher producer prices for cash crop farmers, the limitation of further public debt, and a more efficient system of taxation. These emergency measures also included a drastic devaluation of the Ugandan shilling by 90 percent. Obote accepted the IMF's stipulations unconditionally. In return, Uganda received IMF loans that enabled at least the beginning of a rehabilitation of the transport system and the importation of necessary spare parts and intermediate products for agriculture and industry. In 1982 and 1984 there were two further development programs that indicated priority projects on the basis of sector-specific policies, which were accepted by the World Bank and the conference of donor countries as a framework for further loans.

Some of these measures produced the anticipated results: smuggling abroad was considerably reduced; agricultural production was stepped up; public income increased; and prices appeared to be stabilized. In 1984, however, this positive development came to an end. The inflation rate began to climb rapidly; in addition, Uganda's national debt increased dramatically, in part as a result of the influence of unfavorable developments in the world economy, while a renewal of internal conflicts largely destroyed the consolidation that had been reached up to that point. In view of the continuing difficulties in the supply situation, there was never much doubt as to the magendo's supremacy (ACR1980/81–1984/85ff; Kamunto 1986).

Before it came to power, the NRM had already formulated a strategy for rebuilding Uganda through a "Ten Point Programme." Settling military conflicts was given absolute priority as a decisive prerequisite for political consolidation and for a rebuilding of the economy. With regard to domestic policy, the program listed the following central goals: building a parliamentary democracy that was to be augmented at all levels by Resistance Councils; restoring public safety through a politicized army and police force; integrating all former parties into the NRM in order to promote a national consensus; and eliminating the magendo and corruption. Without the removal of corruption it would be impossible to bring wide areas of the parallel economy back into official, controllable channels and set in motion a permanent process of development. With regard to the economic system, the NRM aspired to a mixed economy with strong private elements, an independent, integrated economy that has at its disposal diversified agriculture and industrial capacities in import substitution, basic materials, and the processing of agrarian raw products. Furthermore, the restoration of social services and the rebuilding of the education and health systems were to begin immediately (Museveni 1986:44ff). At the celebrations for the first anniversary of the NRM government in January 1987 president Museveni admitted that there had been little success in the economic field so far. The economic profile of the NRM had proved to be very diffuse at this stage (*Weekly Review* January 30, 1987:20). The split rate of exchange introduced in May, which had been applauded by the IMF and the donor countries, was withdrawn again in September 1986 with the passing of a strongly deficit budget (ARB, Economic Series, September 1986:8360ff). Doubts were aroused as to the sincerity of the regime's commitment to the private sector, after state departments had taken over trade in important and notoriously scarce goods such as sugar, salt, soap, and hoes. Barter agreements with countries such as Libya, Cuba, and North Korea were intended to alleviate Uganda's problems with the shortage of basic supplies and industrial goods (ARB. Economic Series, May 1987:8658).

Since IMF loans were promised in May 1987, the outlines of the NRM's economic policy have become clearer. In June 1987 the currency reform, planned since 1986, was carried out; one hundred old Ugandan shillings were now worth one new shilling and at the same time the new shilling was devalued in relation to the dollar by 76.6 percent (ARB, Economic Series, May 1987:8672). Although the new budget was certainly aimed at deficit reduction, and noticeable alterations in wage and price structures and in the tax system show a serious attempt to solve structural problems, there are no signs yet that this policy may have any permanent success. As there has been little change in either galloping inflation or the inadequate supply situation, discontent has been mounting.

SOCIAL BASES

Social Structure

Between 1969 and 1980 Uganda's population increased from 9.5 million to 12.6 million inhabitants. In 1970 there was a male working population between fifteen and sixty-five years of age of approximately 2.5 million; in 1980 it was approximately 3.2 million. Population density ranges from the most thickly populated districts of Bukedi in the East and Kigezi in the West (each has more than 160 inhabitants per square kilometer) to the thinly populated Karamoja region in the Northeast (approximately ten inhabitants per square kilometer). Average population growth is approximately 3.2 percent (in 1969 it was 2.7 percent) per year. The urbanization rate leapt from 4 to 7.8 percent during the 1970s but by 1980 it had dropped to 7 percent.

During the onset of industrialization the number of Europeans trebled, to at least eleven thousand between 1949 and 1959, and the number of Asians doubled to approximately seventy-two thousand (0.8 percent of the entire population) (Jørgensen 1981:188). A few Asian families formed an endogenous part of the haute bourgeoisie, but on the whole this section of the bourgeoisie maintained its exogenous character (Jørgensen 1981:288). Although Obote gave all expelled Asians the chance to return after 1980 and offered to restore their property to them, only six thousand Indians were living in Uganda in 1984 (ACR 1984–1985:405). The number of Europeans has been reduced to a few hundred since 1970, because of the continual armed conflicts and the expulsions decreed by Amin.

Almost 60 percent of the population are members of a Christian church; approximately 35 percent are Catholics and approximately 20 percent are Anglicans. The Islamic faith is professed by 8 percent of the inhabitants, mainly in the North and in West Nile District. About a third are followers of traditional religions. With more than forty clearly definable peoples, Uganda is, ethnically speaking, a highly heterogeneous country. The Baganda form the largest individual group with about 2 million people and comprise 16 percent of the entire population. The other Bantu peoples, whose share of the population ranges from 3 to 8 percent each, make up a further 50 percent of all inhabitants. The Nilotic groups, whose share is approximately 26 percent of the population, include the Acholi (4 percent) and the Langi (6 percent). The central Sudanese groups, forming about 6 percent, are concentrated particularly in West Nile District.

Just before independence the rural population of Buganda consisted of 2 percent large farmers with more than 10 regular employees, 45 percent prosperous small- and middle-holders, some of whom permanently employed one or two agricultural laborers, about 30 percent subsistence peasants working on a family basis, and about 20 percent laborers without their own land. Among the Nilotic peoples of the northern region the proportion of subsistence economy was well over 80 percent (Wrighley 1959). Studies of individual cases have confirmed that in the 1980s the patterns of stratification have been largely maintained in both regions. In the North the proportion of the agrarian petite bourgeoisie is still not much more than 15 percent. Thus, little has been done since 1960 to remedy the lack of development in the North (Mamdani 1984a, 1984b; see Diagram 8 and Table 59). A large section of the rural workers, particularly in Buganda, consisted of emigrants from Rwanda (*banyaruanda*), and its capacity for conflict as a rural proletariat was therefore limited. Other rural workers emigrated from the North, sometimes on a seasonal basis. One of the main motives of the secession movement in Buganda was to make use of this reservoir of labor without being obliged to share the wealth with the North in the interests of regional equality (Jørgensen 1981:192).

Amin's tyranny, the destruction during the civil war, and the frequent plunderings and raids by marauding soldiers are only superficial causes of the leveling of rural society. The impoverishment of the progressive smallholders was caused in the first place by a high quota of extraction, put into effect by central marketing institutions such as the Uganda Coffee Board with the aid of state-fixed producer prices. The producers' share in coffee revenues sank from 29 percent in 1974 to just under 15 percent in 1977 (Fendru 1985; Opio-Odongo 1987:72f). Wealthier farmers were able to resort to alternatives such as smuggling goods with their own vehicles or giving up part of their cash crop production in favor of more-lucrative food production for the urban market. Poorer cash crop producers could respond only by returning to subsistence farming (Mamdani 1984a, 1984b; Jørgensen 1981:303).

In the nonagrarian sectors social differentiation was principally affected by additional racial factors. A considerable proportion of the petite bourgeoisie of merchants and tradesmen consisted of members of the Asian population. Of the fourteen thousand retailers in 1966, 75 percent were Africans, but they handled just under a third of the entire trade. Thus the group of African retailers and tradesmen were among those who benefited from Amin's economic war against the Asian population. Fifty-one percent of those in dependent employment, who comprised about 7 percent of the working population both in 1960 and 1980, worked in the service sector, 21 percent were employed in agriculture, and 28 percent in manufacture. The proportion of the nonagrarian proletariat was always very small. The fall in industrial production, after 1971 particularly, affected unskilled workers, who received only the minimum wage laid down by the state. Whereas their cost of living rose by 530 percent between 1971 and 1977, the minimum wages were increased by only 41 percent. After 1974, therefore, many urban workers returned to agrarian subsistence production. Skilled workers were at least able to maintain the same standard of living (Elliot 1977; Jørgensen 1981:299).

The salariat greatly increased during the 1960s. Staff policy in the public sector and the distribution of work permits for foreigners in private enterprises were aimed at the employment of Ugandan citizens wherever possible. In 1967, 90 percent of those employed in the public sector and 64 percent in the private sector were Ugandans (Elliot 1977:20f). At the same time the proportion of Asians at higher administrative levels rose from 5.7 percent in 1954 to 13.4 percent in 1967. As the majority of highly qualified Africans were Baganda, the employment of more Asians at these levels meant a gradual reduction of the traditionally high proportion of Baganda in senior administrative posts. Thus, the salariat also benefited when the Asians were expelled (Jørgensen 1981:247). There was no change, however, in the salary structure that had been taken over from the colonial administration. The annual salary of a middle-ranking civil servant was UShs 12,000 in 1969 and that of a higher-ranking civil servant was UShs 36,000. Three-fifths of the population, on the other hand, did not earn more than the annual minimum wage of UShs 1,800 (Jørgensen 1981:239).

Kampala, where 40 percent of all employees lived in 1970, was the major goal of those who migrated to the towns. Since the metropolis was expanding more rapidly than the modern sector, however, the unemployment rate rose to 35 percent (Elliot 1977:2ff,14). Since the 1960s the relatively high crime rate and especially a particular form of organized armed robbery (kondoism) have reflected the enormous social conflicts in Kampala. The magendo economy, well established since Amin's time, has probably absorbed a large proportion of the subproletariat. As far as the structure of the magendo is concerned, it is estimated that about fifty to one hundred "big bosses" (mafuta mingi) control about twenty-five hundred "entrepreneurs" (magendoists), each of whom is independent but closely linked to the bosses. The basis consists of a host of 200,000 people, the *bayaye*, who are employed as street vendors, messengers, drivers, money changers, or workers within the magendo system (Green 1981).

Political Culture

The Buganda Agreement of 1900 institutionalized the rivalry between the Anglican and Catholic churches as a political factor. Protestants were usually appointed as chiefs by the kabaka and received large estates (mailo land). Most of the chiefs outside Buganda were also Protestant. Islam, on the other hand, which spread to Uganda from Sudan, had been driven back into the North with military force in the 1880s. The local administration posts that were occupied by the chiefs on behalf of the colonial administration were not available to Muslims, apart from a few exceptional cases (Senteza-Kajubi

1987:30f). The churches were able to control political socialization by means of state-supported mission schools, which for a long time monopolized the education system. The political-social power of each church was reflected in the political values, attitudes, and forms of behavior that the pupils were taught (Welbourn 1965). At the same time these schools put Muslims at a great disadvantage, as they were not allowed to use these education facilities. They usually had no access to employment requiring a certain amount of schooling, and this explains their relatively high share of the petty retail trade and their low social standing.

The Buganda Agreement also reinforced Buganda's status as an autonomous unit in contrast to the other regions that Great Britain had united to form the Protectorate of Uganda. The rise of its prosperous small and middle peasantry was based mainly on the Busulu and Nvujjo Law of 1928. This ruling, which brought many advantages for the peasants, was valid only inside Buganda. For the richer rural population, the defense of their material possessions became linked with the struggle to obtain a special status for Buganda (Jørgensen 1981:192). From the 1920s onward the tradition of the Bugandan monarchy and the use of the kabaka as a symbol of integration became the ideological basis for the agrarian petite bourgeoisie in Buganda (Mamdani 1976:120ff).

The prominent position of the kingdom of Buganda among the four neighboring monarchies conformed to the strategy of *divide et impera* upon which the British notion of indirect rule was based. As a reward for the subjugation of Bunyoro, Buganda was allowed in 1896 to annex part of Bunyoro, the so-called lost counties. The bitterness that resulted in Bunyoro and among the inhabitants of the lost counties, who suffered many disadvantages, was still present after 1960. British intervention also caused comparatively prolonged conflicts in other parts of the country (Kasfir 1976), which continued up to and after independence in the form of ethnic-regional rivalries and presented a considerable obstacle to all attempts to build up a national consensus (Senteza-Kajubi 1987:29ff.; Mamdani 1976:42f). The discrepancy between relatively highly-developed kingdoms and "rulerless" egalitarian-segmentarian societies in precolonial times was further reinforced by the division of labor introduced by the colonial power. This discrepancy also had a great effect on the images that the various ethnic groups had of themselves and on what they expected from the others. Whereas the Baganda controlled the African part of the administrative apparatus and the colony's economy, the Acholi and Langi in particular were recruited into the colonial army, and, up till the late 1920s, they were not allowed to cultivate cash crops. The northern peoples' sense of inferiority toward the South of Uganda on the one hand, and attitudes of arrogance, pride, and domination toward the North, especially on the part of the Baganda, on the other, formed the background for all manner of intrigues, which had important effects on political conflicts (Mudoola 1987:58ff).

Since the Legislative Council was not made accessible to Africans until the 1940s, and even then only to a few, there was never a forum capable of performing integrating functions. In the entirely local fora of political debate a national identity was not able to develop, and Uganda's political culture continued to be characterized by an extraordinarily high degree of hostility and mistrust among various ethnic groups (Mittelman 1975). This fragmentation of social forces led to the formation of fractions and cliques in virtually every institution, egotistic battles for positions of power, and various methods of personal gain in public posts. After independence, Obote, too, was unable to resist the temptation of using mere tactics and populist slogans in order to stay in power. This did not help to settle conflicts; on the contrary, it intensified and prolonged them (Mudoola 1987:56f). Under these circumstances Uganda was never able to make decisions that would have led to the formulation of truly national development goals, aims, and corresponding policies. Obote's regime forsook all chances of using such goals to mobilize the population in its favor and press ahead with constructing a national identity. Instead of establishing long-term harmony between the aims of the regime and the values of the population, and in this way acquiring a permanent basis of legitimacy and confidence, Obote resorted to the tactics of gratifying particular interests (e.g., the lost counties issue) in order to uphold his regime on the basis of specific supports (Khiddu-Makubuya 1985).

Lack of success both in political stabilization and the establishment of public safety, and demoralization in all state institutions, shook the population's confidence equally quickly in the interim governments of 1979/80 and Obote's second regime between 1980 and 1984. In view of the very long armed struggles, nearly all forms of social solidarity beyond one's immediate family and a minimum of mutual trust in social relations now seem to have disappeared. Ugandan society today resembles Hobbes's "war of all against all" more than that of any other African state. In the South of Uganda, at least, the NRM appears to have succeeded in starting to change this trend.

INPUT STRUCTURES

Intermediary Groups

Trade unions. In 1964 strike laws were passed that permitted labor disputes only after an exhaustive process of mediation. This was Obote's reaction to a wave of wildcat strikes initiated in 1963 by members of the UPC youth organization and the UPC-influenced trade union organization. When the Federation of Uganda Trade Unions (FUTU) was founded in 1964, the more radical trade unionists and left-wing UPC General Secretary John Kakonge lost their basis. At the same time, interest in the trade unions diminished considerably. The number of members decreased from ninety-six thousand in 1964, when membership was at its peak, to sixty-five thousand in 1966 (Mamdani 1976:281ff.; Jørgensen 1981:226f).

Until the state crisis of 1966 there were two opposing trade union organizations, the FUTU and the Uganda Trade Unions Congress (UTUC). Obote then enforced their unification by law, forming the Uganda Labour Congress (ULC). The subsequent trade union elections were won not by the formerly radical functionaries who were loyal to the UPC but by representatives of the moderate UTUC, which received most of its support from urban employees. In 1968, however, Eriabu Kibuka, a former FUTU leader and member of the UPC, proclaimed himself general secretary of the ULC with official backing. At the same time the government ensured that it had a right of veto in the appointment of all ULC functionaries.

On the occasion of the nationalizations in May 1970 Obote announced a general ban on all strike action. He did not succeed in subduing the strikes, however, which had flared up at intervals since 1969 over demands for an extensive rise in the minimum wage. During Amin's dictatorship the trade unions lost the basis for any effective activity: first, workers who took part in a strike were in constant fear that the army or other armed forces would be sent in; second, in this generally insecure state of affairs anyone drawing particular attention to himself was in danger of his life. Between 1980 and 1984 the new National Organization of Trade Unions did not progress beyond an initial rebuilding of organizational structures and a programmatical elucidation.

Agricultural organizations. In the 1960s the cooperatives, which served as an organizational basis for the petite bourgeois cash crop producers, succeeded, with massive state support, in acquiring increasingly large shares in the marketing and processing stages of coffee and cotton. The Co-operative Law of 1963 guaranteed complete autonomy in all financial and management matters for these institutions, which had previously been under the supervision of the colonial authorities. Instead of the usual profits there were now large deficits, as a result of management errors (investment errors, unjustified distribution of dividends) and financial irregularities. Obote tried to gain a certain amount of state control with a new law in 1970, but in doing so he antagonized the agrarian petite bourgeoisie to an even greater extent (Mamdani 1976:230ff., 277f).

At first, the agricultural organizations were hardly affected by Amin's coup, but the magendo economy, which had first developed as a result of the state's toleration of coffee smuggling, soon infiltrated this sector as well. It was almost impossible for the producers to avoid its dominant position in the transport sector, and even today the majority of farmers who do not have their own transport and therefore have to rely on official marketing organs receive only a fraction of the potential revenues (Green 1981).

Religious communities. Soon after independence the fragmentation of political forces led to organizational rifts and prolonged conflict within religious communities. The two Anglican dioceses in Buganda, for example, demanded a joint special status after 1965. In order to weaken the traditional Muslim League, which was close to the KY, the UPC supported the foundation of a second Muslim organization after 1966. The discord in these two cases only came to an end when Amin threatened to use force (Mamdani 1976:285ff). Anglican bishops, under the leadership of Archbishop Janan Luwum, made a first attempt in 1976/77 to protest gross abuses of human rights; Luwum was murdered by Amin's underlings in February 1977. It was not until after 1980 that representatives of the Christian churches joined with Muslims in taking up the offensive once again and, in view of the innumerable outrages committed by undisciplined troops, urged that human rights should be observed (ACR 1976–1977:379ff.; ACR 1980–1981:310).

The Press. With the exception of the Amin era, Uganda has since independence always had an extraordinarily varied press that includes both official party organs and newspapers that have party connections (e.g., the *Citizen*, which is loyal to the DP), government organs (at present, *New Vision*), and several newspapers published by independent entrepreneurs. Since 1979 there has been an astonishingly high degree of freedom for the press (see ACR 1983–1984:304f). Journalists' working conditions, however, are often precarious in view of the very high number of detentions under every regime and the frequently very poor standards of public safety. Yet the press publishes remarkably open accounts of the situation in northern Uganda, for example, whenever there is any information available (ARB, Political Series, December 1986:8318).

Military organizations. The militarization of society during the years of Amin's dictatorship provided a background for the activities of organized rebels, mostly based in particular regions or ethnic groups, who opposed the legitimacy of the various governments. As in the situation after 1981, various armed organizations declared war on the present regime in 1986/87. In 1986 the NRM managed to integrate the three other active freedom movements against Obote—the UNRF, UFM, and the Federal Democratic Movement (Fedemu)—in the all-party cabinet and to join their troops with the NRM's National Resistance Army (NRA). Purges among the coopted officers, and conflicts arising from a collaboration characterized by tactical tricks and attempted domination, finally led to the withdrawal of these groups by June 1987 from the alliance with Museveni (*Weekly Review*, June 26, 1987: 42f).

The Uganda People's Democratic Movement (UPDM), led by Otema Alimadi, a former prime minister under Obote, has accused the NRM of massive violations of human rights and denounced Museveni's apparent pro-

Libyan course and the betrayal of Ugandan interests to Libya, Cuba, and North Korea. The Fedemu, relatively close to the UPDM, supports the return to the semifederal constitution of 1962 and the reinstatement of the ethnic monarchies. The UFM, whose leader Andrew Kayiira was arrested during his cabinet membership in September 1986 because of a planned coup and was later murdered under mysterious circumstances, had already renounced the coalition with Museveni in March 1987. In the North of Uganda the formerly scattered remains of the Uganda National Liberation Army, which Obote had recruited mainly from this region, are gaining strength. In the regions under its control it appears as the representative of ethnic groups living there or enforces support from the population (ARB, Political Series, September 1987:8608).

These groups, together with other newly founded organizations and secret unions such as Force Obote Back Again, which appeared briefly in the headlines in connection with murderous attacks, are a threat to public safety, which in the South at least is otherwise more or less guaranteed. Part of the unrest in the Northeast is caused by the Karamojong living in this area who have a tradition of cattle-raiding. Now that they have formed large gangs and are equipped with modern submachine guns and rifles, however, their attacks often involve much bloodshed. The NRA's inability to protect the population with any efficiency contributes to the erosion of its authority in these areas (*Weekly Review* , October 31, 1986:17f).

Party System

The parties that entered the National Assembly in 1962 had been formed in the 1950s during the course of the violent political conflicts that resulted from Buganda's demands for secession. In the UPC, ethnic groups from the North combined with some of the eastern and western Bantu peoples. Their opposition to the Baganda and their membership in the Protestant church served as a common factor. The party was dominated in a socioeconomic sense by retailers who were more national-minded (Apter 1961:316ff.; Gertzel 1974:34). The second-largest party, the DP, defined itself as the representative of the Catholic population. Through this party the chiefs of Buganda who had lost their power hoped to win the support of the largely Catholic smallholders. The DP's mainstay in the North were the civil servants who had been educated in Catholic schools. Buganda's mainly Anglican large farmers and higher administration officials, on the other hand, joined forces in the KY (the party name means "kabaka above all") movement, which also received support from many traditionally oriented smallholders in Buganda (Welbourn 1965; Low 1971; Weyel 1976:69ff.; Mamdani 1976:208ff).

From the very beginning the internal structure of the UPC resembled a federation of regional parties ruled over by provincial "sovereigns." The

UPC, which was not founded until 1960, lacked both a fully developed organizational structure and an internal cohesion sufficient to curb the federative tendencies and bitter struggles over party lines. Instead of substantive discussions of the major issues there were intrigues, rivalries, and opportunistic alliances, often dictated by purely parochial disputes (Mujaju 1976b). In this way Grace Ibingira, leader of the party's right wing, succeeded in ousting Kakonge, who wanted to transform the UPC into a mass party along the lines of the TANU, from his post as general secretary in 1964, thus crucially weakening the left wing of the party (Jørgensen 1981:224ff).

The UPC-KY coalition broke up over the lost counties question, after Obote succeeded in holding a referendum in 1964 with the aim of separating these areas from Buganda. After 75 percent of the population involved had voted against remaining a part of Buganda, the KY changed its tactics. It formally dissolved its party in 1965 and recommended that its members join the UPC. Together with Ibingira it now influenced the UPC's course inside Buganda and tried in 1966 to overthrow prime minister Obote by parliamentary means. After the attempted coup Obote had five ministers, including Ibingira, taken into custody, and from then on he began to govern with authoritarian methods. In 1969, at the beginning of his move to the left, Obote finally banned the opposition party, the DP, which had already been greatly handicapped and weakened since 1963 as numerous members left to join the other parties. His ideological offensive, however, did not progress beyond the early stages. The UPC had in the meantime lost all political substance and was no longer in a position to carry out a widespread mobilization of the population for Obote's program (Mabirizi 1986; Jørgensen 1981:221ff). Amin's military dictatorship brought this stage of the one-party system to an end.

After the parties had been reintroduced under Muwanga in 1980, a party system developed that was similar to the constellation of the 1960s. Largely unchanged in their socioeconomic and ethnic-religious bases, the UPC and DP were founded again, together with a slightly changed KY, now the Conservative Party. The UPM, which received its support from Ankole, Museveni's homeland, and from younger, educated Ugandans, was the only other newly formed party with any prospects of success. During the election campaign of 1980 the UPC had extensive resources at its disposal (trucks, advertising material, widespread organization, etc.), which had been financed by donations, including some from the wealthy Indians expelled by Amin. In addition the party had its own daily newspaper, *Uganda Times* (Nsibambi 1987:14f). From an organizational point of view, the DP was at a decided disadvantage, but it derived considerable strength from the use of informal church structures and the ownership of a well-known daily newspaper, *Munno*. In the event, the DP managed to gain fifty-one seats, compared with seventy two for UPC and one for the UPM (ACR 1980–1981:363ff).

In spite of the somewhat precarious situation as far as safety was concerned, Obote adhered to the multiparty system until 1985. The DP opposition, which had some individual contacts with the UFM, was accused of failing to distance itself from this group. Detentions, murders, flight abroad, and defection to the UPC all served to reduce both the number of DP members in Parliament and the power of the legal opposition until the middle of 1985 when Obote was overthrown once again (see ACR 1981–1982:304, 1984–1985:293f).

From the outset, the NRM claimed that it could offer a political haven to followers of all the leading parties ("broad-based government"). In order to prevent a revival of the former party constellation, all parties were "suspended" for the space of four years, which meant that it was forbidden to organize political activity outside the NRM. Before the suspension, however, Museveni had integrated representatives of all parties in his cabinet. Officially they are there as individuals, but party political loyalties still exist and the public is well aware of them. Accusations from UPC circles of injustices ranging from persecution to detentions and murder show that this experiment has been successful only in part (*Weekly Review* June 26, 1987:42). There is still an opportunity for a broad spectrum to express its opinions within the NRM, however, ranging from the emphatically conservative groups to the radical socialist ones. Indeed, this is one of the main reasons for the lack of clarity regarding the NRM's development policies. The future situation will depend on whether the considerable pluralism within the NRM can be transformed into a system of functioning national parties or whether it will develop into a one-party system, serving as a platform for widely varied political forces (Medard 1986:29f).

CENTRAL POLITICAL SYSTEM

Institutional Aspects

The exceptionally complicated constitution of independence, which corresponded formally to the Westminster model, was drafted under the influence of Great Britain's support for Buganda's interests. It established in 1962 the dual status of Buganda, which enjoyed numerous rights of autonomy within the federal state but whose monarch was also the federal state's president. Obote's coup against the kabaka in 1966 may have solved one of Uganda's serious constitutional problems, but it also concentrated a great many competences in the hands of the head of state within the presidential system. After drawing up a centralized constitution, Parliament reinstated another major law in 1967, the Public Order and Security Act, which was to be consequential for the future. This act allowed for the possibility of detentions; that is, arrests that could be ordered by the president without the control of the courts. The brief period of a legalized one-party system, which began in 1969 with the banning of all parties other than the UPC, came to an end after Amin's coup in January 1971. The legitimation of this one-party system in specially regulated elections, planned to further the national consensus, was forestalled by the coup.

The institutional structure of Amin's regime, which consisted of a cabinet and Defence Council, had never been fully realized up till April 1979. The Defence Council, formally the highest state organ, could dismiss ministers and suspend all cabinet decisions at any time but never achieved its intended significance. Amin's personal dictatorship was disguised only very thinly by these two bodies (ACR 1974–1975:306).

The interim governments of 1979/80 were headed by presidents who had been appointed by the UNLF. At the Conference of Moshi, however, it had been decided that the leading and representative organs of the UNLF, which always contained the whole spectrum of opposition to Amin, should make all far-reaching political decisions. The many weaknesses of this structure resulted in parliamentary elections being called in December 1980 and the formal reinstatement of the 1967 constitution (ACR 1979–1980:348ff.; Sathyamurthy 1986:658ff).

The NRM has declared that, after a four-year transitional period wherein the political situation must be stabilized and appropriate institutions built up, the new regime will also be replaced by a new constitution and an elected, legitimate government. In January 1986 Museveni, after being sworn in as president, selected the first ministers for his cabinet and founded as the highest organ the National Resistance Council, which is made up of high-ranking officers of the armed forces and political representatives of the NRM. The cabinet, supplemented by prominent representatives of the suspended parties and leaders of other rebel organizations, has developed into an all-party government. DP politicians such as Paul Ssemogerere, minister of the interior, occupy central posts, although NRM representatives dominate numerically. The cabinet is headed by the political leader of the NRM, prime minister Doctor Samson Kisekka, who lived in exile in Nairobi until 1986. There is also an attempt to maintain a certain amount of ethnic equilibrium (Medard 1986:17ff). The council, which decides central political issues, was extended later to become an interim Parliament. In September 1986 president Museveni appointed all thirty-two cabinet members as ex officio members of the council, thus extending it further to about fifty people. After the national council had been further augmented by coopted members of the regional Resistance Councils (RC), it finally consisted of one-hundred members at the beginning of 1987.

Since the beginning of 1986 the NRM has been governing with a hierarchy of RCs, whose lower ranks comprise all the members of a rural or urban community, a factory, or other large works. They elect an executive committee, which in turn sends representatives to the executive committee of the next-highest level of organization. These people's committees are responsible in a "basic democratic" sense for all local issues, and they are intended to keep a check on jurisdiction and administration and contribute toward the maintenance of public safety. In this way the RCs are supposed to ensure that legal norms are observed in all administrative processes, thus supplementing the state leadership's attempts to bring order into the weary and disorganized administrative apparatus. Museveni's critics compare the RCs to the Libyan People's Committees and suspect that they are intended to prevent the transition to a pluralistic system for as long as possible. Whether they can exist parallel to the organs of a parliamentary democracy in the long run, or whether they will become the pillars of an authoritarian system depends on the future constitution, which is to be based on the results of discussion among all social forces within the framework of the RCs and the national council (Medard 1986:22f., 32f).

Both the high standards and the independence of the legal system, which had been typical for Uganda until 1971, were maintained to a remarkable degree during the years of the military dictatorship. Courageous judgments, even in some cases where crimes had been committed or instigated by state organs, were by no means rare. Incidents such as the murder of Uganda's highest judge, Benedicto Kiwanuka, who was kidnaped from his court by soldiers in 1972, clearly show, however, that representatives of the legal system were not exempt from the widespread repression. The courts' powers were greatly limited by the low standards of police inquiries, the involvement of police and security forces in criminal activity, and the far-reaching regulations that allowed political opponents to be detained without trial or ensured that the repressive apparatus could nearly always escape punishment for its own crimes. As a result an increasing number of citizens ceased to appeal to the courts, whose judgments were frequently ignored by the state (see Kabwegyere 1987:19f).

Actual Power Structure

Between 1962 and 1964 cabinet and Parliament enjoyed a status of considerable importance, under a prime minister who had been granted a relatively strong position in the constitution. Five of the fifteen ministers were members of the KY, the smaller coalition partner. The prime minister's support from his own party was very limited, due both to its structure as an alliance of locally influential dignitaries and its considerable political heterogeneity. Defections from other parties, usually motivated by the promotion of individual careers, and the dwindling of the opposition downgraded Parliament after 1966 almost to the point of insignificance. Obote's isolation at the top became evident during his move to the left. Although sanctioned by a UPC congress, the manifesto and the attempted revival of the UPC along populist lines were virtually Obote's personal work

(Mamdani 1976:269f). Since he had used the army against the kabaka and now had to rely upon it constantly because of the state of emergency in Buganda, the armed forces had become a decisive power factor. In view of the amount of power incorporated in the presidency, Uganda's political system changed from the end of 1969 into an authoritarian one-party system (Jørgensen 1981:252ff).

In Amin's military regime, the Defence Council, appointed as the highest state organ, was formally responsible for all political decision-making. As the council was dominated by Amin, however, who altered its composition at will by periodically dismissing officers who had fallen out of favor and continually appointing new ones, it was not in a position to perform a function of corporate leadership. Members of the cabinet whose competences were reduced to the implementation of policies were in an even more precarious situation. About half of the ministers, including Amin's closest advisers in the period up till 1976 (the minister for finance, internal affairs and defense, Charles Oboth-Ofumbi, and the foreign minister, Wanume Kibedi), did not survive Amin's dictatorship. Amin's real basis of power consisted of the ethnic group from which he himself came, the Kakwa, and cliques of devoted followers from West Nile District. Members of these circles, often relatives such as General Mustafa Adrisi, took over important posts at the head of special army units and security corps for long periods. From the ranks of the Kakwa and the Nubians, a minority group of Arabic origin comprising 0.6 percent of the population, Amin recruited his military and economic oligarchy, which soon attained wealth and power (Jørgensen 1981:276ff.; ACR 1971/72:72ff).

The policies of the interim cabinets under Lule, Binaisa, and Muwanga were dominated by the attempt to preserve, outwardly at least, the unity of the Moshi agreements, where all political forces had joined together against Amin in 1979, but at the same time to create as suitable a starting point as possible for each prime minister's own fraction, whether it was Lule's conservative, Buganda-loyalist wing of the DP or Binaisa's and Ssemo-gerere's centrist wing of the DP or the the UPC. In each case the change was instigated by the Tanzanian leadership. As it wished to withdraw its troops from Uganda as quickly as possible, Tanzania urged a rapid consolidation of the state of affairs, and whenever a regime was threatening to go too far in the other direction, Tanzania withheld its support (ACR 1980–1981:359ff.; Sathyamurthy 1986:66ff).

During Obote's second regime, the army leadership under General David Oyite-Ojok, a Langi, and General Tito Okello, an Acholi, once again played a central role, determined by security problems including the control of the armed forces. The threat to the ethnic equilibrium that became evident after Oyite-Ojok's death in an accident and after a plot by Muwanga, who also held a key position and represented Obote's basis in Buganda, finally led to Obote's overthrow (ACR 1984–1985:392f).

As a leader of armed units in the battle against Amin and in the bush war against Obote and Okello, Museveni had gained almost absolute authority within the NRM. The relationship of the coopted cabinet members to the older NRM cadres inside the national council has been very difficult to assess so far. After the withdrawal of the Fedemu, UFM, and UNRF from the alliance with the NRM, the basis of the the NRM regime has been largely reduced to its collaboration with the DP. Since the DP does not have its own military section, it is considered to be politically lightweight at the present time in Uganda and has no option but to cooperate with Museveni. This means, however, that complete control over all the armed forces, which the NRM agrees is a prerequisite for any political stabilization, is becoming increasingly doubtful.

OUTPUT STRUCTURES

Administrative Structure and Behavior

Both organizational structure and the methods of the administrative apparatus changed after independence in two ways. The racially classified salary structure was formally abolished, although senior cadres in the administration received the same salary as their European predecessors; namely, about twenty times the official minimum wage. In 1959 the proportion of Africans at higher administrative levels was already just over 25 percent. They had received their education at Christian schools for the elite and some had studied at Makerere University. In 1967 nearly 80 percent of the higher functionaries were Africans and about 14 percent were Asians. By 1970 the bureaucracy had expanded by 60 percent. Against a background of crumbling social control, the appointment of new civil servants depended not so much on the applicants' qualifications as on a consideration of political criteria and patronage systems; thus the efficiency of the apparatus was undermined by corruption and nepotism (Jørgensen 1981:239f., 248).

After the coup there began a general process of demoralization in the bureaucracy, caused by the elimination of well-qualified, honest administrative functionaries who, if they showed the slightest resistance to Amin, were dismissed and, frequently, murdered, if they had not already fled the country (Kabwegyere 1987:15). The administrative reform of 1973, which divided Uganda into semifederal provinces with, all together thirty districts, primarily followed Amin's strategy for maintaining power. At the head of each province there was a governor. These were mostly officers who Amin no longer wanted in a position of military power but who he wished to keep within his sphere of influence. The provincial administration soon degenerated into a sinecure in which the holders were able to enrich themselves without restraint by raiding the civilian population. In addition there were constant changes of personnel and halfhearted attempts by Amin to control the desintegrated bureaucracy. At the end of the seventies there was virtually no functioning administration that could extend beyond the torso of the central ministries (ACR 1974–1975:308; Jørgensen 1981:307ff).

In the attempt to establish the UPC's control over the public sector, Obote, in his second period of office, failed almost completely to recognize the necessity of ensuring the bureaucracy's acceptance and efficiency by a certain measure of party-political neutrality. Membership in the UPC became an essential condition for a post in the civil service. Furthermore, the bureaucracy's efficiency was diminished by salaries that were totally inadequate in view of the galloping inflation and that forced all civil servants to resort to supplementary sources of income.

One of the essential tasks of Museveni's regime, therefore, is to build up structures that can be accepted as legitimate, and to recruit honest, upright functionaries at all levels of the administration. In its attempt to do so, the NRM has put great hopes on the control of the administration by the RCs, as well as on the selection of suitable administrative cadres by the RCs, who can fall back on the experience of local communities. In the areas that were already under the NRM's control in 1985, the RCs proved their worth. After its victory the new regime had no choice but to take over the existing administrative apparatus, including the commissioners who Obote had installed at district level. The new government provided each of them with a special district assistant, however, whose task was to control the actions of the official administration, organize the formation of RCs, and coordinate their activities (Medard 1986:20f).

Structure and Behavior of the Repressive Apparatus

The approximately one thousand–strong colonial army that Uganda took over at independence, including an officer corps whose senior staff were all Europeans, consisted of 60 percent Acholi and Langi. In 1964, against a background of massive internal conflicts, Obote submitted entirely to the demands of mutineering units who were discontented with pay, promotion, and equipment. Under these circumstances it did not take long for the former Corporal Amin to rise to the rank of general chief of staff. The state of emergency since 1966, the large number of detentions since 1967, and the actions against critics and opponents taken by the General Service Unit, a special unit immediately responsible to Obote, all characterize a regime whose power was already based chiefly on its repressive potential.

Amin's economic war of 1972, as a result of which important economic posts were given to members of the army, and the administrative reform of 1973, after which posts in the administration, including those of provincial governors, were given exclusively to army officers, led to a further militarization of society. Amin tried to ensure the army's loyalty by continually replacing his senior officers and by appointing Nubians and Kakwa to key positions. Massacres, purges, and the persecution of entire ethnic groups such as the Acholi, Langi, and Madi were the result of a strategy that was constantly aimed at playing off one group against another. In addition there were several greatly feared security services—the State Research Bureau, the Public Safety Unit, and the Military Police—that were not only directed against the population as organs of state repression but also kept each other in check. A Palestinian bodyguard and mercenaries from Zaire, Sudan, and other places completed the system that enabled Amin to govern the country with extreme brutality until 1979 (Jørgensen 1981:273ff.; ACR 1977–1978:439ff).

The spectrum of violence ranged from massacre and murder, planned or initiated by the state leadership, to the disappearance of both prominent and ordinary citizens, to a great number of raids by members of the military. Private crime also thrived in this environment. Human rights organizations estimate that there were up to 500,000 victims of the Amin era; in at least thirty thousand cases, according to the strictest criteria, and almost certainly a great many more, the repressive apparatus and its masters in the state leadership were directly responsible. Repression was aimed not only at particular ethnic groups but also, especially after the student unrest of 1976, at the educated Christian elites; for example, members of universities, doctors, lawyers, functionaries of various organizations, and so forth (Jørgensen 1981:309ff.; ACR 1976–1977:377ff).

The start of guerrilla activity against Obote in February 1981 by the NRM and the UFM, which was associated with the DP, meant another great setback for the attempts to bring peace to the country. The army, which was sent in to defend the regime, had been hastily recruited, inadequately trained, and was largely undisciplined. Especially in the Luwero Triangle, northwest of the capital, there were renewed large-scale massacres, devastation and looting by marauding troops. A large number of detentions, tortures, and political murders were also recorded during Obote's second regime. After the coup in 1985 over twelve hundred people were freed from just one facility, Luzira Prison near Kampala, most of them having been detained without legal grounds. In 1985, both before and after the coup, the catastrophic human rights situation in Uganda was characterized by torture, rape, massacres, and abductions by the army and security forces (AI 1986). Foreign military aid, whether through the presence of Tanzanian troops from 1979–1981 or through British and North Korean military advisers from 1980–1985, could do little to change the situation (see, e.g., ACR 1982–1983:309ff., 319).

After 1970 the central role of the armed forces was also displayed by size, which expanded from nearly fifteen thousand members to about twenty-two thousand (see Table 55). In 1971, 20 percent of the budget was being spent on defense, but by 1979 the share had risen to 25 percent. Adding in stationing costs for Tanzanian troops, Uganda was spending more than a third of its entire budget on defense by 1982. After Tanzania's withdrawal, official army and paramilitary units reached a level of twenty-two thousand men in arms once again, because of a renewed outbreak of civil war, especially in the Luwero Triangle, and the military budget with its share of 25 percent of the total budget remained the greatest single expenditure.

The rehabilitation of public safety, which faces enormous practical problems if only because of the number of arms in circulation, is absolutely fundamental to further development. In order to keep his own forces under control, Museveni employed new methods. He recruited soldiers for the NRA by letting the village elders select suitable young men, who were then enlisted in areas close to their villages. The social control exerted in these cases by their own local communities has prevented excesses. At present, therefore, one can say that there is a certain degree of confidence in the army in the southern and western regions, including the capital. If single offenses occur, they are dealt with internally. In the North and East of the country, however, where this kind of confidence does not yet exist, the civil war continues, and attacks by various NRA units on civilians have reduced their acceptance. In addition, detentions are no longer restricted to violent forces who are an acute danger to public safety, but also affect individuals who are critical of the NRM policies without resorting to armed force.

TIME SERIES ANALYSIS

Political indicators. The political indicators reflect a development that included peaceful demonstrations before 1964 (see Table 48) but was later chiefly characterized by violent events. A large number of strikes accompanied the escalation of domestic conflicts before 1964 when the small, non-agrarian proletariat felt that its hopes regarding independence had not been fulfilled, and again between 1969 and 1971 when employees suffered severe cuts in real wages. Only the larger mutinies, Obote's attempted intervention in 1972, and the unrest at Makerere University in 1976/77 appear in the data of Taylor and Jodice (1983b) (see Tables 47, 49, and 50). Since the establishment of indices for human and civil rights, Uganda has been classified in the category for the greatest violation of these normative standards (see Table 3).

Macroeconomic indicators. In the first decade of independence Uganda registered a positive development on the whole, with an average annual GDP growth of 4.5 percent in 1962–1966 and 4 percent in 1966–1970, but it began to slow down when the balance of payments crisis started in 1969. The expulsion of Asians, which meant a great loss for the country's economy, together with the first oil crisis between 1973 and 1975, led to an annual reduction in the GDP of 2 percent. Uganda did not benefit to any great extent from the coffee price boom in 1976/77, as production continually decreased in bulk, and a considerable part of the harvest was smuggled abroad. The weak economy was affected even more greatly by the second oil crisis and the deterioration of economic conditions. There was a pronounced decline in production which could be attributed to the war against Amin. In the second decade after independence there was thus a considerable drop in marketed agrarian production (35 percent) and industrial production (73 percent). As the subsistence economy did not follow this trend, the overall GDP decreased by only 19 percent. Between 1981 and 1984, when Uganda received aid in agreement with the IMF to rebuild its infrastructure, there was a definite recovery due both to the improved external conditions and to progress in the attempt to combat smuggling. After average growth rates of 5 percent, this development turned to stagnation in 1985 when the civil war became more intense. Although the security situation had much improved in southern Uganda since January 1986 and there was a more optimistic attitude among the citizens, the GDP decreased once again by 5.5 percent in 1986 because of the enormous amount of destruction before the takeover (see Table 7).

In the mid-1960s Uganda was still one of the more progressive states in Africa, economically speaking, with a textile industry, for example, that included all stages of production, from the cultivation of cotton to the manufacture of textiles intended chiefly for the East African market. In 1970 its manufacturing industries (processing of cotton, coffee, tea, and sugarcane, production of food and luxury goods, building materials, etc.) constituted 9 percent of GDP; after 1980, however, it was only 4 percent (see Tables 11 and 12). The lack of qualified staff, the shortage of suitable spares (which could no longer be bought because of a lack of foreign currency), and the deterioration of public safety have all been responsible for this retardation since 1972. The agrarian sector's share of GDP, which was 52 percent in 1970, rose to 75 percent during the 1980s. More than 90 percent of the population depend on agriculture, just as in 1960 (see Tables 11 and 12). Due to increasing terrorism, internal strife, and the lack of motivation for export production among the producers, the proportion of subsistence production rose from 30 percent in 1970 to 36 percent in 1980. In 1986 the nonmonetary sector still constituted about a third of GDP. The rebuilding of the transport system, a key sector, since 1986, and the foreign reserves that Uganda now has at its disposal after an agreement with the IMF and the World Bank in May 1987, are providing the first important steps to an economic recovery. It remains to be seen whether the campaign against the extended magendo, including smuggling, which is so detrimental to the official economy, will have more success than it did in 1986, when it was still fairly ineffectual.

After high inflation during the Amin era had caused high real wage losses, particularly among the lower-income groups, the hyperinflation between 1979 and 1981 brought about a drastic reduction in the real income of agrarian producers and employees as well. Attempts to balance these losses with higher producer prices and wage rises, for example an increase of up to 500 percent in civil service wages in 1984, were soon rendered useless by the continuing hyperinflation. As an inflation rate of 200 percent has also been estimated for 1987, the proposed wage increase of 50 percent can represent only the first step in an essential revision of the wage structure (see Table 15). Because of the continual deterioration of purchasing power and serious supply problems, the population became increasingly discontented with the economic achievements of the the NRM regime during the course of 1986. The high devaluation, finally carried out in May 1987, and the currency reform are intended to rectify the imbalance and pave the way for a permanent solution.

Social indicators. Due to political unrest, Amin's tyranny, and the civil wars later on, the time series show some inconsistencies. This has a considerable effect on the value of the information given by the PQLI, which reflects the arrest of social development during the Amin regime with an index rating of 40 in 1975 but shows sudden progress in development up till 1980 with an index rating of 55 (see Table 28). This rating does not take into consideration, however, that the life expectancy in 1980 was still indicated to be relatively high at fifty-four years, but in 1981, after the new census, it turned out to be only forty-eight years (see Table 17). Because of gaps in the data for the time after 1980, the second single indicator, infant mortality, also appears to be applicable only in a limited way, too (see Table 18). The literacy rate shows a steady increase from 25 percent in 1974 to 52 percent in 1980 (see Table 19). Other data on education and health, however, demonstrate how much the quality of life was affected by Amin's rule. The proportion of primary school pupils in any one age group was at the same level in 1980 as it had been in 1960, that is, 50 percent, although it had already gone up to 67 percent in 1965 (see Table 26). The share of secondary school pupils also remained virtually unchanged at 5 percent in 1980 (see Table 27). Medical care, which had reached a comparatively high level in 1970 with a ratio of nine thousand inhabitants to one doctor, has suffered a definite deterioration. After the departure of the European and Asian physicians, this ratio fell to 26,810:1 (see Table 23). The total destruction of buildings and sometimes a catastrophic lack of equipment (medication, bandages, and instruments, but also schoolbooks) characterize the decay of the social infrastructure. Its rebuilding was given as much priority by Obote as by the the NRM's present Ten Point Programme. The calorie consumption per head of the population was reduced from 102 percent in 1970 to 83 percent in 1980 and 78 percent in 1982 (see Table 20). Malnutrition, growing susceptibility to infectious diseases, and the deterioration of water supplies all contribute to the decline in public health. The fertility of the country is presumably the only reason why Uganda did not suffer any severe famines.

EXTERNAL FACTORS

Foreign political relations. Toward the end of the 1960s Uganda's foreign policy with its move to the left followed a specifically antiimperialist course. Uganda, Tanzania, and Zambia formed the so-called Mulungushi Group, which used the forum of international organizations to speak out against Great Britain's support for South Africa and Rhodesia (ACR 1970–1971:195ff). Uganda's basically pro-Western orientation was displayed, however, in the intensive contact between the Socialist International and the the UPC, in the Christian International's support for the DP, and in U.S. groups' support for the conservative wing of the the UPC (Mabirizi 1986:24).

International factors also were involved, indirectly at least, in Amin's coup d'état. Through comprehensive economic and military assistance, Israel had made Uganda its ally as far as Middle East and African policies were concerned and was using it to support the Christian rebels against the Islamic central government in Sudan. When General Ga'afar Numeiri came to power in Sudan at the head of a revolutionary government in 1969, Obote refused to agree to these maneuvers any longer, but Amin, as the head of the armed forces, continued cooperation with Israel. The revelation of this secret collaboration in 1970 became a central element in the legitimacy crisis before the coup (Mamdani 1976:292ff).

After the coup, Amin at first enjoyed full support from Great Britain, Israel, and other Western states. The nationalizations decreed in 1972, the abrupt expulsion of the Asians, and the enormity of the human rights abuses caused most Western states, however, to stop giving Uganda their open support. Great Britain and the United States broke off diplomatic relations, and most development aid was frozen. Amin's erratic foreign policy soon found a reliable supplier of arms in the Soviet Union. After his break with Israel, he won support from Libya and other Arab states by radically pro-Arab policies, and these countries were prepared to supply his regime, by then practically isolated, with financial and military support (Jørgensen 1981:316ff).

Tanzania, which had granted asylum to Obote in 1971 and had permitted an invasion to be launched from its territory, was on the brink of war in 1972 until the situation was settled through the mediation of Somalia (ACR 1972–1973:275f). In the mid-1970s Amin's territorial claims concerning large parts of Kenya had affected relationships with that country so severely that armed conflict seemed imminent. Kenya's trade embargo blocked the entire oil supply to Uganda for a short time in 1976 and almost broke the Amin regime before Uganda finally agreed to withdraw its claims (ACR

1976–1977:386ff). Amin's provocations finally brought about the collapse of the EAC in 1977. This hit Uganda hardest of all, because of both its inland situation and the structure of its trade relations. Against a background of tense relationships with nearly all neighboring states and conflict within his own country that was weakening his position, the dictator gave the order for his army to annex the Kagera region of Tanzania on October 30, 1978 (Jørgensen 1981:318ff.; ACR 1978–1979:425f). After the attack had been repelled, the Tanzanian leaders, under Nyerere, who since 1971 had vigorously refused to recognize Amin, especially within the Organisation of African Unity, decided to support Ugandan resistance armies in their battle against Amin. Since Kenya feared that a Tanzanian hegemony would thus develop in East Africa, it was very reserved toward the interim regimes, but after Obote had been elected, close contacts developed very rapidly. In fact, Obote played a key role in bringing about a reconciliation of the other two former EAC partners. In 1983 he was even able to arrange an agreement over the distribution of EAC funds, from which Uganda had the greatest benefit (ACR 1983–1984:305ff).

Because of his pronounced pro-Western orientation and his openness to IMF policies, Obote could be certain of support from Great Britain until the middle of 1985. In spite of serious human rights abuses, Great Britain did not recall its military advisers. Museveni, on the other hand, who was in search of a country that would provide him with money, arms, and suitable training camps, had tried in vain to gain other international support and finally accepted help from Libya. Libyan plans for a continuous collaboration, including political cooperation, were not pursued with any intensity by the NRM, but they were sufficient to cause tension in Uganda's international relations, especially with Kenya (c.f. *Weekly Review* April 10, 1987:28ff). Museveni tried hard to win the support of Great Britain and other EC countries and come to an arrangement with the IMF and the World Bank (ARB, Economic Series, May 1986:8160). At the same time, the NRM is aiming at close cooperation with all its neighboring states, first in order to encourage regional economic relations, and second to prepare an international basis for the fight against the magendo (ARB, Political Series, April 1986:7997).

In spite of the support Museveni received from Kenya after the middle of 1985, Uganda's relations to its important eastern neighbor remained occasionally strained. The mistrust that marks the relationship the two nations is expressed by each accusing the other of providing support for its opponents and acting as a base for these opponents' conspiratorial activities. Especially, Uganda's economic and military collaboration with Libya, Cuba, and North Korea has strengthened fears within Kenya, with its distinctly pro-Western orientation, that Uganda could become an outpost of subversive forces. In Uganda itself this cooperation is dismissed as a purely pragmatic issue, even if Museveni has occasionally professed his ideological concurrence with Libya's revolutionary leader Mu'ammar Qaddafi. Behind the policy of irritations, provocations, and allegations in the media there are certain objective conflicts of interest, however. Uganda's decision to transfer the transport of coffee and oil from the roads to the railways, for example, has meant savings of U.S. $50 million, but as a result Kenya's transport industry has lost this source of income. It is therefore necessary to consider the sometimes deliberate delays in the transport of goods between Uganda and the port of Mombasa in the light of these problems (see *Weekly Review* May 29, 1987:59f.).

Foreign economic relations. During the 1970s Uganda had regular balance of trade surpluses, which, depending on world economic conditions (e.g., development of terms of trade) or internal factors (emigration of classes with strong purchasing power after 1972, drop in the demand for import goods during the civil wars), fluctuated between $10 million in 1975 and $190 million in 1977. The high transit costs paid to Kenya for all goods coming into Uganda via Mombasa led to a regular deficit of approximately $70–80 million in the balance of payments, however. On the whole, the overall balance with surpluses and deficits of about $50 million kept within remarkably positive limits. In 1980, for example, there were exports of $450 million (approximately 3.5 percent of the GDP) and imports of $340 million (approximately 2.7 percent) (see Table 46). If these figures are compared with those of 1965, when exports constituted 16 percent but imports almost 24 percent of the GDP, then the change in structure, but also the loss of development this conceals, becomes clear (see Tables 34 and 35). The rise in the share of foreign trade from 3.1 percent in 1980 to 10 percent in 1983 was linked with large balance of payments deficits in 1981/82 and a considerable increase in the national debt (see Tables 33 and 34). As public safety again deteriorated in 1985/86, trade volume decreased by half, while debt repayments are presently consuming more than half of the export revenues. The only remaining export commodity of any importance in recent years has been coffee. In the early 1970s it comprised more than half of the export revenues. The share continued to rise until 1981, when it reached the present level of just over 95 percent. The export of cotton (share of exports in 1972: 15.4 percent) and tea (1972: 5 percent) has continually declined to the point of insignificance, because of the deterioration of plantations and processing facilities (see Table 30). The chief imports have been for the public sector—for example, military goods (1980: 21 percent; 1985: 40 percent)—followed by oil products (1980: 25 percent; 1985: 25 percent) and machines or vehicles (1980: 17 percent; 1985: 6 percent) (see Table 31).

Despite the occasional policy disagreements, foreign trade is still mostly directed toward the Western nations. The reduction in the share of the former colonial power, Great Britain, which received 20 percent of exports in 1970 but only 14 percent in 1980, was balanced by other EC states, Japan (7 percent), and the United States (26 percent) (see Table 32). Kenya is becoming increasingly important as a supplier both of mineral oil products from the refinery at Mombasa and of simple, locally manufactured consumer goods (see Table 33). In spite of the collapse of the EAC in 1977, Kenya's share of Ugandan imports rose from 30 percent in 1970 to 39 percent in 1980. Although there is a constant supply of electricity to Kenya from the Owen Falls power station, uninterrupted even in Amin's era, there is a permanent balance of trade deficit with Kenya.

The price for Obote's agreement with the IMF in June 1981 was his acceptance of the IMF's conditions. In the same month Obote floated the Ugandan shilling's exchange rate, and it immediately lost 90 percent of its value. Successive devaluations, which were cushioned with the aid of a split rate of exchange from 1982 to 1984, reduced the ratio to the U.S. dollar from 8:1 in 1980 to 1,400:1 in 1986. On the basis of these agreements Uganda received approximately $1 billion from multilateral institutions, mostly in the form of short-term loans. This made its debt repayments more problematic, although at about $700 million its medium- and long-term public debt is still relatively low. Two-thirds of the loans are now coming from multilateral donors such as the IMF and the World Bank, while Uganda's credits from individual nations have been reduced by a third since 1980, mostly through rescheduling agreements. As a currency reform, first announced in 1986, would have been pointless if foreign loans had failed to bring about a real improvement in the supply of import goods, it was not implemented until another agreement was reached with the IMF in May 1987.

OVERALL SYSTEM EVALUATION

Since independence, Uganda has had eight different regimes, all of which have been characterized by breaks in legitimacy and varying degrees of repression. Its political development has therefore shown gross political instability. Changes of leadership and alterations of basic institutions and norms have so far always been brought about by irregular and forceful means. Uganda's high level of ethnic heterogeneity and a strongly pronounced North–South divide, loaded with religious and political conflict, has meant that the process of nation-building began under extremely unfavorable circumstances. Its political culture was characterized by hostility, bitter rivalry, and a sense of inferiority in the North, and pride and arrogance in the South. Numerous regional conflicts hindered the development of a countrywide independence movement. A common political forum, where at least a minimum of consensus might have been reached, was impossible under such conditions, which were further intensified by specific colonial interventions. Great Britain, however, did not offer much resistance, at the end, to decolonization.

Diffuse support for the national community came in particular from the retailers and the salariat who were politically dominant in the North, and to a far lesser extent from the progressive small and middle peasantry concentrated in Buganda. The attempt to consolidate a bureaucratic bourgeoisie as a power factor after 1967 through nationalizations, and to establish this class as the regime's national basis, was only partially successful because of the considerable regional opposition, mainly from Buganda. The agrarian and nonagrarian bourgeoisie became alienated from the regime because of falling producer prices and a limitation of their activities. Obote's populist move to the left may have heralded an abundance of new sources of income for the salariat and state class, but its egalitarian claims imperiled the material interests of the independent middle classes. The regime failed to secure the confidence of the urban and rural lower classes and received at best a certain amount of specific support from the salariat. Any successes in the field of overall economic development in this period were unable to broaden the basis of confidence in the regime because political and constitutional conflicts persisted.

By 1980, however, at least two problems had disappeared: traditional orientations had almost completely lost their basis among the progressive smallholders of Buganda and thus diminished chances of renewed dominance by the Baganda upper classes, and Amin's economic war had driven the Asians, who had been a very powerful intermediate class economically speaking, but without political influence, from Uganda. Under Amin's rule, however, a new problem emerged, that of the magendo, a phenomenon that took hold on the whole of society and went on to undermine all processes of regular development. The recent readjustment of public salaries is the first step toward halting corruption and an essential factor in stifling the magendo. Like Obote before him, Museveni is also acknowledging the importance of cash crop producers by raising producer prices, which had fallen steadily during the 1960s and under Amin. In the same vein, he is backing a strong sector of small commercial enterprises and giving support to the public sector, where a considerable increase in efficiency is planned. Before any real progress can be made, there must first be an improvement in the supply situation and hyperinflation must be brought to a halt, in order to lay the basis for increases in real purchasing power as an incentive for further sustainable economic growth.

Until 1962, Uganda's parties, which had been formed along numerous, reinforcing lines of cleavage, were still at a stage where they appeared as local groups joined together merely for the purpose of gaining power. The weakness of the political leadership, which was based on a virtually impotent coalition of two totally opposed parties, the UPC and the KY, together with the fact that it was burdened with constitutional conflicts and battles between party factions, prevented the largest political group—the UPC—from being remodeled into a mobilization party along Tanzanian lines. Apart from a few economic interest groups, such as the cooperatives, the input structures within the system were paralyzed. As the de facto two-party system after 1980 had similar problems, it seems reasonable that the present regime is attempting to restrict political opportunities for participation on a broad basis to within the the NRM for an interim period, and at the same time to make use of this forum to transform the political-cultural conditions.

Structural weaknesses in the semifederal constitution of 1962 and the political leadership's inability to overcome these difficulties within the institutional framework blocked essential processes of decisionmaking by 1964 at the latest. After the formal separation of powers, established in 1962, had been undermined—with the exception of the judiciary, which was rooted in British traditions—the formal structures of the 1967 presidential system retained very little significance. Instead of seeking a rational-legal legitimation for the new constitution by going to the polls, and instead of attempting a political reconciliation with Buganda, Obote relied chiefly on repression in order to stay in power. Although this meant the end of Buganda's dual status, the army became the primary power factor within the authoritarian one-party system. The main reason for the failure of Obote's second regime after 1980 was the weakness of the state leadership, whose policies were often impossible to implement in view of the poor safety situation and the failure to keep the armed forces under control. In contrast, the institutional structure of the the NRM regime grew up out of the resistance movement that was loyal to the new leadership. The attempt to attain a fair representation of all ethnic groups in the cabinet and interim parliament—the National Resistance Council—was aimed at broadening the basis of legitimacy without having to resort to elections. Since the broad basis is now threatening to crumble, Museveni's personal integrity and authority, still widely accepted in the South, is becoming an increasingly significant factor.

Apart from the magendo, there is a second central problem: the militarization of society and the lack of control over the various armed forces in Uganda. The constant menace to, and sometimes the complete collapse of, public safety negated some initial achievements during Obote's second term of power. The fact that he was forced to depend on an undisciplined army virtually beyond his control was an additional blow to his flawed basis of legitimacy. One of Museveni's greatest merits has been the building up of a controllable army, at least in the South. The transference of this achievement to the North still seems to be problematic.

Both the problem of control over the repressive apparatus and that of inefficiency and corruption inside the administration increased in severity under Amin. Constant intervention, together with a method of promotion and recruitment oriented exclusively toward the dictator's Machiavellian considerations, had led to the demoralization and dismissal of the few remaining reliable and suitably qualified cadres in the administration and armed forces. In view of the enormity of the destruction, it has been almost impossible for the new political leadership to reintroduce regular processes and constitutional standards in the adminstration. The formation of a second chain of elected institutions (the RCs), which are intended to support the population's interests against the apparatus and to fulfil control functions in the style of revolutionary committees, seems to be more successful as an alternative to Obote's strategy, which chiefly consisted of infiltrating the civil service with the UPC supporters.

The intensification of internal conflicts through the support of rival power blocs and factions by external forces has been a constant factor in Uganda's political development. As a result of its partial collaboration with such countries as Libya, Cuba, and North Korea, the NRM's policies are also in danger of being influenced from outside. In this case, the beginnings of an internal political consenus may again be called into question, and problems in the relationship with Kenya, Uganda's most important neighbor, would certainly be intensified. The conflicts with Kenya and Tanzania under Amin, and the central role Kenya still plays as the major link to the sea, reflect Uganda's special dependence on East African developments. Uganda suffered more than did the others when the EAC collapsed in 1977. Since 1980 the strengthening of regional cooperation has therefore become a top priority in Uganda's foreign policy. In the field of foreign economic relations the unilateral, neocolonial ties to the former colonial power were successfully loosened, but economic recovery and the rebuilding of an infrastructure are more than ever dependent on international loans. Since stabilization can no longer be concentrated on the solution of political problems as in 1980, and an increasing amount of specific support on the basis of economic progress is also needed to consolidate the regime, the agreements reached with the IMF and the World Bank in May 1987 are of great significance.

III
Comparative Studies

6
Paired Comparisons

Following the methodological steps outlined in the introduction, we will first make systematic paired comparisons of the three cases. In this way, their commonalities, but also their specific differences, can be established more clearly and the number of the potential explanatory variables can be reduced considerably.

Since our study is an exploratory one, the network of possible variables was consciously spread wide. With the aid of a checklist derived from the systems model, and on the basis of the data collected in the individual case studies, more than one hundred variables were examined. In cases where the available data did not allow an exact operationalization, estimates of size and quality were made. The individual variables were grouped into areas: precolonial and colonial influence; horizontal and vertical social structure; political culture and input structures; central political system; output structures; orientation of development policy; and foreign relations. In addition, some important political and socioeconomic indicators were compared in time series. In view of the small number of cases, extensive statistical analyses such as correlation, multiple regression, and variance analysis had to be discarded. The fundamental dilemma in such analyses (the discrepancy between a large number of variables and a small number of cases) can thus be resolved only to a limited extent. As, for example, Przeworski and Teune (1970:30) state: "The logic of the most similar systems design is based on the assumption that characteristics shared by one group of systems . . . can be removed one-by-one in quasi-experimental manner. But this is an unrealistic assumption. . . . Social phenomena vary in syndromes and it is difficult to isolate [single] experimental factors." However, since many of the observed variables show a considerable degree of covariance, it is at least possible to identify some of the characteristic syndromes and, in this way, reconcentrate the analysis on a few central factors. Nevertheless, a threshold is eventually reached whereat systematic quantifying statements end. They must therefore be augmented by well-founded qualitative information, based on long experience of these cases but also on intensive discussions with experts on the countries concerned and representatives of relevant groups and organizations in these countries. Once again, Przeworski and Teune (1970:38) state: "In their practical activities, social scientists are actually willing to take the risk of false generalizations rather than satisfy themselves with rigorous inferences about accidental populations."

KENYA AND TANZANIA

The precolonial social and political structures of Kenya and Tanzania have many similarities. The form of colonial administration, too, shows no significant differences, if the relatively short period of German rule in Tanganyika and the special status of Zanzibar are left out of the equation. The relatively strong element of European settlers in Kenya did, however, have a clear influence on its economy and social structure. The decolonization process, too, proved much more difficult and exacerbated the postcolonial class structure through the measures implemented (breakup of the large European estates, settlement programs, commercialization of peasant agriculture). On the other hand, traditions of protest and resistance did develop in the groups that considered themselves unfairly treated (e.g., the oath-taking ceremonies of the Kikuyu).

Ethnic composition—in view of the arbitrary drawing of borders this is also a result of colonial policy—also shows differences. In Tanzania, the five largest groups together account for only about one quarter of the entire population, whereas in Kenya the figure is two thirds. If one then considers the relatively strong economic position of the largest group in Kenya, the Kikuyu, this disparity is emphasized still further. The Kikuyu are still, nevertheless, dependent on potential ethnic and/or class alliances to form a majority. The considerably lower ethnic conflict potential in Tanzania, a result of its splintered nature and its many small ethnic groups, is clearly demonstrated in the largely unproblematic acceptance of an indigenous national language, Kiswahili, which is today widely used all over the country as a lingua franca. Postcolonial economic policy strengthened already existing tendencies. After a transitional phase, Tanzania adopted its own path to socialism: egalitarian traditions were to be continued, dressed in modern clothing, and self-reliance and independence emphasized. In Kenya, too, an orientation to African socialism was initially proclaimed, but in fact a dependent-capitalist development path was chosen. The policy of integration into the world market was consciously continued (increasingly also for progressive small farmers). The share of foreign capital in plantations, industry, and the service sector (finance, foreign trade, tourism etc.) remained high. In Kenya the government restricted its intervention to indicative outline planning and some initial approaches to overall economic management. In Tanzania the government intervened in a strongly regulatory manner and took direct control of wide areas of production, marketing, finance, and foreign trade through parastatal organizations.

From a background of a constantly higher population growth rate—3.9

percent in 1980 in Kenya and 3.3 percent in 1980 in Tanzania—the growth rate of GDP in Kenya from 1967 on was always faster. While Kenya had an above-average annual growth rate of around 6.5 percent until 1973, the rate of growth of GDP in Tanzania, which up until the time of the ujamaa policy had also been around 6.4 percent, fell by 1973 to 4.8 percent. Thus, in 1980 Tanzania had attained a per capita GNP of $280 (1960: $97), so that the gap between the two countries (Kenya's GNP per capita in 1960 was $143, and in 1980, $420) had further widened. Kenya also has an advantage in sectoral economic structure (the agricultural sector's share of GDP was 34 percent in 1980, compared with Tanzania's 54 percent that same year). However, the high proportion of foreign capital in Kenya's industrial sector (50 percent; Tanzania's was about 20 percent) does indicate possible negative influential factors (e.g., uncontrolled capital export). Despite the slowdown of economic growth, however, Tanzania has achieved some major successes in providing social services. Between 1960 and 1980 the PQLI value increased from 24 to 61, reflecting a greater improvement in the quality of life than in Kenya, where the social development index rose by only twenty points, from 35 to 55. The much higher literacy rate in Tanzania and the considerably higher level of secondary school attendance in Kenya illustrates how priorities differ in this respect.

The social structure also clearly reflects different policies. In Tanzania the extent of social differentiation remained relatively small. The share of the population employed in the agricultural sector was over 80 percent. Indeed, because of the decline in other sectors, the relative proportion of GDP of this sector increased. The major part of the population continued to be made up of the agricultural proletaroids, producing mainly for their own consumption. Writers such as Hyden (1980) quite rightly talk about a largely "uncaptured peasantry" in spite of intensive government measures. In the nonagricultural sphere, the proletariat remained relatively small. Despite official policy, there was, however, an increase in the number of self-employed nonagricultural proletaroids, especially in the informal sector. There was also a great increase in the salaried classes—especially in the public sector—and in the state class heading public sector organizations. The proportion of indigenous capitalists and of managers in foreign companies greatly declined. In Kenya, on the other hand, the quasi-caste structure that had existed during the colonial era, based on racial groups, was transformed into a marked peripheral-capitalist class structure. The proportion of the population employed in agriculture declined to around two-thirds, despite an overall high rate of population growth. Within the agricultural sector, the petite bourgeoisie continued to increase, although with considerable regional differences. The agricultural proletariat declined in number, especially on large farms. The nonagricultural proletariat, especially in the industrial sector; the nonagricultural proletaroids, partially in the informal sector; the nonagricultural petite bourgeoisie; and the salaried class: all grew. There was also a marked increase in the state class (top tiers of the administration and parastatals), but this is matched by a considerable, largely Africanized class of managers and capitalists. The growth of a marginalized subproletariat is also clearly evident. As regards land distribution, the GINI index shows Tanzania to be much more egalitarian, with a value of 35, than is Kenya, with a value of 55. A similar picture is presented by the data for income distribution, with the top 5 percent in Tanzania having 33 percent of the income, while in Kenya the income share of the top 5 percent is 46.2 percent. The development of agricultural producer prices explains, however, why the favorable structure of distribution in Tanzania is not matched by a widely distributed mass purchasing power as in Kenya.

Differences in policies followed and in the social structure are also demonstrated in the input area. In Tanzania, intermediary groups were largely subordinated to the party and in some cases actually integrated (as with youth and women's organizations). The unions are dependent on the party, and there is no right to strike. The original rural purchasing and marketing cooperatives were at times prohibited. Organizations of industrialists and the self-employed play a very minor role. The press is largely state-owned, although there is a certain degree of freedom to criticize individuals or corrupt practices. Ethnic organizations, apart from the continuing special status of Zanzibar, are of no particular importance. In contrast, the churches have managed to maintain their independence and certainly do occasionally express criticism. In Kenya, the input terrain is generally much more diverse and largely independent of party and senior government levels. The interests of large farmers in particular are effectively represented (for a long time by the Kenya Farmers' Association, but now by the more broadly based KNFU). However, the relatively high producer prices also benefit the progressive small and medium farmers. Industrial and capital interests, including their foreign representatives, also have relatively open access to the system. While the unions and their umbrella association are organizationally independent, their actual scope for action, including the right to strike, is restricted. Some sections of trade unions (civil servants and teachers) have been prohibited. The ethnic organizations, which for some time had the character of latent political parties—this was particularly the case with the powerful GEMA—were banned in 1980. The press is one of the most diverse and free in Africa, but criticism of the system, and especially of the president, is taboo and can be made only indirectly (e.g., by quotation). The churches—especially the Anglican church, but also smaller Protestant groups—are increasingly becoming the mouthpiece of dissatisfaction for certain groups in the population.

There are characteristic differences in the role of the single party, which is now established in the constitution of both countries. Despite relatively independent ideologies and practices in other regards, Tanzania leans heavily on the organizational structure of a Leninist party. The center of policymaking clearly lies with the NEC and the party leadership in the narrower sense. A strict code of behavior is intended to prevent the party members, and especially the leading representatives, from granting themselves privileges. The modest life-style of the party chairman, Julius Nyerere, set standards in this respect. In the economic crisis of recent years, however, more and more deviations from these standards have been observable, without any strong measures being taken against the miscreants in most cases. In Kenya, on the other hand, KANU, which has been de facto the sole party since 1969 and was constitutionally recognized as such in 1982, was for a long time no more than a shadow. For this reason, some writers occasionally spoke of a "no-party system." The party's role consists merely of exercising some kind of filtering function in the selection of parliamentary candidates. Attempts in recent years to breathe new life into the party organization have resulted in the formal registration of 4 million members, but there is still no significant policy formation within the party involving regular participation of the membership. A disciplinary committee which was formed following the attempted coup in 1982 with the intention of punishing corruption and nepotism and even cases of politically undesirable behavior, has since been dissolved. The real decisionmaking authority still resides with the party chairman and state president, proclaimed without any opposing candidate, and his immediate entourage.

The factual dominance of the executive, and especially of the Office of the President, the position of which has been strengthened in recent years, is conspicuous in Kenya. The cabinet, which reflects a broad ethnic coalition, has, in contrast, only limited significance—as is demonstrated by the frequent reshuffles. Even Parliament, which has formal sovereignty, has only a background role, although it is occasionally the forum of clearly articulated criticism by backbenchers. It is filled largely on a competitive basis. In this way, local and regional conflicts and even those between individuals, families, clans, and villages can be articulated in individual constituencies. However, a very clear preponderance of the rural petite bourgeoisie and other members of the middle and upper classes is discernible here, just as, indeed, the senior levels of politics and administration show tendencies to self-privilege in a clearly clientelist system. In Tanzania, in contrast, the executive has remained subordinated to the party, even although in recent years, since the separation of the party leadership and the president's office a certain amount of dualism, even in respect of concrete political alignments, could not be overlooked. The Tanzanian parliament is even more over-shadowed by the party organization and functions predominantly as an organ of acclamation. It is hardly ever the scene of controversial debates. The judicial organs are formally independent in both states, although some limitations are, in reality, discernible. Preventive detention without trial, originating in the colonial era and questionable in terms of the rule of law, continues to be used in both countries.

The output structures in both countries are shaped to a large extent in the British pattern. In Tanzania, though, they are clearly subordinated to the party, whereas in Kenya the administration has a largely independent role, headed by the Office of the President. Actual behavior, however, is not infrequently different from the model. In Tanzania the efficiency of the bureaucracy is clearly restricted, not least because many civil servants found it necessary to pursue second jobs in the informal sector to secure their existence. In Kenya, on the other hand, greater efficiency goes hand in hand with a greater involvement with private sector interests and possibilities for personal gain, partially legal and partially illegal, especially in the higher echelons. Forms of petty corruption can be observed in both countries to an extent that is difficult to quantify. Nepotism, especially ethnic and regional, seems to be more widespread in Kenya.

The organization of the military also initially followed the British pattern. However, following the mutinies of 1964, in Tanzania it was placed under direct political control by means of careful recruitment and ideological education of soldiers. Now, however, the members of the military also enjoy certain material advantages. In Kenya, on the other hand, the policy of political neutralization of the military was continued by increased professionalism and material benefits. In addition, some real measure of counterbalance was created in both countries in the form of the militia in Tanzania and the paramilitary General Service Unit in Kenya. Both methods of subordinating the military to the civil government have hitherto proved to be relatively effective, even if the respective attempted coups in 1982 and 1983 did show up some limits in this respect. For the future, therefore, political intervention by the military cannot be ruled out in crisis situations that develop in other areas.

Our political events indicators record the extent of manifest political violence by which constitutional standards are disregarded, both by officials and society at large. A comparison of the number of violent disturbances between 1963 and 1977—fifty in Kenya and only one in Tanzania—or the number of deaths in domestic political disputes—363 in Kenya, twenty nine in Tanzania—confirms the finding of greater stability in Tanzania, which is also discernible in a historical-qualitative context. Culmination points of destabilizing tendencies, such as were reached in Kenya in 1969, 1974/75, 1982, and possibly also in 1986/87, have not been experienced by Tanzania. In a comparison of the indices of political rights and political repression (see Table 3) over several years, however, Tanzania has a much worse record, with a far greater number of political prisoners, often running into several hundreds, in comparison with Kenya, with mostly less than thirty.

If the feedback mechanisms of the overall systems are considered, then it is evident that, from an economic point of view, the agricultural surplus extracting character (see Table 1) of the Tanzanian regime is much more pronounced, as is shown by the producer prices for coffee. In spite of generally egalitarian policies, an urban-rural disparity has thus developed, which is damaging to productivity in both areas. The social achievements of the regime, in particular in the areas of health and education, must not be overlooked here, although these too have recently come up against economic limits. In Kenya, the social disparities are generally much more glaring. However, continuing urban-rural family ties, return flows for self-help projects and similar redistributive measures have so far ameliorated this. Since small farmers also benefit from development, self-supporting mechanisms have developed, including the informal sector, partially through increasing mass purchasing power, which have so far kept the dynamic equilibrium of the country on an even keel.

On the political level, things look somewhat different. In Tanzania, favorable background conditions, coupled with the personal integrity of the long-serving state president, Julius Nyerere, and the high esteem in which he was held, contributed to a considerable degree of political stability, in spite of some severe economic crises. The recent constitutional amendment limiting the president to two terms in office, and the possibility of voting no in presidential elections, means that there is some measure of institutional feedback at this level. In Kenya, the competitive character of the political system is restricted to the parliamentary level. In view of the overwhelming power of the president, the unlimited period in office, and the lack of effective electoral mechanisms in this area, potential opposition has no institutionalized form of expression in this regard. In the long term, this is without doubt one of the weak points of the system.

In terms of their foreign relations, both countries are dependent on world economic conditions. The terms of trade in both cases worsened after independence. The basic requirement for increased autonomy is self-sufficiency in food production. This could not be achieved in Tanzania in the crisis years, so that all the efforts at achieving self-reliance were checked. In addition, unrealistic rates of exchange forced a considerable portion of foreign trade into the informal sector (including the smuggling of goods and currency). The level of integration in the world economy is generally much higher in Kenya, so that fluctuations have a stronger ripple effect. In spite of high population growth and increasing scarcity of land, sufficient food production has largely been maintained through higher productivity. The large share of foreign capital and heavy capital outflows—partially through illegal transfers by the indigenous upper income groups, including the Asians, who feel particularly vulnerable—that in 1986 made Kenya into a net exporter of capital, do, however, represent a negative factor in the chances for development.

KENYA AND UGANDA

In respect of ethnic composition there are some parallels between Kenya and Uganda: the overall number of groups is approximately the same, their membership in different families of languages (Bantu and Nilotic, including some pastoral groups) is similar, and their relative size (the five largest groups in Uganda account for approximately half the population) is comparable. However, there is a fundamental difference in the political structure of some of the ethnic groups. In contrast to the mainly egalitarian-segmentarian structure in Kenya and similar structures of the Nilotic groups in Uganda, some of the Bantu in Uganda had developed important monarchies before colonization. Of these, the most prominent was the Kingdom of Buganda, whose role was strengthened in the course of British colonial rule by the feudalization of land in this part of the country, and by British indirect rule through the rulers of Buganda. The anchoring of Buganda's special status in the independence constitution resulted in the first severe state crisis.

In contrast to the settlement policy in Kenya, British colonial power in Uganda concentrated on small and medium farms for the production of cash crops, especially in the southern part of the country, where there were markedly favorable climatic conditions for this. Members of the administration and the military, on the other hand, tended to be recruited more in the North, so that ethnic and economic lines of conflict coincided. This pattern was further exacerbated by the different mission establishments (mainly Catholic in the South and Protestant in the North). This also offers an explanation of the features of the party structure, which was built on these foundations. In Kenya, by contrast, although certain ethnic and economic disparities cannot be denied, these conflict lines did tend to crosscut each other to a much greater extent. Membership of differing churches did not add another conflict-aggravating factor.

After independence in Kenya, a social structure characterized by class differentiation developed, which has so far been kept intact by elements of consociation in the formation of governments, and the inclusion of wider circles of small farmers in the development of the economy. In Uganda there was to a very large extent a disparity between the economic strength of the South and the political dominance of the North (first under Obote, then under Amin, and finally once again under Obote and the Okellos). This political tension stood in the way of uniform development. On the contrary, those in power, who increasingly ruled by naked force, plundered available resources wherever they could. The peasant economy of the South, which was basically sound, was thus pushed back into subsistence and shadow economic activity, including smuggling. Many members of the economically more successful classes lost their lives.

While the growth curve of the GDP in Kenya is predominantly determined by directional changes in international economic trends, and—despite the two oil crises in the 1970s grew by an annual average of 5.6 percent—the turning points of economic development in Uganda coincided with domestic political turning points. Thus, the per capita GNP in

Kenya in current prices rose from $143 in 1970 to $420 in 1980; in Uganda, on the other hand, it rose from $135 in 1970 to only $300 in 1980. The development of the security situation after 1971 played a significant part in this. The 19 percent decline in GDP during the Amin era was balanced out by short-term growth rates of 5 percent per annum between 1980 and 1984. In comparison with Kenya's comparatively favorable sectoral structure (agricultural share of GDP in 1980 was 34 percent), 76 percent of Uganda's GDP was accounted for by agriculture. In the broadly diversified range of Kenya's agricultural exports, coffee accounts for around one-fifth, while since 1976, 80 percent of Uganda's export earnings have been provided by coffee. The PQLI for 1975 shows Kenya, with a rating of 51, to have a much higher quality of life than does Uganda, with only 40. A comparison of school attendance in Kenya (1965: primary 54 percent, secondary 4 percent; 1980: primary 100 percent, secondary 18 percent) with that in Uganda (1965: primary 67 percent, secondary 4 percent; 1980: primary 50 percent, secondary 5 percent) demonstrates the contrasting developments in the two countries.

The political culture, which in Kenya can to some extent build on traditional participatory forms and which has so far enabled some minimal degree of consensus to be achieved, is once again splintered in Uganda and laden with enduring antagonisms. Traditional forms of monarchical political legitimacy, such as existed mainly in Buganda and were given expression by the KY, no longer play any significant role. At the same time, in view of the political upheavals, participatory forms of legitimation could not gain a foothold, even in the North and within the smaller Bantu tribes, where such traditions had in the past existed. Instead, repression and force prevailed. It remains to be seen whether the new government leader, Museveni, can succeed in establishing the support he received in those areas from which he recruited his NRM on a more permanent basis (through the newly created village councils, etc.). The chances of achieving this in the North seem to be as slim as ever. Even putting a stop to the armed disputes and reducing the often criminal and private use of violence would be some kind of success. However, any kind of overall national consensus—no matter how limited—does not seem anywhere near likely. In spite of obvious gaps in the time series data on the political development of Uganda, at least the indicator "deaths arising from political conflicts" quantifies the contrast between the glaring instability of Uganda (thirty thousand and more dead) and its high level of state repression, and the stability of Kenya (around three hundred deaths), whose political system, while frequently shaken by crisis, has never been placed in doubt. In any evaluation of human and civil rights by Amnesty International or Freedom House, Uganda is always placed in the worst category, while Kenya is charged with only relatively minor violations of normative standards.

In contrast to the relatively varied landscape of input structures in

Kenya, the upheavals in Uganda have hitherto not allowed any lasting independent profile to develop in this respect. Even now, everything is in a state of flux and, in the final analysis, any reasoned assessment will depend on the path that the overall political system will eventually take. The tendency in the direction of a socialist military regime (on this concept, see Berg-Schlosser 1984d), which is evident in some sections of the NRM, means that there is a probability of tying labor organizations closely to the regime. On the other hand, in those parts of the country where the NRM has its support, agriculture and the small trade and craft sectors are clearly oriented to petit bourgeois forms, which will eventually find institutional expression in the articulations of these interests. The same applies to the press, which has now bloomed into a much more diverse and spontaneous form, but which still has not established any enduring basis as regards its material conditions.

The activities of political parties have been suspended in Uganda. However, they continue to be present in a latent form in political life, if we disregard the presumably permanent decline in importance of the KY. Political orientations and behavior relate strongly to original DP—or UPC affinities. The renewed legalization of parties would therefore, in all probability, and in spite of bitter experience, lead to the rekindling of the old patterns of conflict. Whether or not the NRM will be able to build up an acceptable alternative to this through the local RCs remains to be seen. In view of the large number of conflict lines in Ugandan society, mainly finding expression in ethnic groups and the churches, a one-party system (which must of course address the demands of inner-party democracy—such as is practiced to some extent in Kenya and Tanzania) does seem to present a more appropriate solution.

Uganda's government claims, as in Kenya, to embody certain elements of consociational democracy. The broad-based government, which includes former DP and UPC representatives as well as a broad political spectrum of opinion of NRM members, is already threatening to crumble. In any case, however, in order to be able to justify the claim to be even a short-term, national alliance, it ought to include respected representatives from the northern and eastern regions. However, it is still the case that security conditions do not allow this. To an even greater extent than in Kenya, therefore, the current political situation is determined by the state president personally. Even if there is much to be said for the seriousness of his attempts to lead the country back to the road to stability and prosperity, and for his personal integrity, scepticism does seem to be in order in view of the extent of the economic and political disorganization.

The fundamental precondition for all further developments remains the military pacification of the country. In the areas from which the NRA draws its recruits, the "subjective" condition for control over armed force seems to be assured, in respect of the NRA's identification with the NRM's objectives and its loyalty to the state president. However, this is far from being the case as regards its operation in the North and East of the country. Even professional standards, such as those prevailing in Kenya, have not so far been met. Whether the assistance given by Libya in this respect will have a favorable effect on such a development must appear dubious. In the NRM heartland, the success of the chosen economic and more general development policy will give impetus to the development of, at least, further specific supports. After military pacification, a regulated economic life must once again become established, which allows private initiatives sufficient room, but which also comes to grips with the shadow economy (magendo) and the foreign trade situation, which remains as precarious as ever. The recent currency reform and the resetting of the exchange rate of the shilling at a more realistic level are first steps—if only very tentative ones—in this direction. Similarly, the agreement with the IMF and other donors can improve the foreign economic position and contribute to the rebuilding of the country's infrastructure. The Kenyan example, especially with regard to appropriate agricultural producer prices, could be a very helpful model in this respect. On the other hand, actual relations with Kenya are still tense, despite its importance for access to the sea and its role as a potentially important regional economic partner. The divergent ideological orientations of the two regimes and the alliances with foreign powers they have entered into have further increased each state's suspicion of the other's support for its domestic opposition.

TANZANIA AND UGANDA

In relation to the colonial scheme of things, some degree of similarity between Tanzania and Uganda is immediately apparent. Neither country developed settler colonies. Instead, the colonial powers decided right from the turn of century to build up production of export crops based on small farmer production. Because of the uncertainties of the British mandate over Tanganyika and also the lack of success of European planters in Uganda, the plantation sector in both countries also remained relatively small. The pressure the German colonial administration applied to force the cultivation of cotton was met with massive resistance by the people of Tanganyika in the Maji-Maji uprising of 1905. Only through the devastation of entire regions did colonial forces put the uprising down in 1907, but the blow to development efforts that this entailed did enable the peoples of Tanganyika to maintain the egalitarian-segmentary structure of their societies relatively intact. As opposed to the situation in Tanganyika, the British colonial power in Uganda was faced with a severe development gap. The egalitarian societies of the ethnic groups in the North contrasted with strongly differentiated societies in the South. The colonial division of labor, which initially restricted the cultivation of cash crops to the more advanced southern kingdoms, reinforced these differences. In addition, the role of Buganda, which occupied a special position vis-à-vis the other parts of the country within the scheme of indirect rule, led to a splintering of political forces.

In both cases, however, the immigrant Asian commercial bourgeoisie, having wrung monopoly rights from the colonial administration, controlled the entire intermediate trade in agricultural raw materials. When the United Kingdom intensified its drive for industrialization in Uganda to a greater extent than in Tanganyika, Indian capital had a share in the investments. The politically isolated Asian ethnic group was thus able to improve its key role in the economy. In comparison with Tanzania, Uganda thus had a considerable industrial potential at the start of its independence. The link between the political instability of Uganda and the decline in its economic potential is plain to see. Amin's economic war, by itself, resembled plunder of productive capital. While Tanzania managed, in spite of internal barriers to development, to achieve an average annual growth in GDP of over 4 percent, the GDP of Amin's Uganda fell by 2 percent per annum. The retrograde development of the sectoral structure was also more marked in Uganda (agricultural share of GDP in 1980 was 54 percent, and subsistence share about 30 percent). In contrast to the greater diversification of Tanzania's export production, 90 percent of Uganda's exports are accounted for by coffee. Extremely high rates of surplus extraction for agricultural exports (see Table 1) and high rates of inflation—far in excess of 50 percent from the early 1970s onward—resulted in a considerably greater decline in real incomes in Uganda than in Tanzania. In the case of Tanzania this decline was to some extent compensated for by better social provisions.

The loss of development that Uganda has suffered as a result of the enduring upheavals and civil wars since independence has led to a situation in which 90 percent of the labor force are still employed in agriculture, as opposed to 80 percent in Tanzania. The greater urbanization of Tanzania has led to strong growth of the group of nonagricultural proletaroids employed in the informal sector, but two-thirds of the Tanzanian population still belong to the group of agricultural proletaroids. The social structure of Uganda, though, is still primarily shaped by the North–South disparity. While agricultural proletaroids make up a good 80 percent of the population in the Northern parts of the country, a good half of the southern population, especially in Buganda, belongs to the agricultural petite bourgeoisie. It is true that even in Buganda the decline into subsistence is discernible, but there are several signs that this leveling is probably only a short-term phenomenon.

The original monarchistic and secessionist orientation of the small and medium farmers of Buganda, who, at 16 percent of the population, also represent the most important economic group, together with other ethnic-regional conflicts and the political overtones of religious differences, has prevented any crystalization of even a minimal national consensus. Rivalries and animosities of this kind led to the splintering of Uganda's politically active middle classes. In Tanzania, on the other hand, a socially and regionally relatively egalitarian social structure combined with a favorable distribution of ethnic groups. Their smaller size did not allow any of the 120 various ethnic groups to dominate the others. A national awareness of unity and strength, which sprang from the Maji-Maji uprising and which, from the 1920s found expression in a countrywide organization, the Tanzania African Association, forerunner of the government party, the TANU, demonstrates favorable political-cultural background conditions.

The response of both regimes to the crisis of legitimacy, which came to a head in both cases with a mutiny of troops and severe disturbances in the trade unions in 1964, was to make institutional changes. In 1967, under the charismatic leadership of Mwalimu Julius Nyerere, the state and party in Tanzania put into practice a concept of development, the ujamaa policy—a resettlement and nationalization program—that was initially relatively easily conveyed. However, the retreat of the small farmers into subsistence in the face of compulsory government measures and overtaxation, does indicate that there were tensions here, too, although these were to some extent smoothed out by the generally much improved provision of social services. In addition, the growth of a large public sector allowed a bureaucratic bourgeoisie to become established as an economic power factor and a firm support for the regime. The leadership code, which was also laid down in 1967, prevented functionaries from using their offices to line their own pockets, and thus retained the broad-based credibility of the ujamaa policy. In Uganda, Obote's attempt after 1967 to shore up his regime by creating a similar bureaucratic bourgeoisie, with the formation of parastatal monopoly trading organizations, was undermined by the Asian commercial bourgeoisie and the progressive small farmers of Buganda. Finally, in 1969 the president, isolated by serious domestic and constitutional conflicts, announced a fundamental change, the move to the left. In many respects, the populist program bore similarities to the Tanzanian Arusha Declaration. As a more or less personal maneuver on Obote's part, it was met with lack of interest by farmers and rejected by other social groups because of its egalitarian aims. Its failure was therefore welcomed virtually countrywide.

The corrections of the agricultural reform, even in the radical phases, demonstrate a coherence that is characteristic of Tanzanian politics. Although the traditionally strong agricultural cooperatives had been dissolved only in 1976 and replaced by parastatal crop authorities, a restrained step away from this policy had already been taken by 1977 with the return to greater promotion of private investment. Reverses and failures were openly acknowledged up to 1982, when the balancing of the budget, the increase in efficiency of the state organizations, and the adjustment of the entire structure of prices by allowing market mechanisms to work, among other measures, were eventually composed into a comprehensive policy of structural reorganization, which has since been gradually implementated. The realization of the necessity to allow producers sufficient profits led to the relegalizing of cooperatives in 1982. The economic liberalization that Tanzania is now undergoing is the culmination of a course correction that has been well prepared over a lengthy period and coordinated among the various elements in the system. The broad base of legitimacy has enabled the regime, in doing this, to accept some delay and a dramatic worsening of the supply situation, rather than be over hastily bound by IMF conditions, which the political leadership regarded as socially destabilizing.

Amin's economic war against Asian ethnic groups in Uganda was aimed, as were the policies of Obote before him, simply at achieving the specific support of the civilian and military beneficiaries of this action. In the long term, though, this "solution" to a structural problem not only involved the destruction of economic resources but also burdened the country with a far more serious problem in the shape of the magendo. The skimming of farm profits by the militarized marketing boards and the immense extent of corruption took on far greater dimensions than in Tanzania. For this reason, Obote wanted to stimulate growth once again in 1980 by increasing producer prices and promoting the small capitalist sector. The urgent need to achieve some quick economic success in order to stabilize his regime and gain some specific supports caused him to accept an IMF loan on conditions that quickly led to a slowdown in growth and an increase in inflation. By 1987, the NRM regime had more time at its disposal to work out programs with similar tendencies and to negotiate better terms, but the pressure is also rising on Museveni to show some economic successes in the 1990s.

The high acceptance and consistent implementation of Tanzania's Arusha Declaration cannot be understood without reference to the extensive apparatus of the TANU and its mobilizing ability. It controls important social areas through mass organizations incorporated into the party (e.g., trade unions, women's and youth organizations) and does not allow the formation of autonomous structures. While the party leadership has secured its power over all sections of the party through a hierarchy of appointed secretaries, internal party feedback mechanisms are installed on all levels by way of regular party elections. Since 1982, a greater separation between the party and the state apparatus is intended to strengthen the party's function as an advocate of the people, especially on a local and regional level. The state-owned press does report openly about abuses and irregular behavior by authorities and individuals. It cannot, however, critically discuss any fundamental questions of principle independently of the political leadership. With the exception of the Amin era, the diversity of the press in Uganda and its relatively great freedom are, by contrast, a constant element in the otherwise dysfunctional input structures of Uganda on a national level. Even after the transformation into a system of two major parties in 1980, which signaled the de facto decline of the basis of the KY, party politics was still dominated by opportunism, official patronage, and individual power struggles. As early as 1964, UPC Secretary General Kakonge, who wanted to lead the UPC along the same path as that taken by the TANU, was forced out of the party by his opponents, who saw their own power threatened. In view of the affinities with the former parties, which are ever present in day-to-day politics, and the dazzling diversity of the NRM, the situation, should it ever in the long term come to a one-party system, is at no time comparable with that of the TANU.

The structural weaknesses in the independence constitution of Uganda blocked decisionmaking processes within the constitutional organs and also any reorganization of these. The special status of Buganda was eliminated by the presidential system installed by a coup. However, the state of emergency in Buganda since 1967 paved the way for a development that led to Amin's military dictatorship. The revised version of this presidential constitution proved to be inadequate to prevent the further disintegration of the political system after 1980. Consociational-democratic structures in Museveni's cabinet, and an interim Parliament, the members of which are legitimated in part by revolutionary forces, in part by an election mandate or by the reputation of representatives accepted by particular political groups, are intended to give the regime time for a process of institution-building. In contrast to this, Tanzania was able in the 1960s to expand and adapt its independence constitution. Since that time, gradual changes have remodeled the constitution as the need arose. Nyerere waited until 1975 before he initiated the unification of the TANU with the ASP in Zanzibar into the CMM, thus setting in motion the process of closer integration of Zanzibar with the mainland from 1977. The new union constitution meant that electoral provisions and the maintenance of the principles of the rule of law were also applied to Zanzibar. From 1964, Nyerere constantly criticized the situation in Zanzibar on both of these points. The limitation of the president's time in office, introduced in 1982, finally paved the way for Nyerere to relinquish a further period of service. Prior to that, the distribution of the three highest state offices between Zanzibar and the mainland had been constitutionally regulated. The parliamentary and presidential elections that have been regularly held on the mainland since 1962 have proved to be effective, if restricted, feedback mechanisms, despite being controlled by the TANU or CCM. The real distribution of weight among the various constitutional organs has given the Tanzanian system the flexibility to be able to tolerate politicians from different camps in its institutions. As a result of this, it has the necessary personnel resources for any change of course, should the need arise.

In Uganda, after 1980, the lack in discipline of the official armed forces and the inability to break the power of armed rebels undermined Obote's basis of legitimacy, which was in any case already fragile because of the manipulated elections. In spite of foreign military advisers, he was unable to gain effective control of the hurriedly recruited army. This seems to have been achieved by Museveni with his NRA in the South for the first time in the recent history of the country. With the politicization of these troops, combined with skilful recruiting procedures, he followed a path that had also been taken by Tanzania following the mutiny of 1964. However, the immediate challenge facing the new regime is the existence of the ethnic-regionally concentrated armed opposition formations, which have characterized Ugandan society since its militarization under Amin.

In the area of bureaucracy, the Tanzanian leadership code, which applies equally to civil servants, prevented the more glaring forms of corruption and nepotism until recently. Conflicts of interest with private economic activities on a large scale were thus largely prevented. However, increased possibilities for self-aggrandizement in the wake of liberalization, and the ever-present drive toward second incomes in the course of the expansion of informal activities, have somewhat tarnished this positive picture in recent times. Although the efficiency of the system suffered to a considerable degree from this, state activities have by no means been paralyzed to the same extent as has been the case in the totally demoralized Ugandan administration after Amin. The disentanglement of Uganda's bureaucracy from the clutches of the magendo is an essential requirement for the return of the country to properly regulated development processes.

Nonalignment, independence, and support for independence movements in the Third World are the major constants of Tanzania's foreign policy. The widely observed dispute between Tanzania and the IMF, which went beyond questions of the instruments to be applied and blew up over the lack of respect for national prestige and the violation of political sovereignty that was perceived by Tanzania's leadership, was a continuation of the self-assured foreign policy line. Tanzania thus differs greatly from Uganda, whose internal conflicts have always been exacerbated by the intervention of external forces and have thus been additionally burdened by the foreign policy rivalries of other powers. Because of its landlocked position in the East African region and its economic structure, Uganda was always more dependent on a functional East African community than were Kenya and Tanzania, but at the same time, always the weaker partner, politically in relation to Tanzania and economically in relation to Kenya, within the alliance. Amin's attempt to solve his internally threatened situation by an attack on Tanzania led to the decision, regarded by Nyerere as problematic but unavoidable, to support the opposition to Amin in the overthrow of the dictator. For a short time, Tanzania thus had a massive influence on Uganda's development. At the present time, the latent conflict between Uganda and Kenya is evidence of the sensitivity of Uganda's neighbors to a policy that has already been at the mercy of foreign powers on several occasions.

7
Overall Comparisons

SUMMARY OF RESULTS

The findings of the individual system evaluations and the paired comparisons can be summarized as follows: the precolonial ethnic structures and the differing effects of colonial policy are still in evidence; the relatively large number of small ethnic groups in Tanzania and their relatively homogeneous structure has been particularly beneficial; the number and relative size of the ethnic groups in Kenya and Uganda are approximately comparable, but the hierarchical structure of the monarchies in southern Uganda, reinforced by British colonial rule, created increased tension with the egalitarian-segmentary ethnic groups in the North and East; and, while in Kenya there was increasing socioeconomic differentiation on a class basis, which to some extent cuts across ethnic lines, the ethnic, economic, and religious divisions in Uganda were mutually reinforcing.

In Tanzania, the social basis enabled a relatively unproblematic transition to independence to be made within the framework of a broadly based national movement, the TANU (the separate development of Zanzibar must be seen as something of an exception, though). In view of the shaping of Kenya as a settler colony, its transition to independence was accompanied by fierce confrontations. The original multiparty system, founded on an ethnic basis, soon changed into an organizationally weakly structured single-party system, dominated by the rising middle and upper classes. In Uganda, by contrast, the mutually reinforcing conflict lines led to the development of a centrifugal multiparty system, which is still latent today, and which has condemned to failure all attempts to surmount these conflict structures in an attempt to arrive at some measure of a broad-based national consensus. The bloody experiences in the decades following independence and the devastation of the economy led to an almost Hobbesian political culture of *homo hominilupus*, which continues to hinder any approach to widespread cooperation and economic consolidation.

The political system of Tanzania is based on an organizationally well-developed single-party structure that, in spite of some centralist elements, has so far had adequate feedback mechanisms, both internal and in parliamentary and presidential elections, to enable it to process new political impulses and any necessary reorientations. The recent restriction of the presidency to two terms is a positive factor. In spite of an extensive eco-

151

nomic crisis in the 1970s and early 1980s, which to some extent was caused by domestic factors, Tanzania was able to maintain its political stability, as the smooth changeover of presidents shows. In Kenya there is a relatively strong orientation of the system to the administration and the executive. By comparison, the single party that existed from 1969 led only a shadowy existence, and, in view of the actual power structure with the president at the top, even more-recent attempts at revitalization must be regarded with scepticism. The system's relatively pluralistic input constellation, including a largely independent press, has also allowed sufficient feedback to date. This is particularly the case with the virtually unrestricted, regular parliamentary elections that have an effect right up to cabinet level. The presidency itself, however, has not thus far been subject to this kind of control. While the changeover, following the death of the first president, followed a constitutional course, the lack of any limit to the presidential term and his reaffirmation by simple acclamation indicate certain "hardening" tendencies (as can also be seen from recent political developments), which in the long term could detract from the political stability that has thus far been enjoyed. In all, in view of the quite rapid socioeconomic development, which has further accentuated class and regional divisions, we must regard Kenya as being in a fairly tension-laden situation that, however, has been kept on an even keel within the framework of the ethnic and class alliances discussed. While in Tanzania and Kenya the element of political stability, based on a considerable degree of legitimacy, has so far prevailed in different ways, even in the face of varying socioeconomic developments, the situation in Uganda must be described as being politically extremely unstable and economically regressive. The new regime can be said to have any broad-based support only in the southern parts of the country. The security situation continues to be precarious and economic development uncertain. A gradual economic consolidation will be required before any politically durable institutional basis can be found in all parts of the country. Even though the new regime has shown some initiatives in this respect, and the desirability of such a development is in the interests of all concerned, any forecasts as to the success of these measures must necessarily be purely speculative in view of the devastation of the country over so many years.

The development policies embarked on in the three countries are closely correlated with their political orientations and value systems. Kenya, with its peripheral-capitalist orientation, undoubtedly has the best performance data. In spite of some fluctuations, economic growth has continued to be considerable and the social indicators have improved markedly. Particular emphasis must be given here to the development of small-farm agriculture in some regions, but also to sections of the nonagricultural sector integrated with this development, in part through the informal economy. In view of the extremely high rate of population growth and to some extent also of worsening social and regional imbalances, the dangers confronting this course cannot be overlooked. Tanzania's own way to socialism, by contrast, shows other types of contradiction. The social provisions of the regime, especially in education and health, have been considerable and have had a great effect in avoiding regional imbalances. However, the transposition of this course to the economic sphere must be regarded as a failure. The rural population could not be won over for extensive collectivization measures under the ujamaa policy; the vast parastatal organizations in production, finance, and marketing proved to be inefficient; the inflated bureaucratic bourgeoisie showed itself to be considerably parasitic; and wide sections of the economy were carried on, if at all, in the informal sector. The course correction that has recently been made in the direction of greater individual incentives and private economic organizational forms in agriculture, retailing, and other areas is, by contrast, showing some initial successes. Socially, Uganda must be characterized as a deterrent case. In spite of a relatively good starting point, the respective indicators are virtually without exception regressive. The economy declined, magendo spread its tentacles, and even the PQLI, which initially had the highest value of all three countries, declined in the 1980s. Whether political rebirth will also be able to bring new economic impulses for the implementation of a mixed economy remains to be seen and will depend on the overall security situation.

All of these developments must, however, also be considered in their respective foreign policy and foreign economic contexts. Tanzania's "own way" was also demonstrated in her foreign policy. The country became an important mouthpiece of the nonaligned countries and selectively maintained a similar distance from central elements of both the First and Second worlds. Its relatively intensive contacts to countries such as China and Yugoslavia, but also to the Scandinavian countries, which did not involve any new one-way dependencies, underlined this policy. The economic weakness that made the country dependent on food imports and worsened the debt situation, did, however, tend in the direction of undermining this position. Giving way to the IMF in 1986, even though the conditions were somewhat less rigid than in numerous other cases, was therefore based in part on rationality and in part on necessity. Kenya, on the other hand, has never seriously questioned its firm links with the Western states, originally predominantly represented by the former colonial power, the United Kingdom, but today primarily by the United States. There has always been a high proportion of foreign capital involved in industry, finance, and foreign trade. In foreign economic policy and foreign policy Kenya has largely followed the course indicated by Western powers, although in recent times a certain amount of differentiation can be observed between the more national elements and those who can rather be termed comprador elements of the indigenous bourgeoisie. Uganda's foreign policy orientation has been just as turbulent as its domestic development. The tense domestic situation led to external attempts at intervention. Powers in both West and East, and also the Arab states and

Israel, had a part in this somewhat macabre game. The current regime aims to steer a more independent course, but its relations with Libya have aroused the suspicions of its neighbor, Kenya, and the situation in the North is still influenced by the relations between the resistance groups and the rebels in southern Sudan and their foreign partners.

Initiatives toward regional cooperation, which are to be greatly welcomed in terms of development policy, have also suffered from the differing foreign policy directions. In the meantime, there has been something of a rapprochement between Kenya and Tanzania in this respect. The border, which was closed for a long period, has been reopened. Cooperation between Tanzania and Uganda is also progressing. The relations between Kenya and Uganda, on the other hand, are still imbued with the mutual suspicion that each country is supporting the other's opposition groups. Yet all three of the states could profit from greater intraregional trade, better traffic connections and so on. This could also take place within the framework of the wider PTA in East and central Africa, which all three countries have now joined. In the longer term, however, a more comprehensive regional structural and industrial development policy needs to be kept in mind, albeit one that would, as far as possible, avoid the development of any one-sided advantages. Political control is also of importance with respect to other aspects of foreign economic policy, in order to counteract any existing misdevelopments and long-term one-sided dependencies. Raw materials continue to make up a large proportion of the exports of all three states. The converse is that all three are dependent on imports of crude oil and manufactured products. There is thus still a high degree of dependence on the considerable world market price fluctuation in these products—an illustration would be the price trends of coffee and crude oil. Since independence, there has been a drastic deterioration in the terms of trade for all three countries. The extent of aboveboard and hidden capital outflows is considerable. This applies especially to a relatively better-developed country such as Kenya, where, for instance, a special part is played by the Asians, with their diverse foreign connections, and also by the activities of transnational corporations. However, private inflows of capital and development aid have been only partially able to offset the trend, and the foreign debt of all three countries has greatly increased over the past few years.

All three countries show a clearly definable development pattern. Tanzania's ujamaa socialism has proved to be politically stable but economically inefficient; the reorientation of recent years does, however, show a step in the right direction. Kenya's peripheral capitalist way has had relatively greater economic successes, and, so far, the political system has been able to smooth out internal tensions. Nevertheless, the higher level of domestic and foreign policy risk involved in this course cannot be overlooked. Uganda's politics and economy, on the other hand, are characterized by extreme turbulence that, somewhat less dramatically, persists to this day. All three development patterns show a considerable degree (in the social-structural factors, the political-cultural patterns, etc.) of self-reproducing elements. Any deviation from the chosen course therefore seems possible only gradually, as can be observed in Tanzania, for example.

ISOLATION OF KEY VARIABLES

Beyond the aspects dealt with in the paired comparisons, the isolation of individual central factors is difficult. In view of the vast number of variables to be recorded and the limitation to three cases, a quasi-experimental design can be of only limited use. This is the methodological justification of the configurative analyses that were at first undertaken. In spite of this necessary reservation, the outlined interaction structure of the various development patterns enables us to determine some key variables, in which the relationships between the political system and development success find concise expression.

One variable of this type is the rate of surplus extraction from agricultural exports (see Table 1). Where the data are available, they exemplify the relative priorities accorded to rural and urban interests in the different states at different times: the rural population makes up by far the largest section in all three countries; all recent approaches to development policy in Africa stress—with varying levels of emphasis—the importance of precisely this sector for a broad, self-supporting development (see, e.g., OAU 1980; World Bank 1986; Brandt et al. 1986); the tilt of a particular policy toward the rural or urban sector is strongly reflected in the data. After what has so far been discussed, it should come as no surprise that Kenya performs best in this respect by a large margin, and Uganda, especially in its darkest phases, performs worst. The recent attempts at reform in Tanzania and Uganda, which do not as yet show up in the statistics, also point in the direction of an improvement of small-scale agricultural producer profits.

A second important bundle of indicators is made up by the actual budget priorities set by each regime (see Table 2). Here, too, there is a clear pattern: expenditure on education and health, by way of strategies to fulfill basic needs, is relatively high in both Kenya and Tanzania. In Tanzania, however, military expenditure (which from an economic point of view is unproductive, since it does not have any capacity effect) is also relatively high, and this does not apply only to the period of the war with Uganda. In Uganda, the military swallowed up by far the greatest part of the national budget (quite apart from the extensive private self-aggrandizement of its members).

Our third group of indicators relates to the direct political feedback character of the particular regime. The actual mechanisms, beyond their existing problems and tensions, are an expression—at least partially and indirectly—of the existing level of legitimacy of the regime, and thus also a major aspect of its long-term political stability. The first indicator of this kind relates to political rights and thus to the opportunity of the population for political participation (see Table 3). The reliability of sources with regard to the cases investigated here in some detail is, however, open to question, insofar as their evaluations are based on parliamentary-democratic, Western standards, which, for example, ignore any differentiated assessment of competitive mechanisms within the one-party system. Nevertheless, the relatively better score for Kenya (although the tensions and dangers we have discussed should not be forgotten) corresponds with our assessment. It is our opinion, though, that Tanzania's score is too negative. The worst score by far, that of Uganda, is well deserved, although the latest developments there could not be included in this indicator. As a complement to this aspect, the real level of repression should also be emphasized as an indicator of a lack of legitimacy. This indicator, which is based on sources such as Amnesty International, underlines the above findings: Kenya and Tanzania, with a certain gradation, perform clearly better and Uganda clearly very poorly.

POSSIBLE GENERALIZATIONS OF RESULTS

The results obtained from these analyses are primarily valid only for the cases themselves. As this study has followed a most similar systems design, at least as far as some basic circumstances were concerned, such as similar geographical-climatic, ethnic, and colonial conditions, a direct comparison on this basis would be possible only with other, similar cases. A simple geographical extension of the region examined (e.g., including Malawi, Zambia, Zimbabwe, etc.) immediately involves a great many other, often-individual factors, however. And our analysis has also shown that, above and beyond some of the specifiable common features, each of the cases has formed its own decisive pattern of development. In our opinion it seems more useful, therefore, to make further comparisons regarding particular types of political systems and their developments. For this purpose there are some macro-quantitative studies available that concern the independent states of black Africa as a whole (see Berg-Schlosser 1987a).

If one classifies the African states into relatively stable political systems with a strongly pluralistic structure (polyarchies), stable African socialist one-party systems, and unstable states characterized by numerous military and other armed interventions (praetorian systems), for which the three case studies serve as prototypes to a certain extent (other possible types and further variations have to be omitted here), the following picture emerges: polyarchies show relatively high average growth rates for the GNP per capita (a very summary indicator, but the most widely used one for economic development) during the first two decades of independence; growth rates in socialist countries are by contrast low, and those of the praetorian systems even poorer. With regard to the PQLI, which considers aspects of the satisfaction of basic needs and their distribution, the situation is different: the socialist states rate comparatively high, followed quite closely by the polyarchies; praetorian systems again appear at the lower end of the scale (see Table 4).

If one analyzes this pattern more closely, a major causal factor is revealed in the budget priorities of the various system types (see Table 5): on the whole, the socialist states have the greatest share of government expenditure in relation to the GDP. High priorities for education and health services are clearly discernible for this type, but military expenditure is also high. The polyarchies are in an intermediate position as far as social expenditures are concerned, but their military budgets are relatively low. In praetorian systems the military expenditure is high, and little is spent in the social field.

If one considers political feedback mechanisms as expressed in the indices of civil liberties and political repression, another clear picture is revealed (see Table 6): the polyarchies have relatively high ratings in both aspects; the socialist states display negative values for civil liberties, but as far as the extent of immediate repression is concerned, they are placed just above the mean; and the military regimes show definitely negative rankings for both indicators.

In the light of this statistical evidence, the results of our comparative case studies are validated in certain respects and may be considered as generalizable, within certain limits, in relation to these particular system types. Yet, these macro-quantitative results can indicate only a very rough pattern. It would be desirable if further systematic, comparative analyses could be carried out, for example including francophone West African states, in order to confirm these results or modify them if necessary.

CONCLUSIONS

Our analysis has attempted, on the basis of the three cases examined, to differentiate among, and map out, the complex interactions between differing types of political systems and the economic and social developments that have occurred in those systems. It was demonstrated that the conflict, which has recently once again featured strongly in the discussion of general development theory, between the stabilization and development functions of the state, is resolvable through a dynamic equilibrium, as the cases of Kenya and Tanzania show in different ways. However, some weak points and problems in these cases, which have a certain degree of general applicability, have been pointed out. For instance, it was demonstrated that political stability is a necessary condition (as in the case of Kenya), but not, on its own, a sufficient condition (for example, the case of Tanzania) for successful long-term economic and social development. The Ugandan case does, however, demonstrate that without political stability there is no possibility of any enduring development.

Above and beyond this, the individual case studies and the systematic comparisons have highlighted some fundamental problems of development policy as well as case-specific problem areas. On a fundamental level, these findings underline the importance of development on a broad, rural basis; that is, progress needs to be made primarily in the small-farm and small-craft sectors and in improving productivity and purchasing power in these areas (see Brandt et al. 1986; Nuscheler 1987). In this respect, Kenya is, within limits, a positive example, and Tanzania over a long period a negative one. The state levy on the marketing of major agricultural products, which was identified as a key variable in our comparative analysis, is a central indicator in this respect. The budget priorities set by each system type (the proportion of expenditure on health, education, and other basic needs), including the regional distribution of these, are of a similar importance. In the same way, the violations of human rights and restrictions on the rule of law by a regime reflect a certain degree of feedback inhibition, blocking any broader-based political participation and thus legitimacy, which, in a dynamic sense, is the factor that in the longer term brings about stability. Institutional solutions modeled entirely on those of Western industrialized countries should not, however, be seen as providing the sole answer, and the possibility, for instance, of including competitive elements in a one-party system and similar innovative institutional approaches should also be considered.

In this way, in view of largely identical external conditions, it was possible to trace and document in each case the importance of the internal political determinants in their various forms for a more general process of economic and social development. Our findings generally supported the domestic economic importance of decentralized, market-based forms of organization and the independent function of effective political feedback mechanisms based on widespread participation. However, these findings should not be regarded as implying the mere confirmation of Western or modernization theory clichés. The countries investigated are still without doubt poor countries in a one-sided dependence on world economic conditions. The real value of their (predominantly) agricultural products against imported products has declined almost consistently since independence. The structural reorganization of their economies, but also a reform of the world economic system in favor of the poorer countries, is still urgently needed. Domestically, public controls are required to avoid private monopolies in industry and finance. Even if African socialist development, as it is has been practiced so far, must largely be regarded as a failure, dependent-capitalist development, without sacrificing the objectives of improving the quality of life of the population at large and maintaining the greatest possible equality of opportunity and political participation, remains a tightrope walk.

Creative initiatives in this regard, which also include innovations in development policy and political-institutional innovations, must primarily come from the concerned countries themselves. Even with the level of dependence and asymmetry of world economic conditions, the major national actors' room for maneuver in this respect and their possibilities for action must not be underestimated. Both Kenya and Tanzania have, in their different ways, developed some approaches to this. Whether the same will be the case after the new beginning in Uganda remains to be seen.

IV

Diagrams and Tables

Diagram 1   Model of Dynamic Interactions Between Political System and Environment

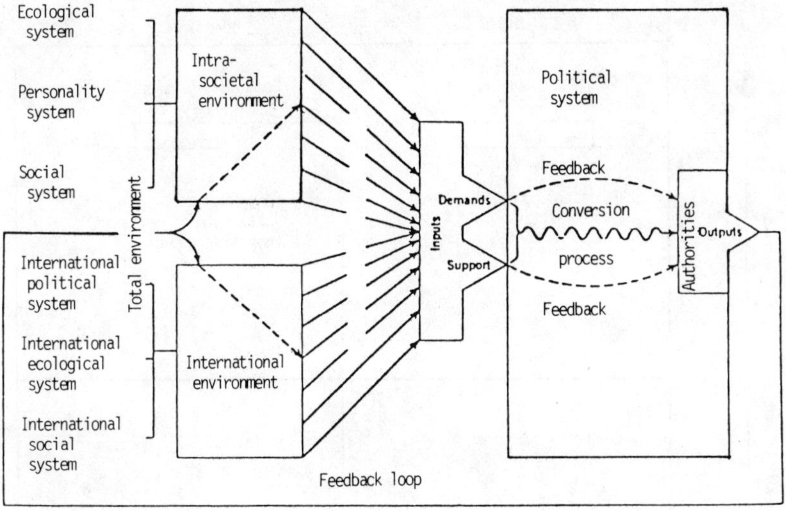

Source: Adapted from Easton 1965:30.

Diagram 2   The Political System in the Context of the Social System

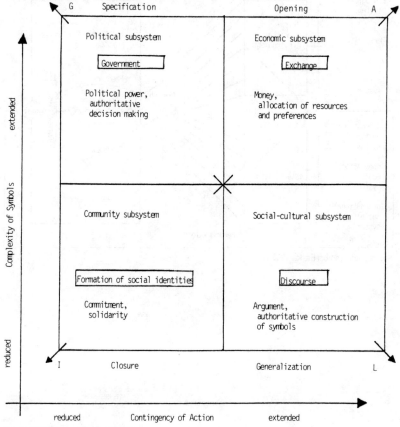

Source: Adapted from Münch 1982:20.
Note: G = Goal attainment
          A = Adaptation
          I = Integration
          L = Latent pattern maintenance

Diagram 3   Model for a Differentiated Class Analysis

Relationship to means of production / Dominant source of income	Private ownership		Decision-making authority	Political control
	Agricultural sector	Nonagricultural sector	private sector	public sector
Capital	Large-scale farmers	Capitalists	Final authority: management	State class
Capital and labor	Agrarian petite bourgeoisie	Nonagrarian petite bourgeoisie	Intermediate: salariat	
Labor	Agrarian proletaroids	Nonagrarian proletaroids	None: proletariat	
No permanent source of income	Subproletariat			

Source: Adapted from Berg-Schlosser 1979b:317.

Diagram 4   Components of Political Culture in a System's Framework

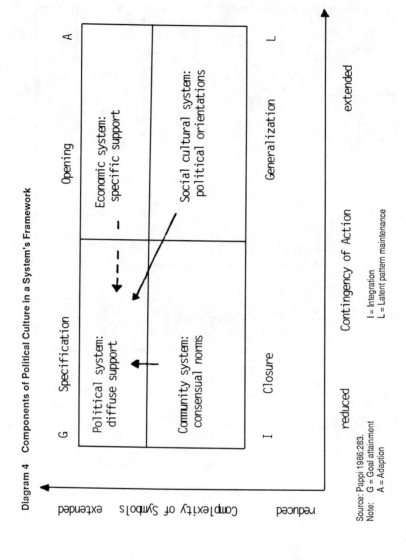

Source: Pappi 1986:283.

Note: G = Goal attainment   I = Integration
        A = Adaption   L = Latent pattern maintenance

Diagram 5   Social Structure of Kenya 1950, 1960, 1970, and 1980

1950

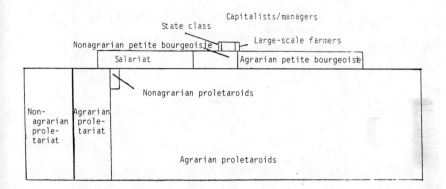

1960

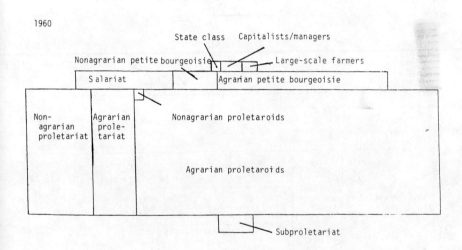

Diagram 5   (continued)

1970

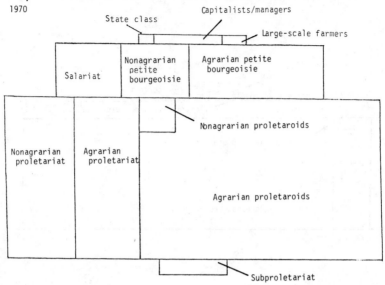

1980

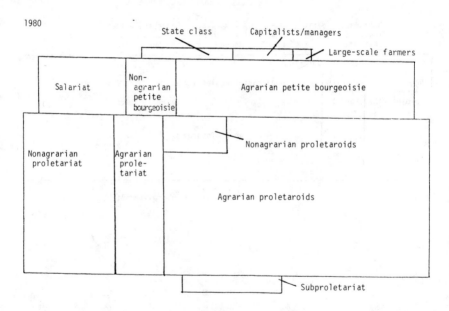

Diagram 6 Intersections of Classes and Ethnic Groups in Kenya 1970 and 1980

1970

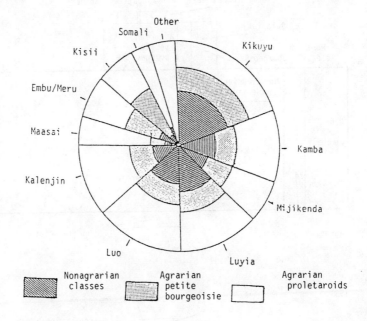

	Nonagrarian classes		Agrarian petite bourgeoisie		Agrarian proletaroids

1980

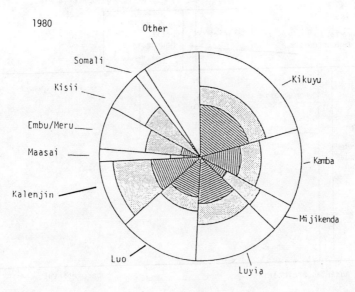

Diagram 7   Social Structure of Tanzania 1967 and 1980

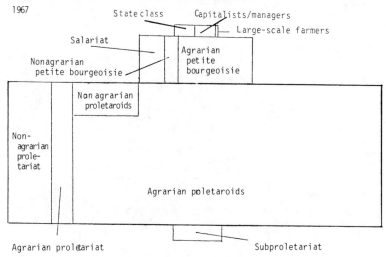

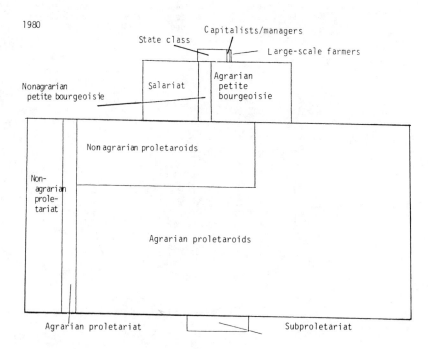

Diagram 8   Social Structure of Uganda 1980

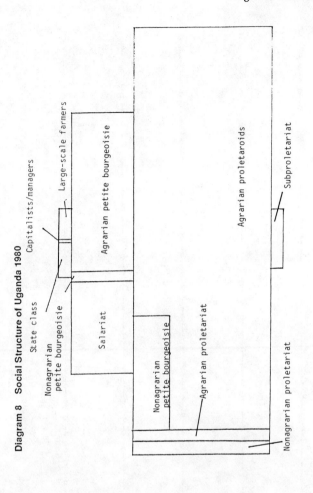

Diagram 9   Political Events in Kenya (Time Series Analysis)

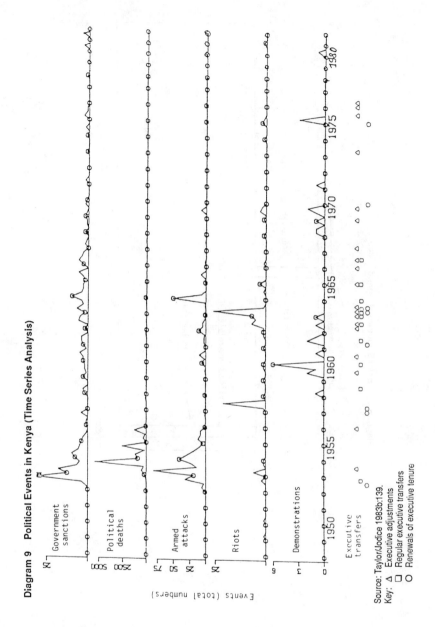

Source: Taylor/Jodice 1983b:139.
Key: △ Executive adjustments
      □ Regular executive transfers
      ○ Renewals of executive tenure

Diagram 10 Political Events in Tanzania (Time Series Analysis)

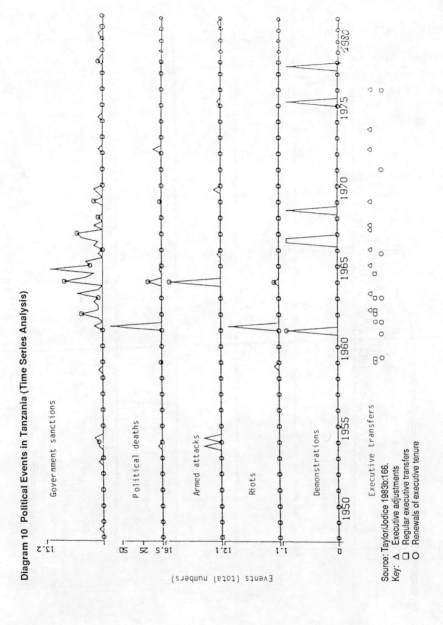

Source: Taylor/Jodice 1983b:166.
Key: △ Executive adjustments
      □ Regular executive transfers
      ○ Renewals of executive tenure

Diagram 11   Political Events in Uganda (Time Series Analysis)

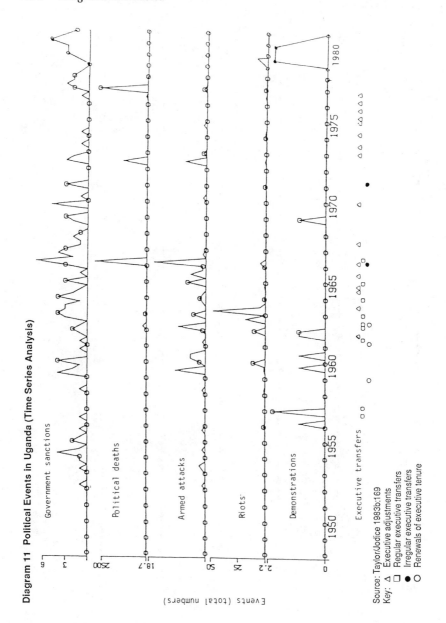

Table 1 Rate of Surplus Extraction, Agricultural Sector, 1974–1978 (Percentage of Export Value Paid to Producers)

	1974	1975	1976	1977	1978
Kenya	92.4	93.6	92.1	92.1	87.7
Tanzania	66.7	60.9	49.5	45.3	49.9
Uganda	28.6	32.4	17.2	14.5	32.3

Source: Wiebe/Dodge 1987:73.

Table 2 Budget Priorities of Central Governments, 1972 and 1982 (in Percentages)

	Kenya		Tanzania		Uganda	
	1972	1982	1972	1982	1972	1982
Defense	6.0	13.2	11.9	11.2	23.1	19.8
Education	21.9	19.9	17.3	12.1	15.3	14.9
Health	7.9	7.3	7.2	5.5	5.3	5.2

Sources: Kenya, *Statistical Abstract* 1982; Kenya, *Economic Survey* 1975; Germany, Office of Statistics, 1984–1986.

Table 3 Political Feedback Factors

	Index of Political Rights	Index of Political Repression
	1979	1979/80
Kenya	5	2
Tanzania	6	3
Uganda	7	5

Sources: Taylor/Jodice 1983a; Berg-Schlosser 1984d.

Note: The index of political rights measures the involvement of the population in the determination of the government and legislation (values 1–7, with 1 as the best score). The second index measures political repression and the violation of the principles of the rule of law, such as the use of torture, the number of political prisoners, and political murders (values 1–5, with 1 as the best score).

Table 4   Level of Development by System Type, 1960–1980

	GNP per Capita Rate of Change	N	POLI Rate of Change	N
Polyarchies	3.6	5	1.7	3
Socialist systems	0.8	4	2.0	4
Authoritarian systems	2.9	8	1.0	6
Praetorian systems	0.6	21	1.2	17
Total	1.6	38	1.3	30

Sources: Taylor/Jodice 1983a; *UN Statistical Yearbook* 1978; World Bank, *World Development Report* 1980–1984.

Note: For this period, Angola, São Tomé, Cape Verde, Mozambique, and Zimbabwe, which became independent later, have not been taken into consideration.

Significance: $p < 0.05$

Table 5   Government Expenditure by System Type (Percentage of GDP)

	General Government Expenditure	Public Education	Public Health	Defense Expenditure	N
Polyarchies	17.35	3.12	1.48	0.57	6
Socialist systems	19.75	5.7	2.15	3.27	4
Authoritarian systems	15.27	4.05	1.32	1.48	6
Praetorian systems	15.21	3.46	1.05	2.64	20
Total	16.15	3.73	1.29	2.09	36

Source: Taylor/Jodice 1983a.

Note: The same cases are considered here that are in Table 1. Because of missing data some means are based on a somewhat smaller N.

Significance: $p < 0.01$

Table 6   Respect for Normative Standards by System Type

	Civil Liberties, 1979	Index of Political Repression, 1979–1981	N
Polyarchies	3.43	1.57	7
Socialist systems	6.12	3.25	8
Authoritarian systems	5.4	3.4	5
Military regimes	5.65	3.48	23
Total	5.25	3.12	43

Sources: Gastil 1980; AI *Annual Reports* 1979–1981; International Commission of Jurists, *The Review,* 1979–1981.

Significance: $p < 0.01$

V
Statistical Appendix

Table 7   GDP, 1960–1984 (Current Prices, in Millions of US $)

	1960	1965	1970	1971	1972	1973	1974	1975	1976	1977	1978	1979	1980	1981	1982	1983	1984
Kenya	730	920	1,604	1,799	2,004	2,372	2,865	3,253	3,405	4,583	5,310	5,280	5,990	6,960	5,340	4,940	5,140
Tanzania	555	790	1,284	1,372	1,558	1,872	2,219	2,581	2,686	3,542	4,216	4,130	4,350	4,350	4,530	4,550	4,410
Uganda	540	1,080	1,323	1,415	1,472		1,993	2,567				8,410	12,790	9,390	8,630	3,360	4,710

Sources: *UN Statistical Yearbook* 1965–1986; World Bank, *World Development Report* 1978–1986.

Table 8   GDP Growth Rates, 1970–1986 (Constant Prices in Percentages)

	1970	1971	1972	1973	1974	1975	1976	1977	1978	1979	1980	1981	1982	1983	1984	1985	1986
Kenya	6.8	7.0	6.8	7.0	3.6	1.2	6.1	7.3	6.7	3.8	3.3	3.5	1.8	3.1	0.9	4.1	4.9
Tanzania	4.5	4.5	5.9	4.4	2.1	4.6	5.3	5.9	5.6	3.1	3.5	-1.7	-3.2	-1.3	2.4	2.4	
Uganda	3.1	2.5	1.2	-1.2	-2.0	-2.2	0.7	1.5	-5.7	-11.3	-3.4	3.9	8.2	4.9	5.2	0.6	-5.5

Sources: Kenya, *Economic Survey* 1976–1986; *Africa Contemporary Record* 1980/1981–1986/1987; Tanzania, *Statistical Abstract* 1986.

Table 9   GNP per Capita, 1960–1984 (in US $)

	1960	1964	1970	1975	1976	1977	1978	1979	1980	1981	1982	1983	1984
Kenya	84	102	143	242	240	270	330	380	420	420	390	340	310
Tanzania	53	61	97	167	180	190	230	260	280	280	280	240	210
Uganda	60	83	135	222	240	270	280	290	300	220	230	220	230

Sources: *UN Statistical Yearbook* 1965–1986; World Bank, *World Development Report* 1978–1986.

Table 10　GDP per Capita, Index of Purchasing Power, 1960–1978

	1960	1963	1970	1975	1977	1978
Kenya	84	102	143	242	320	370
Tanzania	53	61	97	167	220	263
Uganda	60	135	222			

Source: *UN Statistical Yearbook* 1965–1980.

Table 11　Sectoral Distribution of GDP, 1960–1985 (in Percentages)

	1960	1965	1970	1975	1980	1985
Agriculture						
Kenya	38	35	40	30	34	31
Tanzania	57	46	41	41	54	54
Uganda	52	52	52	55	76	
Industry						
Kenya	18	18	14	23	21	21
Tanzania	11	16	16	15	14	12
Uganda	13	13	10	8	6	
Manufacturing						
Kenya	9	11		13	13	12
Tanzania	5	8	10	10	9	7
Uganda	9	8		7	6	
Services						
Kenya	44	47	46	47	45	48
Tanzania	32	40	43	39	33	34
Uganda	35	35	38	37	18	

Sources: World Bank, *World Development Report* 1978–1986; *UN Statistical Yearbook* 1977; Germany, Office of Statistics, 1984–1986.

Table 12　Sectoral Distribution of Working Population, 1950–1981 (in Percentages)

	1950	1955	1960	1965	1970	1977	1978	1979	1980	1981
Agriculture										
Kenya	89	87	86	84	82	78	79	78	78	78
Tanzania	92	91	89	88	86	84	83	83	83	83
Uganda	93	91	89	88	86	84	83	83	83	83
Industry										
Kenya	4	5	5	6	7	9	8	10	10	10
Tanzania	3	3	4	4	5	6	6	6	6	6
Uganda	3	3	4	5	5	6	6	6	6	6
Services										
Kenya	7	8	9	10	11	12	13	12	12	12
Tanzania	5	6	7	8	9	10	11	11	11	11
Uganda	4	6	7	7	9	10	11	11	11	11

Sources: Taylor, 1983a; World Bank, *World Development Report* 1978–1984.

Table 13   Consumer Price Index, All Goods, 1966–1984

	1966	1967	1968	1969	1970	1971	1972	1973	1974	1975	1976	1977	1978	1979	1980	1981	1982	1983	1984
Kenya	96	98	98	98	100	102	100	108	124	147	160	178	219	225	235	268	336	388	423
Tanzania	91	95	96	97	100	105	113	124	149	188	201	227	253	286	372	469	603	766	1,041
Uganda	82	84	82	91	100	116	112	140	234	273	434	730							

Sources: UN Statistical Yearbook 1978, 1984–1985.

Table 14   Consumer Price Index, Food, 1966–1984

	1966	1967	1968	1969	1970	1971	1972	1973	1974	1975	1976	1977	1978	1979	1980	1981	1982	1983	1984
Kenya	97	98	99	98	100	102	100	105	124	150	160	179	225	229	242	273	324	358	392
Tanzania	95	97	98	98	100	106	115	128	174	227	226	260	298	337	426	528	699	890	1,223
Uganda	82	87	81	88	100	125	118	140	245	303	490	880							

Sources: UN Statistical Yearbook 1978, 1984–1985.

Table 15 Inflation Rates, 1970–1986 (in Percentages)

	1970	1971	1972	1973	1974	1975	1976	1977	1978	1979	1980	1981	1982	1983	1984	1985	1986
Kenya	2	3.7	5.4	11.1	15.8	17.8	9.9	11.7	12.3	8.4	12.8	15.9	22	18	10	8	4
Tanzania		1.3	12.9		20	25	8	11	12	25	32.5	25.6	28.9	27.1	36	27	
Uganda		8	1.3	47						200	100	106	27	20	10.3	110	175

Source: Africa Contemporary Record 1970–1987.

Table 16 Investment Rates, 1965–1985 (in Percentages)

	1965	1970	1971	1972	1973	1974	1975	1976	1977	1978	1979	1980	1981	1982	1983	1984	1985
Kenya	12.4			21.8	20.4	19.1	20.2	20.0	21.0	25.0	23.8	23.7	24.0	19.8	18.6	19.5	18
Tanzania		22.5	26.4	21.8	21.8	22.0	21.2	22.0	19.0	20.8	23.1	22.4	21.9	20.2	16.8	14.5	
Uganda													3.3	6.1	8.6	13.0	9.4

Sources: Kenya, Statistical Abstract 1981–1987; Kenya, Economic Survey 1978–1987; Tanzania, Statistical Abstract 1984–1986; Africa Contemporary Record 1980/1981–1987.

Table 17   Life Expectancy, 1960–1984 (Years at Birth)

	1960	1965	1975	1980	1984
Kenya	43	48	50	55	54
Tanzania	37	41	47	52	51
Uganda	43	46	50	54	49

Source: World Bank, *World Development Report* 1978–1986.

Table 18   Infant Mortality, 1960–1984 (in Percentage for First Year of Life)

	1960	1965	1970	1975	1980	1984
Kenya	138	124	119	83	87	92
Tanzania	190	170	162	152	103	111
Uganda	160	126		160	97	110

Sources: *Africa Contemporary Record* 1982–1986; World Bank, *World Development Report* 1978–1986.

Table 19   Literacy Rates, 1960–1980 (in Percentage of Population Aged 15 and Above)

	1960	1974	1975	1976	1977	1980
Kenya	20	40	40	45	50	47
Tanzania	17	63	66	66	66	79
Uganda	25	25	35		48	52

Sources: World Bank, *World Development Report* 1978–1982; Germany, Office of Statistics, 1986.

Table 20 Total Calories per Head, 1960–1983 (in Absolute Amount per Day and in Percentage of Requirements)

	1960	1970	1974	1976	1977	1980	1981	1982	1983
Kenya	1,850	2,261	2,114	2,117	2,032	2,078	2,056	2,056	1,919
	(80%)	(98%)	(100%)	(91%)	(88%)	(88%)	(88%)	(88%)	(83%)
Tanzania	2,440	2,027	2,002	2,003	2,063	2,051	1,985	2,331	2,271
	(106%)	(88%)	(87%)	(86%)	(89%)	(93%)	(83%)	(101%)	(98%)
Uganda	2,240	2,250	2,096	2,096	2,110	1,760	1,778	1,807	2,351
	(97%)	(102%)	(90%)	(90%)	(91%)	(83%)	(80%)	(78%)	(101%)

Source: World Bank, *World Development Report* 1978–1986.

Table 21 Protein per Head, 1960–1974 (in Grams per Day)

	1960	1970	1974
Kenya	64.3	67.3	59.8
Tanzania	68.6	47.3	47.1
Uganda	54.4	54.0	54.0

Source: Taylor 1983a.

Table 22 Piped Water Supply, 1975 and 1980 (in Percentage of Households)

	1975	1980
Kenya	17	
Tanzania	24	50
Uganda	49	

Source: World Bank, *World Development Report* 1979–1982.

Table 23 Inhabitants per Physician, 1960–1981

	1960	1965	1974	1980	1981
Kenya	10,000	12,840	5,800	10,500	10,140
Tanzania	20,000	21,840	20,690	17,560	
Uganda	15,000	11,080	20,800	26,810	24,500

Sources: Germany, Office of Statistics, 1984; World Bank, *World Development Report* 1978–1984.

Table 24 Inhabitants per Staff Employed in Medical Sector, 1960–1981

	1960	1965	1974	1976	1977	1980	1981
Kenya	2,270	1,780	1,300	1,070	1,090	550	990
Tanzania	11,890	2,100	3,180	3,300	3,080	3,010	
Uganda	10,030	3,130	6,870	4,410	4,300	4,080	2,000

Sources: Kenya, *Statistical Abstract* 1982–1984; Germany, Office of Statistics, 1984; World Bank, *World Development Report* 1978–1984.

Table 25 Hospital Beds per 100,000 Inhabitants, 1975–1983

	1975	1977	1978	1979	1980	1981	1982	1983
Kenya	172	156	168	175	174	177	171	156
Tanzania		152					90	
Uganda	128		123	118	113	111		

Sources: Kenya, *Statistical Abstract* 1982–1986; Germany, Office of Statistics, 1984, 1986.

Table 26 Primary School Enrollment, 1960–1983 (in Percentages of Age Group)

	1960	1965	1970	1975	1976	1977	1978	1979	1980	1981	1982	1983
Kenya	47	54	66			86	99	99	108	109	104	100
Tanzania	24	32		57	70	70	70	104	104	105	98	87
Uganda	49	67		53	51	65	50	50	50	54	60	57

Sources: Kenya, *Statistical Abstract* 1982; Germany, Office of Statistics, 1984–1986.

Table 27 Secondary School Enrollment, 1960–1983 (in Percentages of Age Group)

	1960	1965	1975	1976	1977	1978	1979	1980	1981	1982	1983
Kenya	2	4	13	15	17	18	18	18	19	20	19
Tanzania	2	2	3	3	3	4	4	4	3	3	3
Uganda	3	4	6	7	7	5	5	5	5	8	8

Sources: Kenya, *Statistical Abstract* 1982–1986; Germany, Office of Statistics, 1984, 1986.

Table 28 Physical Quality of Life Index, 1960, 1975, and 1980

	1960	1975	1980
Kenya	35	51	55
Tanzania	24	44	61
Uganda	31	40	55

Source: Taylor 1983a.

Table 29 Population in Slum and Squatter Settlements

	Urban Population (%)	Large Towns	Inhabitants (in Thousands)	Large Town Share of Urban Population (%)	Population in Squatter Settlements (% of Large Town Population)
Kenya	9	Nairobi	535	48	33
		Mombasa	255	23	66
Tanzania	8	Dar es Salaam	334	43	50

Source: Grimes/Orville 1976.

Table 30   Export Structure, 1960–1985 (Share of Major Exports in Total Exports)

	1960	1965	1970	1975	1976	1977	1978	1979	1980	1981	1982	1983	1984	1985
Kenya														
Raw materials	80	90	87.2	87	88	90	86	86	84	88	86	87		
Coffee			20.1	16.4	29.3	42.5	33.1		21.0					
Tea			13.4	10.7	10.0	14.9	17.2		12.4					
Fruit and vegetables			2.0	4.8	4.7	4.6	7.6	7.5	4.9	8.3	9.6			
Sisal			1.7	3.4	1.3	0.8	0.9	1.2	1.4	1.6	2.0			
Cashew			0.9	0.5	0.3				0.3					
Industrial production (without oil)			12.0	14.8	10.1	5.6	18.1	20.5	18.4	18.1	17.4	18.7		
Oil products			12.4	22.6	17.9	15.1		20.0	33.3	31.9	27.4	19.7		
Tanzania														
Raw materials	87	87	87	88	91	94	94	83	84	86	87			
Coffee			17.7	17.5		41.4		27.1		29	32	34	39	37
Cotton			13.6	11.2		12.9		11.0		14	14	16	13	12
Sisal			9.7	10.8		5.3		4.9		6	6	3	3	3
Cashew			7.4	7.9		6.4		5.1		6	2	2	8	4
Tobacco			3.2	4.4		3.1		3.3		3	5	6	6	5
Minerals			8.7	6.4		3.2		7.8		12	11	12	9	8
Oil			6.0	5.0				3.1		3	3	5	4	8
Finished products			8.5	8.1		3.0		11.1		11	10	12	9	12
Uganda														
Raw materials	100	99	99	99	100	100	100	99	99	99	99			
Coffee			65	71.7	83.2		89.9	97.7	98.2	98.2	97.7			
Cotton			15.4	10.3	6.0	2.7	5.7	1.7	1.2	0.9	1.0			
Tea			5.0	5.9	3.0	4.3	2.4		0.08	0.1	0.3			
Tobacco			0.5	0.8										
Copper			5.0	3.4	2.0									

Sources: Kenya, *Statistical Abstract* 1982–1986; Tanzania, *Statistical Abstract* 1984–1986; Germany, Office of Statistics, 1984–1986.

Table 31 Import Structure, 1965–1984 (Share of Major Imports in Total Imports)

	1965	1970	1975	1976	1977	1978	1979	1980	1981	1982	1983	1984
Kenya												
Food	14.1	8.3	5.9				5.4	4.4	4.7	5.9	9.0	9
Raw materials (nonfood)	36.5	36.0	29.0				29	28.2	25.0	27.3		3
Oil/oil products	10.5	9.3	26.4				23.7	30.9	36.9	36.9	36.6	20
Machinery/capital goods	9.9	14.7	17.0					17.1				32
Transport equipment	13.2	16.7	12.9				20.2	12.9	9.5	9.5	7.1	13
Tanzania												
Food			16.0	4.3	5.4	3.8	1.8	9.6	9	9	10	9
Raw materials (nonfood)			1.8	2.3	1.7	1.4	1.2	1.2	1	2	3	3
Oil			10.7	21.0	13.0	11.0	13.8	20.7	23	22	22	20
Machinery/transport equipment			26.6	30.9	33.6	38.9	40.7	32.6	40	31	32	32
Chemicals			10.6	12.0	11.5	11.7	10.4	10.7	9	10	11	13
Uganda												
Food			5.5			3.7	10.0	9.8	11.3	3.4		
Raw materials (nonfood)			1.4			0.9	0.5	0.6	0.7	0.6		
Oil			19.3			16.7	31.9	42.3	29.5	29.7		
Machinery/transport equipment			22.1			23.1	40.9	28.9	11.4	11.0		
Chemicals			7.4			8.7	9.7	20.9	4.2	4.0		

Sources: Kenya, *Statistical Abstract* 1982–1986; Tanzania, *Statistical Abstract* 1984, 1986; Germany, Office of Statistics, 1984–1986.

Table 32 Major Destinations of Exports, 1965–1984 (Share in Percentages)

	1965	1970	1975	1976	1977	1978	1979	1980	1981	1982	1983	1984
Kenya												
UK	21.4	20.7	13.2	11.1	12.9	14.9	14.2	11.4	11.1	12.7	14.9	18.4
FRG	15.6	9.5	11.3	13.2	17.8	15.3	14.7	10.9	10.9	11.7	12.9	12.9
France												
All EC				30.8	47.9	45.5	43.6	34.4	33.1	42.4	39.6	45.3
USA	5.6	8.9	4.9	5.7	5.3	4.5	4.0	3.3	3.6	6.2	6.1	5.0
Singapore												
Tanzania				7.2	1.6	0.5	0.8	0.7	0.9	1.0	0.8	1.0
Uganda				8.4	9.1	8.5	9.6	12.9	9.8	10.3	10.4	8.5
Tanzania												
UK	27.4	20.0	12.8		16.9	21.1	16.5	13.8	13.5	7.0	13.0	13.4
FRG	7.4	4.7	8.8		18.1	15.5	17.8	14.5	15.7	17.9	16.9	21.3
Netherlands					4.2	5.4	4.2	5.5	4.6	6.1	7.4	7.0
All EC	42.8	34.9	34.8		49.1	50.6	48.2	42.7	43.1	44.6	48.9	50.0
USA	6.0	9.6	6.1		13.8	11.2	5.1	4.0	2.5	6.8		
India	8.1	7.2	5.5		3.7	0.4	4.8	1.7	6.7	7.4		
Kenya	4.8	6.5	6.3					0.02	1.7	0.3	0.2	1.4
Uganda								2.5	1.7	0.2	0.7	0.7
Uganda												
UK	17.1	20.4	19.8	20.5	18.1	17.7	9.0	14.1	12.0	9.7	11.5	14.1
FRG	3.0	4.6	4.1	4.4	1.9	5.3	5.4	4.2	5.5	6.5	8.3	9.1
France	1.2	0.1	1.6	6.2	5.6	11.2	15.1	12.8	8.1	8.0	9.8	9.5
All EC			35.6	42.4	35.7	38.9	37.2	53.3	40.7	34.6	35.8	
USA	22.4	20.6	23.6	33.4	39.3	22.2	18.6	26.0	35.1	40.3	28.4	22.6
Kenya						1.4	0.5	0.6	0.6	0.4	0.5	0.4

Sources: *UN Statistical Yearbook 1965–1986*; Kenya, *Statistical Abstract 1982–1986*; Tanzania, *Statistical Abstract 1984, 1986*; Germany, Office of Statistics, 1984–1986.

Table 33 Major Suppliers of Imports, 1977–1985 (Shares in Percentages)

	1977	1978	1979	1980	1981	1982	1983	1984	1985
Kenya									
UK			22.5	16.9	16.8	14.9	13.6	16.7	15.9
FRG			11.1	8.1	8.1	8.3	7.9	8.3	8.7
All EC			45.7	37.1	35.4	33.4	32.9	39.2	37.9
USA			5.6	6.3	6.9	5.9	6.3	5.2	7.4
Japan			8.0	9.2	7.9	7.7	9.6	10.6	10.8
Saudi Arabia			8.3	17.5	19.8	14.8	7.6	13.7	13.3
Tanzania									
UK	15.4	18.6	19.6	17.4	14.4	11.6	13.4	12.0	
FRG	11.3	10.7	12.7	9.8	11.3	11.6	12.2	10.8	
All EC	46.1	52.6	50.7	46.2	43.4	40.0			
USA			4.1	6.1	5.7	3.5	3.4	3.9	
Japan	11.1	10.9	7.6	8.6	11.8	8.9	10.7	9.8	
India	5.6	4.0	4.7	2.8	2.9	2.2	1.9	2.1	
China			3.7	0.9	1.8	1.1	1.3	2.1	
Kenya			0.9	0.8	1.0	1.1	1.1	1.0	
Uganda									
UK		23.0	18.3	19.1	14.1	17.7	10.3	13.3	
FRG		11.7	4.9	6.7	9.4	11.2	10.6	6.6	
All EC		51.2	30.9	39.7	33.7	41.0	31.6		
USA		1.2	0.3	2.9	1.0	2.8	1.3	1.1	
Japan		5.8	3.5	4.2	1.4	2.5	4.7	5.9	
India		4.7	5.1	4.6	5.2	5.5	4.9	6.2	
Kenya		36.2	46.7	43.9	32.4	33.9	30.3	35.8	
Tanzania		0.06	6.1	3.7	2.8	2.7	2.4		

Sources: *UN Statistical Yearbook* 1965–1986; Kenya, *Statistical Abstract* 1982–1986; Tanzania, *Statistical Abstract* 1984, 1986; Germany, Office of Statistics, 1984–1986.

Table 34   Export Levels, 1960–1985 (in Percentage of GDP)

	1960	1965	1970	1971	1972	1973	1974	1975	1976	1977	1978	1979	1980	1981	1982	1983	1984	1985
Kenya	15.3	14.2	12.3	24.1	24.6	20.6	23.2	20.4	24.1	27.3	19.2	18.1	19.5	17.7	17.0	17.0	19.2	16.8
Tanzania	27.9	23.2	23.9			22.4	21.3	18.2	18.1	18.1	14.1	14.0	13.6	13.0	10.6	10.8	10.3	
Uganda	22.2	16.2	18.6			16.4	10.8					5.1	3.5	3.4	4.3	10.5	8.5	

Sources: World Bank, *World Development Report* 1978–1986; Germany, Office of Statistics, 1984–1986; *UN Statistical Yearbook* 1965–1986.

Table 35   Import Levels, 1960–1985 (in Percentage of GDP)

	1960	1965	1970	1971	1972	1973	1974	1975	1976	1977	1978	1979	1980	1981	1982	1983	1984	1985
Kenya	10.0	12.4	24.2	33.0	29.8	26.0	37.7	31.1	28.5	29.0	32.1	27.7	36.4	30.7	29.6	23.8	27.1	25.2
Tanzania	19.1	17.2	28.4			29.3	34.8	31.0	21.2	22.7	28.9	26.7	27.3	21.7	18.5	24.7	17.7	
Uganda	36.3	9.1					10.7	7.7				4.3	2.7	4.2	3.9	10.1	8.3	

Sources: World Bank, *World Development Report* 1978–1986; Germany, Office of Statistics, 1984–1986; *UN Statistical Yearbook* 1965–1986.

Table 36   Share of Foreign Trade, 1960–1985 (in Percentage of GDP)

	1960	1965	1970	1971	1972	1973	1974	1975	1976	1977	1978	1979	1980	1981	1982	1983	1984	1985
Kenya	12.7	13.3	18.7	28.5	27.2	23.3	30.5	25.8	23.5	27.2	25.7	26.2	34.1	22.2	24.9	21.7	25.5	21.0
Tanzania	23.5	19.7	26.1			25.9	28.1	24.6	19.2	18.2	18.7	19.5	20.3	19.6	16.8	17.7	14.0	
Uganda	23.8	20.5	13.9				2.9	1.6				3.9	3.1	3.8	4.1	10.1	8.4	

Sources: World Bank, *World Development Report* 1978–1986; Germany, Office of Statistics, 1984–1986; *UN Statistical Yearbook* 1965–1986.

Table 37 Terms of Trade, 1960–1984

	1960	1970	1976	1977	1978	1979	1980	1981	1982	1983	1984
Kenya	112	100	102	123	104	89	76	80	76	74	84
Tanzania	96	100	114	127	104	100	98	100	83	86	89
Uganda	95	100	127	159	106	95	92	75	71	69	86

Sources: World Bank, *World Development Report* 1978–1986.

Table 38 Oil Prices, 1945–1986 (US $ per Barrel)

1945–1959	1960–1972	1973	1974	1975	1976	1977	1978	1979	1980	1981	1982	1983	1984	1985	1986
1.7	1.4	2.7	9.8	10.7	11.6	12.4	12.7	23.0	33	32	30	29	27	25	11

Sources: Brandes et al. 1981; IMF, *Annual Report* 1986; World Bank, *World Development Report* 1978–1988.

Table 39 Coffee Prices, 1960–1984 (US $ per Pound)

1960	1965	1966	1967	1968	1969	1970	1971	1972	1973	1974	1975	1976	1977	1978	1979	1980	1981	1982	1983	1984
1.3	0.4	0.4	0.4	0.4	0.4	0.5	0.4	0.5	0.6	0.9	1.5	1.8	2.1	1.8	2.1	1.5	1.5	1.4	1.5	1.4

Sources: Kebschull et al. 1977; Strahm 1985.

Table 40   Net Credit Flow of Publicly Guaranteed Middle- and Long-Term Loans, 1970–1984 (in Millions of US $)

	1970	1976	1977	1978	1979	1980	1981	1982	1983	1984
Kenya	23	184	136	165	326	335	299	212	80	322
Tanzania	40	102	30	151	198	190	203	221	274	119
Uganda	22	28	−8	22	13	132	32	39	29	37

Source: World Bank, *World Development Report* 1978–1986.

Table 41 Major Donors of Official Development Aid, 1975–1985 (Share in Percentages)

	1975	1976	1977	1978	1979	1980	1981	1982	1983	1984	1985
Kenya											
UK	30.0	21.6	17.7	15.4	6.0	4.7	5.8	6.8	5.4	7.1	8.5
USA	10.9	9.7	9.4	6.1	17.8	14.2	9.8	9.9	8.6	6.9	8.6
FRG	9.7	8.5	9.8	12.4	5.1	5.3	5.5	4.8	5.7	4.5	5.7
Japan	1.8	3.6	5.4	6.0							
IBRD	11.1	20.7	20.3	19.1	22.0	16.5	15.2	15.8	18.1	29.1	23.1
IDA	18.9	19.9	19.6	19.6	18.2	16.0	20.4	18.8	22.7	18.3	23.2
Tanzania											
China						22.6	18.5	16.8	14.1		
USSR						14.6	13.1	12.2	11.6		
USA						5.8	5.7	5.5	5.2		
FRG						11.7	11.5	10.7	10.4		
IDA						14.3	17.4	21.0	22.1		
IMF						10.1	7.9	6.4	4.3		
Uganda											
UK							8.7	2.8	4.1	3.2	3.2
FRG							5.3		0.1	0.7	
Tanzania							25.4	25.9	13.6	10.2	9.9
Zambia							5.0	2.4	1.4	1.2	
IDA/IBRD							15.7	24.9	22.7	29.1	43.4

Sources: Kenya, *Statistical Abstract* 1981–1986; Kenya, *Economic Survey* 1976–1986; Germany, Office of Statistics, 1984–1986; Uganda, Ministry of Planning and Economic Development, *Background to the Budget* 1986–1987.

Table 42   Private Net Direct Investment, 1970–1984 (in Millions of US $)

	1970	1976	1977	1978	1979	1980	1981	1983	1984
Kenya	14	42	54	68	65	61	61	50	54
Uganda	4	–7	1	1	2	3			

Source: World Bank, *World Development Report* 1978–1986.

Table 43 Debt Repayments as Percentage of GDP, 1970–1984

	1970	1976	1977	1978	1979	1980	1981	1983	1984
Kenya	1.7	1.4	1.8	2.4	1.8	2.6	4.5	5.5	6.1
Tanzania	1.2	1.1	1.5	8.2	0.9	1.0	2.1	1.5	1.9
Uganda	0.6	0.2	0.6	3.4	0.3	0.3	0.5	1.9	1.7

Source: World Bank, *World Development Report* 1978–1986.

Table 44   Debt Repayments as Percentage of Exports, 1970–1985

	1970	1975	1976	1977	1978	1979	1980	1981	1982	1983	1984	1985
Kenya	7.9	3.8	4.6	4.0	8.3	7.5	8.8	17.1	20.8	20.6	21.5	27.2
Tanzania	8.2		4.3	7.1	7.4	7.4	18.4	15	15	22	21	
Uganda	3.4		1.6	3.9	2.2	7.4	11.9	3.9				

Source: World Bank, *World Development Report 1978–1988.*

Table 45   Interest Paid for Public Loans, 1970–1984 (in Millions of US $)

	1970	1976	1977	1978	1979	1980	1981	1982	1983	1984
Kenya	11	23	39	45	60	100	116	178	127	144
Tanzania	7	13	22	18	23	31	34	20	36	30
Uganda	4	2	5	1	5	3	2	57	17	30

Source: World Bank, *World Development Report 1978–1986.*

Table 46   Balance of Goods and Services, 1970–1984 (in Millions of US $)

	1970	1976	1977	1978	1979	1980	1981	1983	1984
Kenya	–49	–84	49	–519	–479	–985	–736	–174	–135
Tanzania	–36	–3	–19	460	–480	–548	–533	–256	–354
Uganda	20	–47	66	–130	27	–18	–161		

Source: World Bank, *World Development Report 1978–1986.*

Table 47 Riots, 1948–1982

	1948–1952	1953–1957	1958–1962	1963–1967	1968	1969	1970	1971	1972	1973	1974	1975	1976	1977	1978	1979	1980	1981	1982	Total
Kenya	4	30	20	39	1	6	0	0	0	0	1	3	0	0	0	0	0	1	0	105
Tanzania	0	0	12	1	0	0	0	0	0	0	0	0	0	1	1	0	0	0	0	14
Uganda	0	1	42	61	0	0	0	1	1	0	2	0	1	0	0	6	1	0	0	117

Source: Taylor/Jodice 1983b.

Note: Riots are violent demonstrations or disturbances involving a large number of people and characterized by material damage or bloodshed.

Table 48 Protest Demonstrations, 1948–1982

	1948–1952	1953–1957	1958–1962	1963–1967	1968	1969	1970	1971	1972	1973	1974	1975	1976	1977	1978	1979	1980	1981	1982	Total
Kenya	1	0	15	1	2	4	0	1	0	0	0	3	0	0	0	0	1	0	0	28
Tanzania	0	0	2	2	1	0	0	0	0	0	0	1	0	1	0	0	0	0	0	7
Uganda	0	4	4	0	0	1	0	0	0	0	0	0	0	0	0	4	4	0	0	17

Source: Taylor/Jodice 1983b.

Table 49 Armed Attacks, 1948–1982

	1948–1952	1953–1957	1958–1962	1963–1967	1968	1969	1970	1971	1972	1973	1974	1975	1976	1977	1978	1979	1980	1981	1982	Total
Kenya	43	271	51	74	0	8	0	0	0	0	0	1	1	0	0	0	1	0	1	451
Tanzania	0	10	0	16	0	2	0	0	0	0	0	1	0	0	0	0	0	0	1	30
Uganda	1	5	4	39	0	0	1	0	7	1	1	0	0	1	0	3	0	17	2	112

Source: Taylor/Jodice 1983b.

Table 50 Deaths from Domestic Violence, 1948–1982

	1948–1952	1953–1957	1958–1962	1963–1967	1968	1969	1970	1971	1972	1973	1974	1975	1976	1977	1978	1979	1980	1981	1982	Total
Kenya	171	13,298	206	298	0	18	0	0	1	0	0	38	8	0	0	0	0	0	0	14,038
Tanzania	0	5	66	20	0	2	0	0	7	0	0	0	0	0	0	0	0	0	0	100
Uganda	0	9	258	3,105	0	0	5	1,105	1,865	3,501	10,040	3,700	3,815	2,701	0	0	0	0	0	30,014

Source: Taylor/Jodice 1983b.

Table 51 Political Assassinations, 1948–1982

	1948–1952	1953–1957	1958–1962	1963–1967	1968	1969	1970	1971	1972	1973	1974	1975	1976	1977	1978	1979	1980	1981	1982	Total
Kenya	5	9	0	2	1	0	0	0	0	0	0	1	0	0	0	0	0	0	0	18
Tanzania	0	0	0	0	2	0	0	0	2	0	0	0	0	0	0	0	0	0	0	4
Uganda	0	0	0	0	0	0	2	0	0	0	0	0	0	1	0	0	0	0	0	3

Source: Taylor/Jodice 1983b.

Table 52 Governmental Sanctions, 1948–1982

	1948–1952	1953–1957	1958–1962	1963–1967	1968	1969	1970	1971	1972	1973	1974	1975	1976	1977	1978	1979	1980	1981	1982	Total
Kenya	49	102	64	84	4	5	1	2	0	1	3	5	0	1	2	0	1	4	6	334
Tanzania	6	4	13	67	1	5	0	0	1	0	1	0	0	1	2	0	2	0	0	103
Uganda	1	32	22	58	3	8	1	3	5	1	1	0	1	9	0	4	6	2	3	160

Source: Taylor/Jodice 1983b.
Note: A governmental sanction is an action taken by the authorities to neutralize, suppress, or eliminate a perceived threat to the security of the government, the regime, or the state.

Table 53 **Election Turnout, Percentage of All Registered Voters, 1962–1983**

	1962	1965	1970	1974	1975	1979	1983
Kenya				40.5		65.5	46.59
Tanzania	63.6	76.9	72.25		81.9		

Source: Schönborn 1980:235.

Table 54 **Election Turnout, Percentage of Adult Population, 1962–1983**

	1962	1965	1970	1974	1975	1979	1983
Kenya				37.5		53.6	39
Tanzania	26.5	53.7	57.25		58.95		

Source: Schönborn 1980:235.

Table 55   Repressive Apparatus, 1970–1984

	1970	1971	1972	1973	1974	1975	1976	1977	1978	1979	1980	1981	1982	1983	1984
Military															
Kenya	7,900		6,730	6,730		7,550	7,600	7,700	9,100	12,400	14,750	14,750	16,550		13,650
Tanzania			11,100	11,600	14,600	14,600	14,600	18,600	26,700	51,700	51,850	44,850	40,350	40,350	40,350
Uganda	6,700	12,000	12,600	12,600	16,000	21,000	21,000	22,000				7,500	5,000		
Paramilitary															
Kenya	43,500		1,800	1,800		1,800	1,800	1,800	1,500	2,000	1,800	2,000	1,800		1,800
Tanzania[a]		44,500				47,400	47,400	47,400	47,400	47,400				61,000	61,000
Uganda[a]	7,800												8,000	8,000	23,000

Source: *Africa Contemporary Record* 1969/1970–1986.

Note: [a]Includes militia and police.

Table 56   Number of Strikes and Number of Man-Days Lost, 1960–1986 (in Thousands)

	1960	1965	1970	1975	1976	1977	1978	1979	1980	1981	1982	1983	1984	1985	1986
Kenya	232 (757.9)	200 (345.9)	84 (23.2)	26 (8.8)	44 (26.3)	45 (9.2)	46 (39.3)	54 (33.1)	81 (32.5)	74 (40.3)	100 (26.7)	75 (18.5)	69 (39.4)	150 (29)	121 (168)
Tanzania	203 (1,494.8)	13 (1.8)	3 (0.7)												

Sources: Bigsten 1984; Shivji 1976.

Table 57 Social Structure of Kenya, 1950, 1960, 1970, and 1980

	1950 no. (in 1,000s)	1950 %	1960 no. (in 1,000s)	1960 %	1970 no. (in 1,000s)	1970 %	1980 no. (in 1,000s)	1980 %
State class	0.3	—	1.2	0.1	12.0	0.5	23.7	0.7
Africans	—	—	0.3	—	7.9	0.3		
Asians	—	—	0.2	—	2.5	0.1		
Europeans	0.3	—	0.7	—	1.6	0.1		
Capitalists	1.3	0.1	3.5	0.2	2.9	0.1	4.2	0.14
Africans	—	—	—	—	0.4	—		
Asians	0.3	—	1.0	0.1	2.0	0.1		
Europeans	1.0	0.1	2.5	0.1	0.5	—		
Large-scale farmers	2.0	—	2.0	0.1	1.8	0.1	1.2	0.04
Africans	—	—	—	—	0.9	—		
Asians	—	—	—	—	—	—		
Europeans	2.0	0.1	2.0	0.1	0.9	—		
Managers	1.0	0.1	4.2	0.2	13.0	0.5	14.9	0.5
Africans	—	—	0.1	—	3.1	0.1		
Asians	0.3	—	1.6	0.1	6.0	0.3		
Europeans	0.7	—	2.5	0.1	3.9	0.1		
Nonagrarian petite bourgeoisie	22.1	1.5	23.2	1.2	110.9	4.5	95.7	3.22
Africans	5.0	0.3	10.0	0.5	101.4	4.1		
Asians	16.1	1.1	12.2	0.6	8.8	0.4		
Europeans	1.0	0.1	1.0	0.1	0.7	—		
Salariat	56.5	3.8	91.6	4.9	127.2	5.2	200.7	6.75
Africans	32.8	2.2	48.3	2.7	110.0	4.5		
Asians	17.1	1.1	29.9	1.5	13.0	0.5		
Europeans	6.6	0.5	12.5	0.7	4.2	0.2		
Agrarian petite bourgeoisie (only Africans)	71.9	4.8	97.2	5.3	234.2	9.5	476.6	15.8
Nonagrarian proletaroids	3.5	0.2	1.7	0.1	37.8	1.5	67.1	2.26
Africans	—	—	—	—	30.8	1.2		
Asians	3.5	0.2	1.7	0.1	7.0	0.3		
Agrarian proletaroids	1,035.7	68.9	1,203.2	63.9	1,202.3	48.8	1,295.5	42.33
Nonagrarian proletariat	173.0	11.5	232.2	12.5	345.3	14.0	446.3	15.0
Africans	162.2	11.1	228.4	12.3	341.3	13.9		
Asians	5.8	0.4	3.8	0.2	4.0	0.1		
Agrarian proletariat (only Africans)	136.9	9.1	176.6	9.5	343.6	13.9	260.6	8.84
Subproletariat	—	—	18.0	1.0	34.8	1.4	128.5	4.32
Total (male labor force)	1,504.2	100	1,853.6	100	2,465.8	100	2,974.9	100

Sources: Berg-Schlosser 1979b; Kenya, *Statistical Abstracts* 1981–1986.

Table 58 Social Structure of Tanzania, 1967 and 1980

	Large-Scale Farmers	Agrarian Petite Bourgeoisie	Agrarian Proletaroids	Agrarian Proletariat	State Class	Managers	Capitalists	Nonagrarian Petite Bourgeoisie	Nonagrarian Proletaroids	Proletariat	Salariat	Sub-proletariat	Total Nos.
1967													
Mainland	1,244 (0.045%)	183,947 (6.7%)	1,893,079 (69.1%)	123,870 (4.5%)	10,772 (0.39%)	9,191 (0.3%)	1,425 (0.05%)	23,764 (0.86%)	86,740 (3.16%)	256,870 (9.37%)	57,125 (2.08%)	90,565 (3.3%)	2,738,592
Zanzibar		324 (0.36%)	58,890 (66.99%)	1,259 (1.4%)	301 (0.34%)	313 (0.35%)	324 (0.36%)	1,679 (1.9%)	7,160 (8.1%)	12,844 (14.6%)	1,618 (1.8%)	3,185 (3.6%)	87,897
1980													
Mainland	323 (0.008%)	183,947 (4.6%)	2,705,172 (4.6%)	86,871 (2.17%)	16,709 (0.42%)		1,472 (0.036%)	31,496 (0.79%)	447,554 (11.19%)	289,112 (7.23%)	128,350 (3.21%)	108,199 (2.71%)	3,999,215
Zanzibar (includes Pemba)		277 (0.92%)	44,409 (47.24%)	2,879 (3.06%)	456 (0.485%)	475 (0.505%)	324 (0.34%)	524 (0.56%)	17,241 (22.84%)	21,471 (18.34%)	4,734 (5.04%)	1,535 (1.63%)	94,001

Sources: Tanzania, Bureau of Statistics, *Population Census, 2, 4, 1967*; Tanzania, Bureau of Statistics, *1969 Household Budget Survey: Income and Consumption 1972*; Tanzania, Bureau of Statistics, *Survey of Employment and Earnings 1977–1978*, 1981; Tanzania, Ministry of Finance, Planning, and Economic Affairs, *Statistical Abstract 1984*, 1986.

Table 59 Social Structure of Uganda, 1980

Large-Scale Farmers	Agrarian Petite Bourgeoisie	Agrarian Proletaroids	Agrarian Proletariat	State Class	Managers	Capitalists	Nonagrarian Petite Bourgeoisie	Nonagrarian Proletaroids	Proletariat	Salariat	Sub-proletariat	Total Nos.
10,200 (0.3%)	359,000 (11.2%)	2,202,800 (68.8%)	84,000 (2.6%)	11,200 (0.35%)		200 (0.006%)	17,000 (0.5%)	98,000 (3.1%)	112,000 (3.5%)	210,800 (6.6%)	97,000 (3.0%)	3,200,000

Sources: Mamdani 1976, 1984a, 1984b; Jørgensen 1981.

Bibliography

Aarebrot, F. and Bakka, P.H., 1987: "Die vergleichende Methode in der Politikwissenschaft." In: Berg-Schlosser, D. and Müller-Rommel, F. (eds.), *Vergleichende Politikwissenschaft. Ein einführendes Handbuch.* Opladen, 45–62

Abrahams, R.G., 1985: *Villagers, Villages and the State in Modern Tanzania.* Cambridge

Adams, B.N., 1981: "Uganda Before, During and After Amin." In: *Rural Africana* 11, 15–25

Africa Contemporary Record (ACR). 1968–1988 Annual Survey and Documents. New York, London

Africa Research Bulletin (ARB). 1985–1988 Economic Series, 22–25

Africa Research Bulletin (ARB). 1985–1988 Political Series, 22–25

Akivaga, S.K., Kukundu-Bitonye and Opi, M.W., 1985: *Local Authorities in Kenya.* Nairobi

Almond, G.A. and Powell, G.B., 1966: *Comparative Politics. A Developmental Approach.* Boston

——— 1978: *Comparative Politics. System, Process, and Policy.* Boston, Toronto

Amani, H.K.R. et al., 1984: "Agriculture in Economic Stabilization Policies Perspectives." In: Lipumba, N.H.I. et al. (eds.), *Economic Stabilization Policies in Tanzania.* Dar es Salaam, 112–128

Amey, A.B. and Leonard, D.K., 1979: "Public Policy, Class and Inequality in Kenya and Tanzania." In: *Africa Today* 26, 3–41

Amnesty International (AI), 1979–1981: *Annual Report.* London

———, 1982: *Menschenrechtsverletzungen in Uganda.* Bonn

———. 1987: *Jahresbericht.* Frankfurt/M.

Anker, R. and Knowles, J.C., 1983: *Population Growth, Employment and Economic-Demographic Interactions in Kenya: Bachue-Kenya.* New York

Apter, D.E., 1961: *The Political Kingdom in Uganda.* Princeton

———, 1965: *The Politics of Modernization.* Chicago

Aumüller, I., 1980: *Dekolonisation und Nationwerdung in Sansibar.* Munich, London

Bald, D., 1980: "Koloniale Penetration als Ursache des afrikanischen Widerstandes in Tansania (1905–1907)." In: Pfennig, W., Voll, K., and Weber, H. (eds.), *Entwicklungsmodell Tansania: Sozialismus in Afrika. Geschichte, Ökonomie, Politik, Erziehung.* Frankfurt/M., New York 76–93

Ballot, F., 1986: *Politische Herrschaft in Kenia. Der neo-patrimoniale Staat 1963–1978,* Rheinfelden

Banks, A.S. and Overstreet, W. (eds.), 1983: *Political Handbook of the World.* New York

Baregu, M.L., 1987: "Ideology and Political Stability in Tanzania." Paper presented at the AAPS East African Regional Workshop on Constitutionalism and Political

Stability in the East African Region, Nairobi, Kenya, January 5–7

Barkan, J.D. (ed.), 1984a: *Politics and Public Policy in Kenya and Tanzania*. Revised edition. New York

———, 1984b: "Comparing Politics and Public Policy in Kenya and Tanzania." In: Barkan, J.D. (ed.), *Politics and Public Policy in Kenya and Tanzania*. Revised edition. New York, 3–42

———, 1984c: "Legislators, Elections, and Political Linkage." In: Barkan, J.D. (ed.), *Politics and Public Policy in Kenya and Tanzania*. Revised edition. New York, 71–101

Barkan, J.D. and Holmquist, F., 1986: "Politics and the Middle Peasantry in Kenya: The Lessons of Harambee." Paper presented at a conference on the political economy of Kenya. School of Advanced International Studies. Johns Hopkins University, Washington D.C., April 12–13

Barkan, J.D. and Okumu, J.J., 1978: "'Semi-Competitive' Elections, Clientelism, and Political Recruitment in a No-Party State: The Kenyan Experience." In: Hermet, G. et al. (eds.), *Elections Without Choice*. New York, 88–107

Barkan, J.D. and Okumu, J.J. (eds.), 1979: *Politics and Public Policy in Kenya and Tanzania*. New York

Barve, A.G., 1984: *The Foreign Trade of Kenya. A Perspective*. Nairobi

Bates, R.H., 1980: "Pressure Groups, Public Policy and Agricultural Development." In: Bates, R.H. and Lofchie, M.F., *Agricultural Development in Africa. Issues of Public Policy*. New York, 170–217

Baumhögger, G., 1978: "Überlegungen zu Kenyas politischer Stabilität nach Kenyattas Tod." In: *Afrika Spectrum* 13, 189–208

Baumhögger, G. et al., 1981: *Ostafrika. Reisehandbuch Kenya und Tanzania*. Frankfurt/M.

Bavu, I.K., 1986: "Policy Issues on the Democraticness of One Party Elections." Paper presented at the Joint AAPS/DVPW Symposium at Arnoldshain, West Germany, October 15–17

Berg-Schlosser, D., 1975: "Wahlen in Kenia—Demokratie in einem Entwicklungsland?" In: *Afrika Spectrum* 10, 55–66

———, 1979a: *The Social and Economic Bases of Politics in Kenya—A Structural and Cultural Analysis*. Berkeley

———, 1979b: "Soziale Differenzierung und Klassenbildung in Kenia—Entwicklung und Perspektiven." In: *Politische Vierteljahresschrift* (hereafter, *PVS*) 20, 313–329

———, 1980: "Die Nyayo-Wahlen in Kenya—Ergebnisse und Analysen." In: *Internationales Afrikaforum* 1, 57–62

———, 1981a: "Probleme der nationalen Integration eines Vielvölkerstaates am Beispiel Kenias. In: *Politische Studien. Sonderheft Afrika*, 88–110

———, 1981b: "Zur Funktion von Wahlen im politischen System Kenias." In: Hanisch, R. and Tetzlaff, R. (eds.), *Staat und Entwicklung—Studien zum Verhältnis von Herrschaft und Gesellschaft in Entwicklungsländern*. Frankfurt/M., 199–217

———, 1982a: *"Kenya nach dem Putschversuch. Hintergründe und Perspektiven."* In: *Internationales Afrikaforum* 18, 367–376

———, 1982b: "Modes and Meaning of Participation in Kenya." In: *Comparative Politics* 14, 397–416

————, 1982c: "Uganda." In: Nohlen, D. and Nuscheler, F. (eds.), *Handbuch der Dritten Welt 5. Ostafrika und Südafrika. Unterentwicklung und Entwicklung.* Hamburg, 186–204

————, 1983a: "Vorgezogene Neuwahlen in Kenya—das Ende des `msaliti'"? In: *Internationales Afrikaforum* 19, 381–386

————, 1983b: "Zur Formation endogener Bourgeoisiefraktionen—der Fall der `kapitalistischen Bourgeoisie' Kenias." In: Bruchhaus, E.-M. (ed.), *Afrikanische Eliten zwanzig Jahre nach Erlangung der Unabhängigkeit. (Schriften der Vereinigung von Afrikanisten in Deutschland* 9). Hamburg 113–128

————, 1984a: "African Political Systems—Typology and Performance." In: *Comparative Political Studies* 17, 121–151

————, 1984b: "Afrika zwischen Despotie und Demokratie—Bedingungen und Leistungsfähigkeit der politischen Systeme der Gegenwart." In: *Aus Politik und Zeitgeschichte.* Supplement to *Das Parlament* (7 April), 3–14

————, 1984c: "Die Njonjo-Affäre—ein kenyanisches Watergate." In: *Internationales Afrikaforum* 20, 399–403

————, 1984d: "Third World Political Systems: Classification and Evaluation." Paper presented at the annual meeting of the APSA. Washington, D.C.

————, 1984e: *Tradition and Change in Kenya. A Comparative Analysis of Seven Major Ethnic Groups.* Paderborn (*Internationale Gegenwart* 3)

————, 1985a: :Elements of Consociational Democracy in Kenya." In: *European Journal of Political Research* 13, 95–109

————, 1985b: "Leistungen und Fehlleistungen politischer Systeme der Dritten Welt als Kriterium der Entwicklungspolitik." In: *Konjunkturpolitik—Zeitschrift für angewandte Wirtschaftsforschung* 31, 79–114

————, 1985c: 'Politische Kultur." In: Nohlen, D. and Schultze, R.-O. (eds.), *Pipers Wörterbuch zur Politik 1. Politikwissenschaf. Theorien—Methoden—Begriffe.* Munich, 746–751

————, 1985d: "Zu den Bedingungen von Demokratie in der Dritten Welt." In: Nuscheler, F. (ed.), *Dritte Welt-Forschung. Entwicklungstheorie und Entwicklungspolitik. (PVS* special edition 16), Opladen, 233–266

————, 1987a: "Kriterien und empirische Befunde zur Leistungsfähigkeit afrikanischer Staaten nach der Dekolonisierung." In: Illy, H.F. and Bryde, B.-O., *Staat, Verwaltung und Recht in Afrika 1960–1985.* Berlin, 213–227

————, 1987b: "Politische Kulturen in der Dritten Welt." In: Nohlen, D. and Waldmann, P. (eds.), *Pipers Wörterbuch zur Politik 6. Dritte Welt. Gesellschaft—Kultur—Entwicklung.* Munich, 398–409.

Berg-Schlosser, D., Maier, H., and Stammen, T., 1985: *Einführung in die Politikwissenschaft.* Munich

Berg-Schlosser, D., and Schneider-Barthold, W., 1977: "Wirtschaft und Entwicklung." In: Leifer, W. (ed.): *Handbuch Kenia.* Tübingen, 359–376

Berg-Schlosser, D., and Müller-Rommel, F. (eds.), 1987: *Vergleichende Politikwissenschaft. Ein einführendes Handbuch.* Opladen

Berongo, Y.R., 1984: "The De-Embourgeoisement of Ugandan Society: The First Stage in the Break with International Capitalism." In: *Journal of African Studies* 11, 100–109

Bienefeld, M., 1979: "Trade Unions, the Labour Process, and the Tanzanian State." In: *Journal of Modern African Studies* 17, 553–593

Bienen, H., 1970: *Tanzania. Party Transformation and Economic Development.* Princeton

——, 1974: *Kenya. The Politics of Participation and Control.* Princeton

Biersteker, T.J., 1986: "Self-Reliance in Theory and Practice in Tanzanian Trade-Relations." In: Ravenhill, J. (ed.), *Africa in Economic Crisis.* Basingstoke, 213–253

Bigsten, A., 1980: *Regional Inequality and Development. A Case Study of Kenya.* Westmead

——, 1984: *Education and Income. Determination in Kenya.* Aldershot

Bliss, F., 1986: "Die kulturelle Dimension von Entwicklung. Aspekte eines Defizits im entwicklungspolitischen Instrumentarium." In: *Aus Politik und Zeitgeschichte.* Supplement to *Das Parlament*, (30 August), 28–38

Boeckh, A., 1982: "Abhängigkeit, Unterentwicklung und Entwicklung: Zum Erklärungswert der Dependencia-Ansätze." In: Nohlen, D. and Nuscheler, F. (eds.), *Handbuch der Dritten Welt 1. Unterentwicklung und Entwicklung: Theorien—Strategien—Indikatoren.* Hamburg, 133–151

——, 1985: "Dependencia und kapitalistisches Weltsystem, oder: Die Grenzen globaler Entwicklungstheorien." In: Nuscheler, F. (ed.), *Dritte Welt-Forschung. Entwicklungstheorie und Entwicklungspolitik.* (*PVS* special edition 16), Opladen, 56–74

Boesen, G., Madsen, B.S., and Moody, T., 1977: *Ujamaa—Socialism from Above.* Uppsala

Brandes, V. et al., 1981: *Wie Phönix aus der Asche?* Offenbach

Brandt, H. et al., 1986: *Afrika in Bedrängnis.* Berlin

Brett, E.A., 1973: *Colonialism and Underdevelopment in East Africa. The Politics of Economic Change 1919–1939.* New York

——, 1982: "Staat und Krise in Uganda." In: Elwert, G. and Fett, R. (eds.), *Afrika zwischen Subsistenzökonomie und Imperialismus.* Frankfurt/M., 256–273

Bwengye, A.W.F., 1985: *The Agony of Uganda: From Idi Amin to Obote.* London

Campbell, H. 1983: "The Tragedy of Uganda. A Review of D. Wadada Nabudere's *Imperialism and Revolution in Uganda.*" In: *Mawazo* vol 5 no 1, 70–76

——, 1986a: "The IMF Debate and the Politics of Demobilisation in Tanzania." Paper presented at the Second Triennial Congress of OSSREA, Eldoret, Kenya , July 28–31

——, 1986b: "The Debt Crisis and the Tanzanian Socity." Paper presented at the Economic Policy Workshop on Policies and Strategies for Economic Recovery, February

Carlsen, J., 1980: *Economic and Social Transformation in Rural Kenya.* Uppsala (*Centre for Development Research Publications* 4)

Chango Machyo W'obanda, B., 1985: "The World Bank, IMF and Deepening Misery in Uganda (The Mbale Experience)." In: *Mawazo* 6, 27–49

Chege, M., 1981: "A Tale of Two Slums: Electoral Politics in Mathare and Dagoretti." In: *Review of African Political Economy* 20, 74–88, 121–124

——, 1986: "The Political Economy of Agrarian Change in Central Kenya." Paper prepared for a conference on the political economy of Kenya. School of Advanced International Studies. Johns Hopkins University, Washington D.C., April 12–13

Cliffe, L., 1975: "Underdevelopment or Socialism? A Comparative Analysis of Kenya and Tanzania." In: Harris R. (ed.), *The Political Economy of Africa.* New York

Cliffe, L., Coleman, J.S., and Doornbos, M.R. (eds.), 1977: *Government and Rural Development in East Africa: Essays on Political Penetration.* (Institute of Social Studies: Series on the Development of Societies 2) The Hague

Cliffe, L. and Saul, J.S. (eds.), 1972–1973: *Socialism in Tanzania. An Interdisciplinary Reader. Politics and Policies.* Dar es Salaam

Collier, P. and Lal, D., 1986: *Labour and Poverty in Kenya 1900–1980.* Oxford

Collier, P., Radwan, S., and Wangwe, S., 1986: *Labour and Poverty in Rural Tanzania. Ujamaa and Rural Development in the United Republic of Tanzania.* Oxford

Coplin, W.D. and O'Leary, M., 1982: "Systematic Political Risk Forecasting." In: *Vierteljahresberichte—Probleme der Entwicklungsländer,* 333–340

Coulson, A. (ed.), 1979: *African Socialism in Practice. The Tanzanian Experience.* Nottingham

Cowen, M., 1981: "The Agrarian Problem: Notes on the Nairobi Discussion." In: *Review of African Political Economy* 20, 57–73

Currie, K. and Ray, L., 1984: "State and Class in Kenya. Notes on the Cohesion of the Ruling Class." In: *Journal of Modern African Studies* 22, 559–593

Dahl, R.A., 1971: *Polyarchy: Participation and Opposition.* New Haven

Deutsch, K.W., 1961: "Social Mobilization and Political Development." In: *American Political Science Review* 60, 493–514

De Wilde, J.C., 1980: "Case Studies: Kenya, Tanzania and Ghana." In: Bates, R.H. and Lofchie, M.F. (eds.), *Agricultural Development in Africa: Issues of Public Policy.* New York, 113–169

Dogan, M. and Pelassy, D., 1984: *How to Compare Nations.* Chatham

Doornbos, M.R., 1973: "Changing Perspectives on Conflict and Integration in Uganda." In: Uzoigwe, G.N. (ed.), *Uganda. The Dilemma of Nationhood.* New York, London, Lagos, 313–332

Dowding, K.M. and Kimber, R., 1983: "The Meaning and Use of `Political Stability'." In: *European Journal of Political Research* 11, 229–243

Easton D., 1965: *A Systems Analysis of Political Life.* New York, London, Sydney

———, 1975: "A Re-Assessment of the Concept of Political Support." In: *British Journal of Political Science* 5, 435–457

Eckstein, H., 1982: "The Idea of Political Development: From Dignity to Efficiency." In: *World Politics* 34, 451–486

Elkins, D.J. and Simeon, R.E.B., 1979: "A Cause in Search of Its Effects, or What Does Political Culture Explain?" In: *Comparative Politics* 11, 127–145

Elliott, C.M., 1977: *Employment and Income Distribution in Uganda. Development Studies. Discussion Paper No. 1*

Elsenhans, H., 1981: *Abhängiger Kapitalismus oder bürokratische Entwicklungsgesellschaft.* Frankfurt/M.

———, 1982: "Die Überwindung von Unterentwicklung durch Massenproduktion für den Massenbedarf—Weiterentwicklung eines Ansatzes." In: Nohlen, D. and Nuscheler, F. (eds.), *Handbuch der Dritten Welt 1. Unterentwicklung und Entwicklung: Theorien—Strategien—Indikatoren.* Hamburg, 152–182

———, 1985: "Der periphere Staat: Zum Stand der entwicklungstheoretischen Diskussion." In: Nuscheler, F. (ed.), *Dritte Welt-Forschung. Entwicklungstheorie und Entwicklungspolitik.* (*PVS* special edition 16), Opladen, 135–156

———, 1986: "Dependencia, Unterentwicklung und der Staat in der Dritten Welt."

In: *PVS* 27 Opladen, 133–158

Ergas, Zaki, 1980: "Why Did the Ujamaa Village Policy Fail? Towards a Global Analysis." In: *Journal of Modern African Studies* 18, 387–410

Fallers, L.A. (ed.), 1964: *The King's Men.* Nairobi

Fendru, I., 1985: "The Rural Question and Democracy in Uganda." In: *Mawazo* vol 6, no 1, 50–71

Fortman, L., 1980: *Peasants, Officials and Participation in Rural Tanzania: Experience with Villagization and Decentralization.* Ithaca

Freyhold, M. von, 1977: "The Post-Colonial State and its Tanzanian Version." In: *Review of African Political Economy* 17, 75–89

———, 1979: *Ujamaa Villages in Tanzania. Analysis of a Social Experiment.* London

Friedrich, H.J., 1986: "Der Putsch in Uganda. Neue Köpfe, alte Probleme." In: *Jahrbuch Dritte Welt*, 127–140

Fuchs, D., 1987: "Trends politischer Unterstützung in der Bundesrepublik." In: Berg-Schlosser, D. and Schissler, J. (eds.), *Politische Kultur in Deutschland—Bilanz und Perspektiven der Forschung.* (*PVS* special edition) Opladen, 357–377

Gastil, R.D. (19178–1988). *Freedom in the World* Annual Report, New York

Geiger, T., 1932: *Die soziale Schichtung des deutschen Volkes.* Stuttgart

Germany, Federal Republic of. Department of Export Trade Information, 1984: *Uganda. Wirtschaftsdaten und Wirtschaftsdokumentation.* Cologne

———. Department of Export Trade Information, 1986a: *Kenia. Wirtschaftsdaten. Wirschaftsdokumentation und Projekte.* Cologne

———. Department of Export Trade Information, 1986b: *Tansania. Wirtschaftsdaten. Wirschaftsdokumentation und Projekte.* Cologne

———. Ministry for Business Cooperation, 1986: *Grundlinien der Entwicklungspolitik der Bundesregierung.* Bonn

———. Office of Statistics, Wiesbaden, 1983: *Statistik des Auslandes. Länderkurzbericht Uganda.* Stuttgart, Mainz

———. Office of Statistics, Wiesbaden, 1984: *Statistik des Auslandes. Länderbericht Tansania.* Stuttgart, Mainz

———. Office of Statistics, Wiesbaden, 1985–1988: *Statistik des Auslandes. Ländererbericht Kenia.* Stuttgart, Mainz

———. Office of Statistics, Wiesbaden, 1986: *Statistik des Auslandes. Länderbericht Uganda.* Stuttgart, Mainz

Gertzel, C., 1970: *The Politics of Independent Kenya. 1963–1968.* London

———, 1974: *Party and Locality in Northern Uganda.* London

Gertzel, C., Goldschmidt, M., and Rothschild, D. (eds.), 1969: *Government and Politics in Kenya. A Nation Building Text.* Nairobi

Ghai, D., Godfrey, M., and Lisk, F., 1979: *Planning for Basic Needs in Kenya. Performance, Policies and Prospects.* Geneva

Gingyera-Pinycwa, A., 1978: *Milton Obote and His Times.* New York

Godfrey, M., 1986: *Kenya to 1990: Prospects for Growth.* (*The Economist Intelligence Unit. Special Report No. 1052*) London , 201–221

Godfrey, M. and Langdon, S., 1976: "Partners in Underdevelopment? The Transnationalisation Thesis in a Kenyan Context." In: *Journal of Commonwealth and Comparative Politics* 14, 42–63

Godia, G.I., 1984: *Understanding Nyayo. Principles and Policies in Contemporary Kenya.* Nairobi

Gordon D.F., 1984: "Foreign Relation Dilemmas of Independence and Development." In: Barkan, J.D. (ed.), *Politics and Public Policy in Kenya and Tanzania.* Revised edition. New York, 297–335

Goulbourne, H., 1979: "The Role of the Political Party in Tanzania since the Arusha Declaration." In: Goulbourne, H. (ed.), *Politics and State in the Third World.* London

Green, R.H., 1981: *Magendo in the Political Economy of Uganda: Pathology, Parallel System or Dominant Sub-Mode of Production?* Brighton

————, 1984: "Political-Economic Adjustment and IMF Conditionality. Tanzania 1974–1981." In: Williamson, J. (ed.), *IMF Conditionality.* Cambridge, 347–380

Green, R.H., Rwegasira, D.G., and Arkadie, V. van, 1980: *Economic Shocks and National Policy Making. Tanzania in the 1970s.* The Hague

Grimes, O.F. and Orville, F., 1976: *Housing for Low-Income Urban Families.* London

Gukiina, P.M., 1972: *Uganda. A Case Study in African Political Development.* South Bend, Ind., London

Gulhati, R. and Sekhar, U., 1980: "Industrial Strategy for Late Starters: The Experience of Kenya, Tanzania and Zambia." In: *World Development* 10, 947–972.

Hanisch, R. and Tetzlaff, R. (eds.), 1981: *Staat und Entwicklung. Studien zum Verhältnis von Herrschaft und Gesellschaft in Entwicklungsländern.* Frankfurt/M.

Harbeson, J.W. and Rothchild, D., 1981: "Rehabilitation and Rural Development in Uganda: A Preliminary Assessment." In: *Rural Africana* 11, 1–14

Hart, M., 1978: "Uganda." In: Werobel-La Rochelle, J.M. et al. (eds.), *Politisches Lexikon Schwarzafrika.* Munich, 475-485

Hartmann, Jeanette, 1986a: "The Debate of the Two Socialisms in Tanzania (1962–1982)." Paper presented at the Second Triennial Congress of OSSREA, Eldoret, Kenya, July 28–31

————, 1986b: "The State and Agriculture in Tanzania." Paper Presented at the Ninth SAUSSC Conference, "The Food Question in Southern Africa. Problems and Prospects," Dar es Salaam, June 2–6

Hartmann, Jürrgen, 1987: "Vergleichende Regierungslehre und vergleichende politische Systemforschung." In: Berg-Schlosser, D. and Müller-Rommel, F. (eds.), *Vergleichende Politikwissenschaft. Ein einführendes Handbuch.* Opladen, 25–44

Hazlewood, A., 1978: "Kenya: Income Distribution and Poverty—an Unfashionable View." In: *The Journal of Modern African Studies* 16, 81–95

————, 1979: *The Economy of Kenya. The Kenyatta Era.* New York

Heinrich, T.J., 1985: "Adjustment or Structural Change in Crisis Management Policy of Tanzania." In: *Verfassung und Recht in Übersee* 18, 195–207

Hermet, G. et al., (eds.), 1978: *Elections Without Choice.* New York

Heyer, J., 1981: "Agricultural Development Policy in Kenya from the Colonial Period to 1975." In: Heyer, J. et al. (eds.), *Rural Development in Tropical Africa.* New York

Hilbert, R., 1981: *Ausländische Direktinvestitionen als Entwicklungsdeterminanten Kenias.* Frankfurt/M.

Hill, F., 1978: *Ujamaa. Mobilization and Participation in Tanzania.* London

————, 1979–1980: "Administrative Decentralization for Development, Participation and Control in Tanzania." In: *Journal of African Studies* 6, 182–192

Hofmeier, R., 1978: "Kenia." In: Werobel-La Rochelle, J.M. et al (eds.), 1978: *Politisches Lexikon Schwarzafrika.* Munich, 161–181

———, 1980: "Die Tanga-Region—Regionaler Schwerpunkt der deutschen Entwicklungshilfeprogramme in Tansania." In: Pfennig, W., Voll, K., and Weber, H. (eds.), *Entwicklungsmodell Tansania: Sozialismus in Afrika. Geschichte, Ökonomie, Politik, Erziehung.* Frankfurt/M., New York, 310–339

———, 1981a: "Staatliche Entwicklungsplanung in Tanzania. Instrument zur sozialistischen Transformation von Wirtschaft und Gesellschaft oder Hilfsmittel zur Stärkung der Staatsbürokratie? In: Hanisch, R. and Tetzlaff, R. (eds.): *Staat und Entwicklung.* Frankfurt/M, 433–472

———, 1981b: "Die tanzanischen Wahlen von 1980: Bestätigung des Ujamaa-Kurses oder Ausdruck wachsender Unzufriedenheit?" In: *Afrika Spectrum* 2, 143–162

———, 1982a: "Kenya." In: Nohlen, D. and Nuscheler, F. (eds.), *Handbuch der Dritten Welt 5. Ostafrika und Südafrika: Unterentwicklung und Entwicklung.* Hamburg, 131–152

———, 1982b: "Tanzania." In: Nohlen, D. and Nuscheler, F. (eds.), *Handbuch der Dritten Welt 5. Ostafrika und Südafrika: Unterentwicklung und Entwicklung.* Hamburg, 162–185

Hofmeier, R. and Schneider-Barthold, W., 1983: *Makro-ökonomische Rahmenbedingungen der entwicklungspolitischen Zusammenarbeit mit Tansania.* Unpublished manuscript

Hofmeier, R. and Schönborn, M. (eds.), 1987: *Politisches Lexikon Afrika.* Munich

Holmquist, F., 1980: "Defending Peasant Political Space in Independent Africa." In: *Canadian Journal of African Studies* 14, 157–167

———, 1983: "Correspondent`s Report: Tanzania`s Retreat from Statism in the Countryside." In: *Africa Today* 30, 23–35

———, 1984a: "Class Structure, Peasant Participation. and Rural Self-Help." In: Barkan, J.D. (ed.), *Politics and Public Policy in Kenya and Tanzania.* Revised edition. New York, 171–197

———, 1984b: "Self-Help: The State and Peasant Leverage in Kenya." In: *Africa* 54, 72–91

Holt, R.T. and Turner, J.E., 1970: *The Methodology of Comparative Research.* New York

House, W.J., 1981: "Nairobi's Informal Sector: Dynamic Entrepreneurs or Surplus Labour?" In: Killick, T. (ed.), *Papers on the Kenyan Economy. Performance, Problems and Policies.* Nairobi, London, Ibadan, 357–368

House, W.J. and Killick, T., 1981: "Inequality and Poverty in the Rural Economy, and the Influence of Some Aspects of Policy." In: Killick, T. (ed.), *Papers on the Kenyan Economy. Performance, Problems and Policies.* Nairobi, London, Ibadan, 157–179

Huntington, S.P., 1968: *Political Order in Changing Societies.* New Haven

Huntington, S.P. and Domínguez, J.I., 1975: "Political Development" In: Greenstein, F.I. and Polsby, N.W. (eds.), *Handbook of Political Science 3. Macropolitical Theory.* Reading, Mass., 1–114

Hurwitz, L., 1973: "Contemporary Approaches to Political Stability." In: *Comparative Politics* 5, 449–463

Hyden, G., 1980: *Beyond Ujamaa in Tanzania: Underdevelopment and the Uncaptured Peasantry.* Berkeley
————, 1984: "Administration and Public Policy." In: Barkan, J.D. (ed.), *Politics and Public Policy in Kenya and Tanzania.* Revised edition. New York, 103–124
————, 1986: *Capital Accumulation, Resource Distribution, and Governance in Kenya: The Role of the Economy of Affection.* Unpublished manuscript
Hyden, G. and Leys, C., 1972: "Elections and Politics in Single Party Systems: The Case of Kenya and Tanzania." In: *British Journal of Political Science* 10, 389–420
Ibingira, G.S., 1980: *African Political Upheavals Since Independence.* Boulder, Colo.
Iliffe, J., 1979: *A Modern History of Tanganyika.* Cambridge
Illy, H.F. et al., 1980: *Diktatur—Staatsmodell für die Dritte Welt?* Freiburg
International Commission of Jurists, 1979–1981: *The Review,* Geneva
International Labour Office, (ILO) (ed.), 1972: *Employment, Incomes and Equality. A Strategy for Increasing Productive Employment in Kenya. Report of an Inter-Agency Team.* Geneva
————, 1982: *Basic Needs in Danger: A Basic Needs Oriented Development Strategy for Tanzania.* Addis Ababa
————, 1985: *Informal Sector in Africa. Jobs and Skills Programme for Africa.* Addis Ababa
International Monetary Fund (IMF), 1986: *Annual Report 1986.* Washington D.C.
Jackson, R.H. and Rosberg, C.G., 1982–1983: "Why Africa's Weak States Persist: The Empirical and the Juridical in Statehood." In: *World Politics. A Quarterly Journal of International Relations* 35, 1–24
————, 1983–1984: "Personal Rule. Theory and Practice in Africa." In: *Comparative Politics* 16, 421–442
Jørgensen, J.J., 1974: *The Political Economy of Uganda.* Oslo
————, 1981: *Uganda. A Modern History.* New York
Kaase, M., 1983: "Sinn oder Unsinn des Konzepts ʻPolitische Kulturʼ für die vergleichende Politikforschung, oder auch: Der Versuch, einen Pudding an die Wand zu nageln." In: Kaase, M. and Klingemann, H.D. (eds.), *Wahlen und politisches System. Analysen aus Anlaß der Bundestagswahl 1980.* Opladen, 144–171
————, 1985: "Systemakzeptanz in den westlichen Demokratien." In: Matz, U. (ed.), *Aktuelle Herausforderungen der repräsentativen Demokratie.* Cologne, 99–130
Kabwegyere, T., 1974: *The Politics of State Formation. The Nature and Effects of Colonialism in Uganda.* Nairobi, Dar es Salaam, Kampala
————, 1987: "The Politics of State Destruction in Uganda since 1962: Lessons for the Future." In: Wiebe, P.D. and Dodge, C.P. (eds.), *Beyond Crisis. Development Issues in Uganda.* Hillsboro, Kans., 11–24
Kahama, C.G., Maliyamkono, T.L., and Wells, S., 1986: *The Challenge for Tanzania's Economy.* London, Portsmouth, N.H., Dar es Salaam
Kamau, J. and Cameron, A., 1979: *Lust to Kill: The Rise and Fall of Idi Amin.* London
Kamunto, E.R., 1986: *Uganda's Macro-Economic Policies 1981–1985: A Preliminary Assessment of Economic Performance.* Unpublished manuscript
Kaplinsky, R., 1980: "Capitalist Accumlation in the Periphery—the Kenyan Case Re-Examined." In: *Review of African Political Economy* 19, 83–113
Karugire, S.P., 1980: *A Political History of Uganda.* London

Kasfir, N., 1976: *The Shrinking Political Arena. Participation and Ethnicity in African Politics, with a Case Study of Uganda.* Berkeley, Calif.
Kebschull, D. et al., 1977: *Das integrierte Rohstoffprogramm.* Hamburg
Kenya, Republic of. *Economic Survey 1975–1988*
———. 1975–1980: *Provincial Statistical Abstract. Central Province*
———. 1975–1980: *Provincial Statistical Abstract. Coast Province*
———. 1975–1980: *Provincial Statistical Abstract. Eastern Province*
———. 1975–1980: *Provincial Statistical Abstract. Nyanza Province*
———. 1975–1980: *Provincial Statistical Abstract. Rift Valley Province*
———. 1975–1980: *Provincial Statistical Abstract. Western Province*
———. 1979–1983: *Development Plan*
———. 1984–1988: *Development Plan*
———. 1979–1980: *Employment and Earnings in the Modern Sector*
———. 1980–1988: *Statistical Abstract*
———. 1981: *The Integrated Rural Surveys 1976–79. Basic Report*
——— 1981: *Kenya Population Census 1979*, 1
———. 1984–1988: *Baringo District Development Plan*
———. 1984–1988: *Kakamega District Development Plan*
———. 1984–1988: *Kericho District Development Plan*
———. 1984–1988: *Kwale District Development Plan*
———. 1984–1988: *Narok District Development Plan*
———. 1984–1988: *Nyeri District Development Plan*
———. Office of the President, 1984: *District Focus for Rural Development*
———. 1984–1988: *South Nyanza District Development Plan*
———. 1984–1988: *Trans-Nzoia District Development Plan*
——— 1986: *Report on Small Scale Enterprises (Formerly Informal Sector) in Rural and Urban Areas of Kenya 1973–1982*
———. 1986: *Sessional Paper No.1 of 1986 on Economic Management for Renewed Growth*
———. 1986–1988 *Kisii District Development Plan*
———. 1986 *Ministry of Finance and Ministry of Planning and National Development: Budget Rationalization Programme*
Khapoya, V.B., 1980: "Kenya under Moi: Continuity or Change?" In: *Africa Today* 27, 17–32
Khiddu-Makubuya, E., 1985: "The Rise of the Authoritarian State in Uganda." In: *Mawazo* vol 6, no 1, 10–26
———, 1987: "The Constitution and Human Rights in Uganda. An Overview." Paper presented at the AAPS East African Regional Workshop on Constitutional-ism and Political Stability in the East African Region, Nairobi, Kenya, January 5–7
Killick, T. (ed.), 1981: *Papers on the Kenyan Economy. Performance, Problems and Policies.* Nairobi, London, Ibadan
———, 1984: "Kenya, the IMF, and the Unsuccessful Quest for Stabilization." In: Williamson, J. (ed.), *IMF Conditionality.* Cambridge, 381–413
Kim, K.S., Mabele, R.B., and Schultheiβ, M.J. (eds.), 1979: *Papers on the Political Economy of Tanzania.* Nairobi
Kitching, G., 1980: *Class and Economic Change in Kenya. The Making of an African Petite Bourgeoisie 1905–1970.* New Haven, London
———, 1985: "Politics, Method and Evidence in the `Kenya Debate'". In: Bernstein,

H. and Campbell, B.K. (eds.), *Contradictions of Accumulation in Africa.* Beverly Hills

Kiwanuka, S., 1979: *Amin and the Tragedy of Uganda.* Munich

Klein, H.G., 1980–1981: *Entwicklung, Entwicklungspolitik und kirchliche Entwicklungsarbeit in Tansania.* Aachen

Konde, H.S., 1984: *Press Freedom in Tanzania.* Dar es Salaam

Kreditanstalt für Wiederaufbau (ed.), 1984: *Entwicklungspolitik in Tansania. Ursachen der Krise und Ansatzpunkte für deren Lösung—Länderkurzinformation.* Frankfurt/M.

Kurian, G.T. (ed.), 1982: *Encyclopedia of the Third World.* Revised edition. 3 vols. London

Langdon, S., 1977: "The State and Capitalism in Kenya." In: *Review of African Political Economy* 16, 90–98

———, 1981: *Multinational Corporations in the Political Economy of Kenya.* London, Basingstoke

Leifer, W. (ed.), 1977: *Kenya (Geographie, Vorgeschichte, Geschichte, Gesellschaft, Kultur, Erziehung, Gesundheitswesen, Wirtschaft, Entwicklung).* Tübingen

Leo, C., 1984: "The Peasantry and the Bourgeoisie: Class Struggle or Class Alliance." Paper prepared for delivery at the Canadian African Studies Association Conference, April 11

Leonard, D.K., 1984: "Class Formation and Agricultural Development." In: Barkan, J.D. (ed.), *Politics and Public Policy in Kenya and Tanzania.* Revised edition. New York, 141–170

Leys, C., 1974: *Underdevelopment in Kenya. The Political Economy of Neo-Colonialism 1964–1971.* Berkeley, Los Angeles

———, 1979: "Development Strategy in Kenya since 1971." In: *Canadian Journal of African Studies* 13, 295–320

Lijphart, A., 1977: *Democracy in Plural Societies.* New Haven

Linz, J.J., 1975: "Totalitarian and Authoritarian Regimes." In: Greenstein, F.J. and Polsby, N.W. (eds.), *Handbook of Political Science* 3. *Macropolitical Theory.* Reading, Mass. 175–411

Linz, J.J. and Stepan, A., 1978: *The Breakdown of Democratic Regimes.* Baltimore

Livingstone, I., 1986: *Rural Development, Employment and Incomes in Kenya.* Aldershot, Brookfield

Löwenthal, R., 1963: "Staatsfunktionen und Staatsform in den Entwicklungsländern." In: Löewenthal, R. (ed.), *Die Demokratie im Wandel der Gesellschaft.* Berlin, 164–192

Lofchie, M., 1978: "Agrarian Crisis and Economic Liberalisation." In: *Journal of Modern African Studies* 16, 451–478

Low, D.A., 1962: *Political Parties in Uganda 1949–1962.* London

———, 1971: *Buganda in Modern History.* London

Low, D.A. and Smith, A. (eds.), 1976: *History of East Africa.* 3 vols. Oxford

Mabirizi, D., 1986: "The Historical Basis and Content of One-Party Politics in Uganda 1965–71." Paper presented at the Joint AAPS/DVPW Symposium at Arnoldshain, West Germany, October 15–17

Maganya, E.N., 1986: "The State, Land Reform and Peasant Production. Some Reflections on the Tanzanian and Mozambican Experience." Paper presented at the Ninth SAUSSC Conference, "The Food Question in Southern Africa.

Problems and Prospects," Dar es Salaam, June 2–6

Makokka, J., 1985: *The District Focus. Conceptual and Management Problems.* Nairobi

Mamdani, M., 1976: *Politics and Class Formation in Uganda.* Nairobi, Ibadan, Lusaka

——, 1983a: *Imperialism and Fascism in Uganda.* Nairobi, Ibadan, London

——, 1983b: "The Nationality Question in a Neo-colony: An Historical Perspective." In: *Mawazo* vol 5, no 1, 36–54

——, 1984a: "Analyzing the Agrarian Question: The Case of a Buganda Village." In: *Mawazo* vol 5, no 3, 47–64

——, 1984b: "Forms of Labour and Accumulation of Capital: Analysis of a Village in Lango, Northern Uganda." In: *Mawazo* vol 5, no 4, 44–55

——, 1986: "Peasants and Democracy in Africa." In: *New Left Review* 156, 37–61

Martin, D., 1978a: *General Amin.* London

——, 1978b: "The 1975 Tanzanian Elections: The Disturbing Six Per Cent." In: Hermet, G. et al. (eds.), *Elections Without Choice.* New York, 108–128

——, 1984: "Elections in Kenya and Tanzania: Some Methodological Remarks." In: *CREDU Newsletter* 14, 3–16

Mascarenhas, A., 1979: "After Villagization—What?" In: Mwansasu, B.U. and Pratt, C. (eds.), *Towards Socialism in Tanzania.* Toronto, Dar es Salaam, 145–167

Mawhood, P., 1983: "The Search for Participation in Tanzania.' In: Mawhood, P. (ed.), *Local Government in the Third World: The Experience of Tropical Africa.* Chichester, 75–106

Mazrui, A.A., 1975: *Soldiers and Kinsmen in Uganda. The Making of a Military Ethnocracy.* Beverly Hills, London

Mbithi, P. and Rasmusson, R., 1977: *Self Reliance in Kenya: The Case of Harambee.* Uppsala

Medard, J.F., 1986: *The Creation of a Political Order in Uganda.* Nairobi

Menzel, U., 1987: *Auswege aus der Abhängigkeit.* Frankfurt/M.

Menzel, U. and Senghaas, D., 1986: *Europas Entwicklung und die Dritte Welt. Eine Bestandsaufnahme.* Frankfurt/M.

Meyns, P., 1978: *Nationale Unabhängigkeit und ländliche Entwicklung in der 3.Welt. Das Beispiel Tanzania.* Berlin

Mhina, A.K., 1986: "The State and the Food Problem in Tanzania." Paper presented at the ninth SAUSSC Conference, "The Food Question in South Africa. Problems and Prospects," Dar es Salaam, June 2–6

Migot-Adholla, S.E., 1984: "Rural Development Policy and Equality." In: Barkan, J.D. (ed.), *Politics and Public Policy in Kenya and Tanzania.* Revised edition. New York, 199–232

Miller, N.N., 1984: *Kenya. The Quest for Prosperity.* Boulder, Colo.

Mittelman, J.M., 1975: *Ideology and Politics in Uganda—From Obote to Amin.* London

Mohiddin, A., 1981: *African Socialism in Two Countries.* London

Moi, D. arap, 1986: *Kenya African Nationalism. Nyayo Philosophy and Principles.* London, Basingstoke

Moore, B. Jr., 1966: *Social Origins of Dictatorship and Democracy. Lord and Peasant in the Making of the Modern World.* Boston

Morrison, J.C. et al., 1972: *Black Africa—A Comparative Handbook.* New York

Mosley, P., 1986: "The Politics of Economic Liberalization: USAID and the World Bank in Kenya 1980–1984." In: *African Affairs* 85, 107–114

Mramba, B.P., 1984: "Rural Industrialisation and Self-Reliance. The Case of Tanzania." In: Chuta, E. and Sethurama, S.V. (eds.), *Rural Small-Scale Industries and Employment in Africa and Asia: A Review of Programmes and Policies.* Geneva, 25–46

Msambichaka, L.A. and Bagachwa, M.S., 1984: "Public Sector Enterprises in Tanzania. Problems and Constraints." In: *Vierteljahresberichte—Forschungsinstitut der Friedrich-Ebert-Stiftung*

Msambichaka, L.A., Ndulu, B.J., and Amani, H.K.R.,1983: *Agricultural Development in Tanzania. Policy Evolution, Performance and Evaluation. The First Two Decades of Independence.* Bonn

Mudoola, D., 1985: "The Pathology of Institution-Building." In: Kiros, F.(ed.), *Challenging Rural Development.* Trenton, N.J., 117–128

———, 1986: "The Pathology of Institution-Building: The Uganda Case." Paper presented at the Second Triennial Congress of OSSREA, Eldoret, Kenya, July 28–31

———, 1987: "The Problems of Institution-Building: The Uganda Case." In: Wiebe, P.D. and Dodge, C.P. (eds.), *Beyond Crisis. Development Issues in Uganda.* Hillsboro, Kans., 55–64

Münch, R., 1982: *Basale Soziologie: Soziologie der Politik.* Opladen

Mujaju, A.B., 1973: "The Demise of the UPC Youth League and the Rise of NUYO in Uganda." In: *Africa Review* 3, 291–307

———, 1976a: "The Political Crisis of Church Institutions in Uganda." In: *African Affairs* 75

———, 1976b: "The Role of the UPC as a Party of Government in Uganda." In: *Canadian Journal of African Studies* 10, 443–467

———, 1986: *Consensus and the Party System in Uganda.* (Political Science Monographs Series 1) Kampala

Munishi, G.K., 1987: "Tanzania's One Party Democracy and the Place of Unofficial Election Campaigns: The Case of the 1985 General Elections." Paper presented to the AAPS East African Regional Workshop on Constitutionalism and Political Stability in the East African Region, Nairobi, Kenya, January 5–7

Museveni, Y., 1986: *Selected Articles on the Uganda Resistance War.* Kampala

Mutiso, G.C., 1975: *Kenya. Politics, Policy and Society.* Nairobi

Mwansasu, B.U., 1979: "The Changing Role of Tanganyika African National Union." In: Mwansasu, B.U. and Pratt, C. (eds.), *Towards Socialism in Tanzania.* Toronto, Dar es Salaam, 169–192

Mwansasu, B.U. and Pratt, C. (eds.), 1979: *Towards Socialism in Tanzania.* Toronto, Dar es Salaam

Nabudere, D.W., 1980: *Imperialism and Revolution in Uganda.* London, Dar es Salaam

———, 1986: "The One-Party State in Africa: Its Philosophic Roots." Paper presented at the Joint AAPS/DVPW Symposium at Arnoldshain, West Germany, October 15–17

Nacht, M., 1982: "Stability in Third-World Countries: Five Guidelines, Five Questions." In: *Vierteljahresberichte—Probleme der Entwicklungsländer,* 345–350

Neubert, D., 1986: *Sozialpolitik in Kenia.* Münster

Ng'ethe, N., 1984: "The State and the Evolution of the Peasantry in Kenyan Agriculture: A Summary of Well-Known Issues." In: *Mawazo* vol 5, no 3, 18–34

Njonjo, A.L., 1981: "The Kenya Peasantry: A Reassessment." In: *Review of African Political Economy* 20, 27–40

Nohlen, D. and Nuscheler, F. (eds.), 1982a: *Handbuch der Dritten Welt 1. Unterentwicklung und Entwicklung: Theorien—Strategien—Indikatoren.* Hamburg

——, 1982b: *Handbuch der Dritten Welt 5. Ostafrika und Südafrika. Unterentwicklung und Entwicklung.* Hamburg

——, 1982c: "Indikatoren von Unterentwicklung und Entwicklung. Probleme der Messung und quantifizierenden Analyse." In: Nohlen, D. and Nuscheler, F. (eds.), *Handbuch der Dritten Welt 1. Unterentwicklung und Entwicklung: Theorien— Strategien—Indikatoren. Hamburg,* 451–485

Nohlen, D. and Sturm, R., 1982: "Über das Konzept der strukturellen Heterogenität." In: Nohlen, D. and Nuscheler, F. (eds.), *Handbuch der Dritten Welt 1. Unterentwicklung und Entwicklung: Theorien—Strategien—Indikatoren.* Hamburg, 92–116

Noormohamed, S.O., 1985: "Development Strategy for the Informal Sector: The Kenyan Experience." In: Ndegwa, P. (ed.), *Development Options for Africa in the 1980s and Beyond.* Nairobi, 186–193

Norcliffe, G., Freeman, D., and Miles, N., 1984: "Rural Industrialisation in Kenya." In: Chuta, E. and Sethurama, S.V. (eds.), *Rural Small-Scale Industries and Employment in Africa and Asia: A Review of Programmes and Policies.* Geneva, 9–24

Nsibambi, A., 1987: "The 1980 Elections in Uganda." Paper presented at the AAPS East African Regional Workshop on Constitutionalism and Political Stability in the East African Region, Nairobi, Kenya, January 5–7

Nuscheler, F., 1978: "Uganda." In: Nuscheler, F. and Ziemer, K. (eds.), *Politische Organisation und Repräsentation in Afrika.* Berlin, 2299–2329

—— (ed.), 1985a: *Dritte Welt-Forschung. Entwicklungstheorie und Entwicklungspolitik. (PVS* special edition 16) Opladen

——, 1985b: "Einleitung. Entwicklungslinien der politikwissenschaftlichen Dritte Welt-Forschung." In: Nuscheler, F. (ed.), *Dritte Welt-Forschung. Entwicklungstheorie und Entwicklungspolitik. (PVS* special edition 16) Opladen, 7–25

——, 1987: *Lern- und Arbeitsbuch Entwicklungspolitik.* Bonn

Nuscheler, F. and Ziemer, F. (eds.), 1978: *Politische Organisation und Repräsentation in Afrika.* 2 vols. Berlin

Nyunya, O.J.D., 1987: "Regional Interactions and Political Stability in Eastern Africa." Paper presented at the AAPS Eastern African Regional Workshop on Constitutionalism and Political Stability in Eastern Africa, Nairobi, Kenya, January 5–7

Oberndörfer, D. and Hanf, T. (eds.), 1986: *Entwicklungspolitik.* Stuttgart

Odhiambo, A.E.S., 1986: "Democracy and the Ideology of Order in Kenya." Paper prepared for a conference on the political economy of Kenya. Johns Hopkins University, Washington D.C. School of Advanced International Studies. April 11–12

Offe, C., 1969: "Politische Herrschaft und Klassenstrukturen." In: Kress, G. and Senghaas, D. (eds.), *Politikwissenschaft.* Frankfurt/M., 155–189

Ohe, W. von der et al., 1982: *Die Bedeutung sozio-kultureller Faktoren in der*

Entwicklungstheorie und-praxis. Munich

Okello, C.A., 1986: "IMF Conditionality and the Alleviation of Poverty in Sub-Saharan Africa. The Ugandan Case." Paper presented at the Second Triennial Congress of OSSREA, Eldoret, Kenya, July 2–5

Okoth-Ogendo, H.W.O., 1981: "Land Ownership and Land Distribution in Kenya's Large Farm Areas." In: Killick, T. (ed.), *Papers on the Kenyan Economy. Performance, Problems and Policies.* Nairobi, London, Ibadan, 329–338

Okumu, J.J. and Holmquist, F., 1984: "Party and Party-State Relations." In: Barkan, J.D. (ed.), *Politics and Public Policy in Kenya and Tanzania.* Revised edition. New York, 45–69

Olsen, M.E., 1981: "Comparative Political Sociology." In: *International Journal of Comparative Sociology* 22, 40–61

Olson, M., 1965: *The Logic of Collective Action.* Cambridge, Mass.

Olusanya, G.O. 1987: "Constitutionalism and Political Stability in the East African Region—A Historical Perspective." Paper presented at the AAPS Eastern African Regional Workshop on Constitutionalism and Political Stability in Eastern Africa, Nairobi, Kenya, January 5–7

Ominde, S.H. (ed.), 1984: *Population and Development in Kenya.* Nairrobi, London, Ibadan

Opio-Odongo, J.M.A., 1987: "The Agricultural Cooperative Movement and the Emasculation of Producer Members in Uganda." In: Wiebe, P.D. and Dodge, C.P. (eds.), *Beyond Crisis: Development Issues in Uganda.* Hillsboro, Kans., 65–78

Organisation of African Unity (OAU), 1980: *Lagos Plan of Action for the Economic Development of Africa 1980–2000.* Addis Ababa

Orora, J.H.O. and Spiegel, H., 1979: "'Harambee'-Selbsthilfe Entwicklungsprojekte in Kenya." In: *Internationales Afrikaforum* 15, 55–63

Overholt, W.H., 1982: "Assessing Political Risk: An Overview." In: *Vierteljahresberichte—Probleme der Entwicklungsländer,* 321–331

Oyugi, W.O., 1983: "Local Government in Kenya: A Case of Institutional Decline." In: Mawhood, P. (ed.), *Local Government in the Third World: The Experience of Tropical Africa.* Chichester, 107–140

————, 1986: "Two Decades of Decentralisation Effort." In: *Cahiers africains d'administration publique* 26, 133–161

Pappi, F.U., 1986: "Politische Kultur. Forschungsparadigma, Fragestellungen, Untersuchungsmöglichkeiten." In: Kaase, M. (ed.), *Politische Wissenschaft und politische Ordnung. Analysen zu Theorie und Empirie demokratischer Regierungsweise. Festschrift zum 65. Geburtstag von Rudolf Wildenmann.* Opladen, 279–291

Peterson, S., 1986: "Neglecting the Poor. State Policy toward the Smallholder in Kenya." In: Commins, S.K. et al. (eds.), *Africa's Agrarian Crisis: The Roots of Famine.* Boulder, Colo., 59–83

Pfennig, W., Voll, K. and Weber, H. (eds.), 1980: *Entwicklungsmodell Tansania: Sozialismus in Afrika. Geschichte, Ökonomie, Politik, Erziehung.* Frankfurt/M., New York

Picard, L.A., 1979–1980: "Socialism and the Field Administrator: Decentralization in Tanzania." In: *Comparative Politics* 12, 439–457

Pratt, C., 1976 *The Critical Phase in Tanzania 1945–1968. Nyerere and the Emergence of a Socialist Strategy.* Cambridge

Prunier, G., 1983: "Le magendo. Essai sur quelques aspects marginaux des échanges commerciaux en Afrique orientale.' In: *Politique africaine* 9, 53–62

Przeworski, A. and Teune, H., 1970: *The Logic of Comparative Social Inquiry*. New York

Putterman, L., 1986: *Peasants, Collectives and Choice: Economic Theory and Tanzania's Villages*. Greenwich

Pye, L.W., 1968: "Political Culture." In: Sills, D.C. (ed.), *International Encyclopedia of the Social Sciences* 12. New York, London 218–225

Raikes, P., 1975: "Ujamaa and Rural Socialism." In: *Review of African Political Economy* 3, 33–52

Ravenhill, J., 1979: "Regional Integration and Development in Africa: Lessons from the East African Community." In: *Journal of Commonwealth and Comparative Politics* 17, 227–246

————, 1980: "Comparing Regime Performance in Africa. The Limitations of Cross-National Aggregate Analysis." In: *Journal of Modern African Studies* 18, 99–126

Rayfield, G., 1982: "Political Risks: A Corporate Perspective." In: *Vierteljahresberichte—Probleme der Entwicklungsländer*, 341–344

Reichel, P., 1981: *Politische Kultur der Bundesrepublik*. Opladen

Rokkan, S., 1970: "Methods and Models in the Comparative Study of Nation-Building." In: Rokkan, S., *Citizens, Elections , Parties: Approaches to the Comparative Study of the Processes of Development*. Oslo, 46–47

Rosberg, C.G. and Friedland, W.H. (eds.), *African Socialism*. Stanford

Rosberg, C.G. and Nottingham, J., 1966: *The Myth of "Mau-Mau:" Nationalism in Kenya*. New York

Rothchild, D., 1973: *Racial Bargaining in Independent Kenya. A Study of Minorities and Decolonization*. London

Rüland, J. and Werz, N., 1985: "Von der `Entwicklungsdiktatur' zu den Diktaturen ohne Entwicklung—Staat und Herrschaft in der politikwissenschaftlichen Dritte Welt-Forschung." In: Nuscheler, F. (ed.), *Dritte Welt-Forschung. Entwicklungstheorie und Entwicklungspolitik*. (PVS special edition 16) Opladen, 211–232

Ruloff, D., 1987: *Politische Risiko-Analyse und Dritte Welt*. In: *PVS* vol 28, no 3, 259–279

Rweyemamu, J.F., 1973: *Underdevelopment and Industrialization in Tanzania*. Nairobi

Sartori, G., 1970: "Concept Misformation in Comparative Politics." In: *American Political Science Review* 69, 1033–1053

Sathyamurthy, T.V., 1975: "The Social Base of the Uganda People's Congress, 1958–70." In: *African Affairs* 74, 442–460

————, 1986: *The Political Development of Uganda: 1900–1986*. Aldershot

Saul, J.S., 1979: *The State and Revolution in Eastern Africa*. London

Schönborn, M., 1978: "Tansania." In: Werobel-La Rochelle, et al. (eds.), *Politisches Lexikon Schwarzafrika*. Munich, 428–448

————, 1980: "Ein-Partei-Demokratie in Tansania." In: Pfennig, W., Voll, K., and Weber, H. (eds.), *Entwicklungsmodell Tansania: Sozialismus in Afrika. Geschichte, Ökonomie, Politik, Erziehung*. Frankfurt/M., New York, 213–240

Segall, M.H., Doornbos, M.R., and Clive, D., 1976: *Political Identity: A Case Study from Uganda*. Syracuse, N.Y.

Senghaas, D., 1986: *Die Entwicklungsproblematik. Überlegungen zum Stand der*

Diskussion. Unpublished manuscript

Senteza-Kajubi, W., 1987: "The Historical Background to the Uganda Crisis, 1966–1986." In: Wiebe, P.D. and Dodge, C.P. (eds.), *Beyond Crisis: Development Issues in Uganda.* Hillsboro, Kans., 25–40

Shimwela, N.N.P., 1984: "Tanzania: Some Reflections on the Deepening Economic Crisis." In: Lipumba, N.H.I., Msamichaka, L.A., and Wangwe, S.M. (eds.), *Economic Stabilization Policies in Tanzania. Dar es Salaam,* 96–111

Shivji, I.G., 1976: *Class Struggles in Tanzania.* Dar es Salaam, London

———, 1983: "Working Class Struggles and Organisation in Tanzania, 1939–1975." In: *Mawazo* vol 5, no 2 , 3–24

———, 1986: *Law, State and the Working Class in Tanzania. 1920–1964.* London, Portsmouth, N.H., Dar es Salaam

Simonis, G., 1985: "Der Entwicklungsstaat in der Krise." In: Nuscheler, F. (ed.), *Dritte Welt-Forschung. Entwicklungstheorie und Entwicklungspolitik. (PVS* special edition 16) Opladen, 157–183

Simson, U., 1986: "Kultur und Entwicklung. Die kulturellen Bedingungen wirtschaftlich-gesellschaftlichen Handelns in der Dritten Welt." In: *Aus Politik und Zeitgeschichte.* Supplement to *Das Parlament,* 19 (April), 3–11

Skarstein, R. and Wangwe, S.M., 1986: *Industrial Development in Tanzania: Some Critical Issues.* Dar es Salaam

Stewart, F., 1979: "The Tripartite Agreements in Kenya." In: Ghai, D. and Godfrey, M. (eds.), *Essays on Employment in Kenya.* Nairobi

———, 1981: "Kenya: Strategies for Development." In: Killick, T. (ed.), *Papers on the Kenyan Economy. Performance, Problems and Policies.* Nairrobi, London, Ibadan

———, 1986: *Economic Policies and Agricultural Performance. The Case of Tanzania.* Paris

Strahm, R.H., 1985: *Warum sie so arm sind.* Wuppertal

Svensson, P., 1986: "Stability, Crisis and Breakdown: Some Notes on the Concept of Crisis in Political Analysis." In: *Scandinavian Political Studies* 9, 129–139

Swainson, N., 1977: "The Rise of a National Bourgeoisie in Kenya." In: *Review of African Political Economy* 16, 39–55

———, 1980: *The Development of Corporate Capitalism in Kenya 1918–1977.* London

Syahuke, M., 1983: "The Origin and Development of the Rwenzurur Movement 1900–1962." In: *Mawazo* vol 5, no 2, 60–75

Tamarkin, M., 1978: "The Roots of Political Stability in Kenya." In: *African Affairs* 77, 297–320

Tanga Regional Planning Office, 1985: *Tanga Integrated Rural Development Programme (TIRDEP). Regional Development Strategy.* Tanga

Tanzania, United Republic of. Bureau of Statistics, 1969: *1967 Population Census 1. Statistics for Enumeration Areas*

———. Bureau of Statistics, 1970: *1967 Population Census 2. Statistics for Urban Areas*

——— Bureau of Statistics, 1971: *1967 Population Census 4. Economic Statistics*

——— Bureau of Statistics, 1972.: *1969 Household Budget Survey 1. Income and Consumption*

——— Bureau of Statistics, 1981: *Survey of Employment and Earnings 1977–1978*

——— Bureau of Statistics, 1982: *1978 Population Census 4. A Summary of Selected Statistics*

——— Bureau of Statistics, 1984: *Economic Indicators of Tanzania*

———. Ministry of Finance, Planning and Economic Affairs, 1982: *Structural Adjustment Programme for Tanzania*. Dar es Salaam

———. Ministry of Finance, Planning, and Economic Affairs, 1986: *Statistical Abstract 1984*. Dar es Salaam

———. 1986: *Speech by the Minister for Finance, Planning, and Economic Affairs, Ndugu C.D. Msuya, when Presenting the Annual Plan and the Estimates of Revenue and Expenditure for the Financial Year 1986/87 to the National Assembly on 19th June 1986*

Taylor, C.L. and Jodice, D.A., 1983a: *World Handbook of Political and Social Indicators 1. Cross-National Attributes and Rates of Change*. New Haven, London

———, 1983b: *World Handbook of Political and Social Indicators 2. Political Protest and Government Change*. New Haven, London

Taylor, C.L., Jodice, D.A., and Koonce, W.A., 1980: "A Systematic Approach to Political Indicators." In: Taylor, C.L. (ed.), *Indicator Systems for Political, Economic and Social Analysis. (Publication of the Science Center, Berlin, 22)* Königstein, 117–133

Thomas, B.P., 1985: *Politics, Participation and Poverty. Development through Self-Help in Kenya*. Boulder, Colo.

Tordoff, W., 1967: *Government and Politics in Tanzania*. Nairobi

Uganda, Republic of. Minister of Finance, 1986: *Budget Speech. Delivered at the Meeting of the National Resistance Council*, August 23, 1986

Uganda, Republic of. Ministry of Planning and Economic Development, 1986: *Background to the Budget 1986–1987*. Kampala

Ulbrich, W., 1971: *Kenya. Voraussetzungen und Möglichkeiten der industriellen Entwicklung. (Afrika Industrieberichte 16)* Hamburg

UN Statistical Yearbook, 1965–1986

Verba, S., Nie, N., and Kim, J., 1978: *Participation and Political Equality*. Cambridge

Warner, W.L., 1960: *Social Class in America. A Manual of Procedure for the Measurement of Social Status*. New York

Weber, M., 1964: *Wirtschaft and Gesellschaft*. Cologne

The Weekly Review 1985–1988

Welbourn, F.B., 1965: *Religion and Politics in Uganda 1952–62*. Nairobi

Were, G. (ed.), 1983: *The Underprivileged in Society: Studies on Kenya. (Journal of Eastern African Research and Development* 13) Nairobi

Werobel-La Rochelle, J.M. et al. (eds.), 1978: *Politisches Lexikon Schwarzafrika*. Munich

Weyel, V., 1976: *Interaktionen von Politik und Religion in Uganda nach 1875*. Munich

———, 1983: "Uganda. Macht und Lehen. Präkoloniale und koloniale Bestimmungsfaktoren der Innen- und Außenpolitik." In: *Europa-Archiv* 14, 421–430

Wiebe, P.D. and Dodge, C.P. (eds.), 1987: *Beyond Crisis: Development Issues in Uganda*. Hillsboro, Kans.

Willets, P., 1975: "The Politics of Uganda as a One-Party State 1969–1970." In: *African Affairs* 74, 278–299

Wirth, H., 1985: *Aspekte des Zusammenhangs von Entwicklungshilfe und Entwicklungsplanung in Tanzania.* Bonn

World Bank, 1978–1988: *World Development Report.* Washington D.C.

———, 1986: *Toward Sustained Development.* Washington D.C.

Wrighley, C.C., 1959: *Crops and Wealth in Uganda.* Kampala

Würkner, R.A., 1982: *Systemstabilisierung durch Afrikanisierung? Probleme und Folgen der administrativen Umgestaltung des Handels in Nairobi.* Munich 1982

Young, C., Sherman, N.P., and Rose, T.H., 1981: *Cooperatives and Development. Agricultural Politics in Ghana and Uganda.* Madison, Wisc.

Zwanenberg, R.M.A. van, 1975: *An Economic History of Kenya and Uganda 1800–1970.* London

Index of Persons
and Organizations

About the Book
and the Authors

With the failure of both modernization and dependency approaches to account meaningfully for the increasing differentiation among Third World countries in the last decade, more specific political factors and the role of the state in social and economic development have attracted renewed interest. In this context, this study explores why the three East African states, under similar regional and external conditions, have taken such differing development paths since their independence.

Drawing on fieldworld in Kenya, Tanzania, and Uganda on thier comprehensive statistical analyses, the authors investigate the factors that have contributed to the emergence of each of the three systems and assess its respective performance with regard to a wide range of social and economic indicators. Methodologically situated between broader macro-quantitative studies that necessarily lack depth and detail and single case studies that do not lend themselves to meaningful integration in a theoretical framework, their work has allowed the isolation of some key variables that account for an important part of the observed varianced. Their results underline the importance of the ongoing debate about Africa's political and economic problems and point to some possible remedies for African regimes.

Dirk Berg-Schlosser is professor in the Institute of Political Science, Philipps-University, Marburg, West Germany. He has concluded extensive field research in East Africa during the past 20 years and has published numerous books and articles on Africa and on Third World political systems. Rainer Siegler is a reserach associate at the Philipps-University Institute of Political Research.